The Essential Guide to

Catholic Prayer and the Mass

by Mary DeTurris Poust

A member of Penguin Group (USA) Inc.

ALPHA BOOKS

Published by the Penguin Group

Penguin Group (USA) Inc., 375 Hudson Street, New York, New York 10014, USA

Penguin Group (Canada), 90 Eglinton Avenue East, Suite 700, Toronto, Ontario M4P 2Y3, Canada (a division of Pearson Penguin Canada Inc.)

Penguin Books Ltd., 80 Strand, London WC2R 0RL, England

Penguin Ireland, 25 St. Stephen's Green, Dublin 2, Ireland (a division of Penguin Books Ltd.)

Penguin Group (Australia), 250 Camberwell Road, Camberwell, Victoria 3124, Australia (a division of Pearson Australia Group Pty. Ltd.)

Penguin Books India Pvt. Ltd., 11 Community Centre, Panchsheel Park, New Delhi—110 017, India

Penguin Group (NZ), 67 Apollo Drive, Rosedale, North Shore, Auckland 1311, New Zealand (a division of Pearson New Zealand Ltd.)

Penguin Books (South Africa) (Pty.) Ltd., 24 Sturdee Avenue, Rosebank, Johannesburg 2196, South Africa

Penguin Books Ltd., Registered Offices: 80 Strand, London WC2R 0RL, England

International Standard Book Number: 978-1-61564-075-1
Library of Congress Catalog Card Number: 2010912365

13 12 11 8 7 6 5 4 3 2

Interpretation of the printing code: The rightmost number of the first series of numbers is the year of the book's printing; the rightmost number of the second series of numbers is the number of the book's printing. For example, a printing code of 11-1 shows that the first printing occurred in 2011.

Printed in the United States of America

Publisher: *Marie Butler-Knight*
Associate Publisher: *Mike Sanders*
Senior Managing Editor: *Billy Fields*
Executive Editor: *Randy Ladenheim-Gil*
Senior Development Editor: *Christy Wagner*
Senior Production Editor: *Janette Lynn*
Copy Editor: *Jan Zoya*
Technical Adviser: *Monsignor William Benwell*
Cover/Book Designer: *Rebecca Batchelor*
Indexer: *Angie Bess Martin*
Layout: *Rebecca Batchelor*
Proofreader: *John Etchison*

To my father and mother, Salvatore and Irene DeTurris, for planting the seeds of faith that have blossomed into my lifelong spiritual journey.

Nihil Obstat: Rev. John N. Fell, S.T.D.

Imprimatur: ✠ Paul G. Bootkoski,
Bishop of Metuchen,
October 29, 2010

We Catholics believe in the power of prayer to change lives and the world. In her engaging new book, Mary DeTurris Poust lovingly walks us through many of the Church's rich and diverse traditions of prayer, breathing new life into ancient, beloved devotions, and pointing the way toward more modern methods of prayer as well. Perhaps most valuable of all, Mary breaks down the parts of the Mass—the ultimate prayer—to enhance the reader's understanding and appreciation of this Sunday banquet at which we are all called to gather regularly as a family, united with the sacrifice of Christ on the cross. As Saint Paul confessed, "none of us know how to pray as we ought." This book is sure a help.

✠ Timothy M. Dolan
Archbishop of New York
President, United States Conference of Catholic Bishops

Contents

Appendixes

Introduction

Prayer can be private. Prayer can be public. It can be repetitious or have no words whatsoever. But no matter how or where we pray, one thing is indisputable: prayer is personal. Everything from our family upbringing to our personalities to our lived faith experiences influences how we choose to pray. As a result, no two people pray alike.

We may approach God through poetry or prose, through art or nature, through silence or song. There's no right or wrong way to pray. Sometimes the most difficult thing about prayer is just getting started.

That's where this book comes in. In the pages and chapters that follow, you will find practical, hands-on information about prayer in general and Catholic prayer specifically. You can start at the beginning and read straight through, or you can open to whatever subject and section suits your need or mood at the moment. When you've read through the entire book, you can continue to use it as a prayer book and spiritual guide.

When I sat down to write this book, I knew the experience would become my pathway to deeper prayer in my own life. And it has done just that, often in surprising ways. What I didn't know at the outset, however, was that I would end this book with a pilgrimage to Rome—my first. My 10-day visit to the Eternal City provided me with a unique opportunity to put some of the prayer methods in this book into practice in new ways.

As I visited one church after another, marveling at the Michaelangelos and Caravaggios hanging alongside more ordinary works of art in buildings that were nothing short of awe-inspiring, I found myself lifting up family members and friends again and again in intercessory prayer (which I discuss in Chapter 1).

As I waited for the pope to arrive for a Wednesday morning audience, I joined the Jesuit priest sitting next to me in a spontaneous recitation of Morning Prayer, and there, amid the chaos of a crowd of thousands, I found a moment of sacred silence, thanks to the ancient tradition of the Liturgy of the Hours (which we explore in Chapter 7).

As I sat in the darkened church of Santa Maria in Trastevere on a Friday night and sang Vespers in halting Italian with the help of some young strangers sitting next to me, I felt the power of prayer shared in community (which I discuss in Chapters 3 and 19).

As I traveled to Subiaco, just 30 miles outside Rome, I stood in silent wonder in the cave where St. Benedict lived as a hermit in 500 A.D. and where he planted the first seeds of Western monasticism (which I discuss in Chapter 22).

Of course, you don't have to go to Rome to experience the power of Catholic prayer. In fact, you don't even have to leave home. Prayer can be experienced right where you are at this moment. It cannot be confined to a page or a place or a person, unless that person is Jesus Christ. Prayer happens when we least expect it but most need it, whether we are alone or in a group, when we are at home or in a foreign land. Prayer is at our disposal every minute of every day.

You'll see, as you read through this book, that you have everything you need to nurture and develop a life of prayer in your own sacred space, among your own family, and within your own church community.

Whether you've been praying for years or are just getting started, my hope is that this book will inspire you to go a little bit deeper. When you're done reading this book, I hope you'll turn back to a prayer that spoke to you and say the words until they echo in your heart and soul. Or perhaps you'll put the book aside and enter into the silence of meditation or contemplation.

My wish for you is that this book will give you the spiritual push you need to experience the kind of deep prayer that gives rhythm to your day and meaning to your life.

How This Book Is Organized

This book is divided into five parts:

Part 1, Drawn to Prayer, provides a primer on the meaning of prayer and the way to pray. The first three chapters explore the reasons behind certain prayers, different prayer methods, sacred spaces to nurture prayerfulness in your own life, and more. Think of this as a broad how-to section on prayer.

Part 2, The Way to God, gets more specific while covering the basics of Catholic prayer. In these five chapters, you discover the most common prayers every Catholic learns, starting in early childhood, as well as the equally important but more complex methods of prayer, such as the Liturgy of the Hours and contemplation. When you're through with this section, you'll have a firm foothold in the life of Catholic prayer.

Part 3, Mary and the Saints, delves into an area of prayer that is perhaps most recognizable. This is the popular piety that's often most closely associated with Catholics: prayers and devotions to the Blessed Mother and the many saints of Catholic history. From the Rosary and novenas to specific prayers by some of the most well-known saints, Part 3 offers a way to approach God in prayer through those who've done it best.

Part 4, Prayer's High Point: The Mass, focuses on the ultimate Catholic prayer. The Mass is often not seen as a prayer in and of itself, and yet it is the apex of Catholic prayer life. The chapters in this part take you through the Mass piece by piece, prayer by prayer, giving you insights into the reasons behind parts of the Mass as well as suggestions for getting more involved in liturgy. Part 4 includes the language of the Mass according to the new translation of the missal, effective Advent 2011, marking the first major changes to the Mass since the 1960s.

Part 5, Following the Path of Prayer, provides a detailed look at the methods and means for setting all of life to the rhythm of prayer, through both modern and ancient traditions. From the Church year to praying with icons and fasting to learning to see every moment as a prayer, Part 5 offers hands-on tools for infusing your everyday life with elements of prayer.

In the back of the book I give you a glossary of terms you might not be familiar with, a directory of many of the prayers you'll hear and say as a Catholic, along with a list of further resources to continue your journey with Catholic prayer and the Mass.

Essential Extras

Throughout this book, you'll find special messages to help you understand certain aspects of prayer more fully. Here's what to look for:

Definition

Look to these sidebars for definitions and explanations of words or phrases that might be confusing or unfamiliar.

Prayer Practice

Reading about prayer is one thing; actually praying is another. Here you'll find practical tips for weaving the spiritual into your daily life.

Wisdom for the Journey

These sidebars offer interesting information as well as quotes and observations about prayer from saints and other holy men and women from throughout history to the present.

Misc.

You'll also see a fourth, name-changing sidebar that presents anecdotes, interesting facts, case histories, or other extended background information you should know.

Acknowledgments

This book never would have come into being without the encouragement and enthusiasm of my editor, Randy Ladenheim-Gil, executive editor for Alpha Books/Penguin Group. She believed in my idea but, more importantly, she believed in me, and I am so grateful for her support. Thank you to my agent, Marilyn Allen, and everyone at Alpha who worked on this book, especially Christy Wagner, my development editor; Jan Zoya, my copy editor; and Janette Lynn, my senior production editor.

As with any book on the Catholic faith, getting the theology and spirituality just right is critical, and so I am thankful for the expertise and advice of my technical adviser, Monsignor William Benwell, vicar general of the Diocese of Metuchen, New Jersey, whose professional insights and personal friendship have been a gift.

Every book I write impacts my family in a major way, especially my children, who often have to spend long hours at home while I write rather than doing the fun stuff they would prefer. Thank you to Noah, Olivia, and Chiara for being such great kids and such dedicated fans. Of course, the biggest thank you has to go to my husband, Dennis, who always rallies around me when I take on a book project and never minds all the extra work it means for him. As if that's not enough, he serves as my personal editor, reading every word and making spot-on suggestions all along the way. I am blessed to have the family I do.

My own Catholic spiritual life was built prayer by prayer over the course of my lifetime. I have to thank all those family members, friends, and fellow Catholics who have shared devotions, prayers, and spiritual practices with me so I could, in turn, share them with you. A special thank you to my aunt and godmother Margaret Robertson, whose personal prayer life incorporates so many of the devotions covered in this book. Her help has been invaluable.

Prayer life without community would be incomplete, and so I am grateful to the communities of which I am fortunate to be a member—St. Thomas the Apostle Parish in Delmar, New York; my Cornerstone sisters; my spiritual friends; and my Catholic press and media colleagues—for providing me with a spiritual home and for praying with me and for me. I am inspired by the faith I have witnessed in so many deeply spiritual people I've been blessed to know.

Finally, thank you to all those people who believe in the power of prayer and use it. With hearts and voices joined in word and song, service and silence, we lift up one another and make this world a better place one prayer, one person at a time.

Special Thanks to the Technical Reviewer

The Essential Guide to Catholic Prayer and the Mass was reviewed by an expert who double-checked the accuracy of what you'll learn here, to help us ensure that this book gives you the essentials on Catholic prayer and the Mass. Special thanks are extended to Monsignor William Benwell.

Monsignor Benwell is vicar general of the Diocese of Metuchen, New Jersey. He has been a priest for more than 30 years and has served the diocese as a pastor and in a variety of administrative posts. In addition to a licentiate in canon law, he holds degrees in history and pastoral theology.

Trademarks

Part 1

Drawn to Prayer

Prayer can mean different things to different people. In truth, prayer is as individual as our genetic code. What works for one person may not work for another. And yet, no matter what method we use, what words we say, or whether we say any words at all, prayer always has the same goal: to connect us in a deeper way with our Creator.

Catholic prayer, in particular, has its own rhythms and rituals. Over the course of Catholic Christian history, certain prayer methods have developed, giving us a wide array of prayer options from which to choose. Pick 10 Catholics out of a group and ask them about their prayer lives, and you're likely to get 10 very different answers. The bottom line is that there is no single prayer path to God. As long as you're constantly striving to make a connection through some form of prayer, you'll keep moving forward.

The chapters in Part 1 look at prayer in a general way—why prayer is important, basic types of prayer, how to create an atmosphere of prayer, and how to begin your own prayer routine. From there we set out into the deep to explore an endless expanse of Catholic prayer where there's something for everyone.

chapter 1

Understanding Prayer and Devotion

A look at the human desire for divine connection

Using Jesus as a prayer role model

The elements that make Catholic prayer distinct

A guide to types of prayers

Prayer can calm our soul, center our heart, and feed our spiritual hunger. For some, prayer is a never-ending conversation with a God who feels very close by. For others, prayer is a cry for help in a time of need. We may say our prayers in a group; sing our prayers at Mass; whisper our prayers in the darkness; or wait, unspeaking, for God to come to us in the silence of our heart.

Regardless of how you view prayer or use prayer, one thing is certain: prayer is a critical element of any spiritual life. We wouldn't expect to foster a deep relationship with a friend if we didn't share regular conversations about important things in our lives. And so it is with God, our ultimate friend. If we want to connect, if we want to know God in the deepest sense humanly possible, we cannot do it without prayer.

Unfortunately, getting into a regular prayer routine isn't always easy. It's a lot like exercising. We know if we get out there and do it, we'll be better for it. Just as walking a few miles every day makes our physical hearts stronger, praying for even a few minutes every day makes our spiritual hearts stronger. Still, in today's busy world, prayer can seem unproductive, like a leisure activity. How can we take time out to sit—or kneel, or walk—in prayer when there's laundry to do, a lawn to mow, and bills to pay?

And yet, since time immemorial, prayer has been considered a critical activity for people of every faith. It is the path to spiritual growth, the way to God, the heart of a lifelong pilgrimage.

Prayer Through the Ages

We don't have to be theologians or religion professors to recognize that prayer didn't start with Catholics specifically, Christians in general, or even our Jewish forebears. For as long as people have been walking this earth, there's been a drive to connect with something greater than us, with God. We're hardwired for it. And prayer is really the only way for us to reach out to God. Over the course of history, humans of every background and every faith have come up with ways to pray, be it structured or spontaneous.

From prebiblical times to the present, evidence exists of a deep desire to connect with the divine. We humans are tactile people, after all. In order for us to make that enormous leap toward heaven, we need things—be it candles and incense in a Catholic church, prayer wheels in a Tibetan monastery, pilgrimages to Mecca, or Passover Seder meals—to help us bridge the divide between heaven and earth.

wisdom for the journey

How to pray? This is a simple matter. I would say: Pray any way you like so long as you do pray.

—Venerable Pope John Paul II, twentieth century

No matter what outward signs and rituals we use to make that connection, however, prayer remains at the heart of it. The incense, the candles, and the statues cannot lead us toward God on their own. We need the words, the music, or the silence of prayer for that to happen. We need regular time with God, ongoing conversations, formal or informal, to make any real progress.

One afternoon when I was complaining about something fairly insignificant, my young daughter said, "Why don't you just talk to God?" I looked at her quizzically because I couldn't figure out why she'd made a connection to God from what I'd been saying. Then she mentioned another time when I was frazzled and driving and talking out loud to God. I stopped and thought about it. She was right. Often when I'm rushing around or worried about something, I talk to God. I typically don't say some poetic formal prayer but rather speak conversationally as though I'm sharing my worries with my closest friend or confidant—only this confidant is Creator of the universe!

I'm not unusual, of course. I'm just like countless other men and women throughout history who have followed the need, the urge to connect with God. We are on a quest, a journey that takes us to a place we can't imagine or locate on a map, a place both in the deepest recesses of our heart and the farthest reaches of the universe.

Following Christ's Example

Catholic prayer has its roots firmly planted in Judaism. Jesus was an observant Jew, so it makes sense that we would trace our own spiritual path back to his Jewish faith. We reflect on Scripture from the Old Testament, knowing that the stories we read and the Psalms we sing are the very same ones Jesus read and sang throughout his own life.

Our faith and our prayer life are centered on Jesus, God incarnate, fully human *and* fully divine. And yet, Jesus himself learned about traditional prayer the old-fashioned way—praying at the synagogue, joining his family in prayer at home, and studying Scripture.

Scripture doesn't tell us much about Jesus' life between his birth in Bethlehem and his public ministry as an adult. But in one brief scene, when Jesus was 12, we read about him staying behind in the temple in Jerusalem after his parents had left. Even there, in that quick glimpse into Jesus' early adolescence, we get a view of some basic aspects of his young prayer life. He was on pilgrimage to Jerusalem with his family. He was listening to the teachers in the temple. He was doing all the things an observant Jew of his time would do.

Later, in the New Testament, we get a clear view of the way Jesus prayed. He not only prayed in the temple and synagogue, but he also often spent time alone with God. He withdrew to the desert. He fasted at times. He was silent at times. And then, at other times, he prayed surrounded by his community of followers. Jesus is our role model, the pathway to the Father, and we can look to him not only for the words to say, but also the way to pray.

> When you pray, go to your inner room, close the door, and pray to your Father in secret. And your Father, who sees in secret will repay you … Your Father knows what you need before you ask him. (Matthew 6:6–8)

In this passage from the Gospel of Matthew, we hear Jesus telling us to pray in private, to retreat from the hustle and bustle of life, and to encounter a Father who knows us better than we know ourselves. But private prayer is just one part of the spiritual equation.

Later in the same Gospel, Jesus says, "Where two or three are gathered together in my name, there am I in the midst of them." (Matthew 18:20) So communal prayer is also critical. It's not enough to pray alone.

Jesus provides us with a great starting framework for a life of prayer. It can and should be a blend of private and communal, silent and vocal. It can and should be offered amid the busyness of life and in the starkness of whatever desert we might find ourselves in. It can and should be an experience that's not simply about moving our lips and hands but about moving our hearts and spirits as well.

wisdom for the journey

Before you speak, it is necessary for you to listen, for God speaks in the silence of the heart.

—Blessed Mother Teresa of Calcutta, twentieth century

What Makes Prayer "Catholic"?

If all Christians believe in Jesus and all Christians pray, what makes a prayer specifically Catholic? Several markers, of sorts, are unique to Catholic prayer, although some things overlap with other Christian denominations here and there. After all, we are one big Christian family, so even our differences have some common ground.

Our prayers are always directed toward God and joined with Jesus his Son, just as any Christian prayer would be, but we Catholics approach prayer in some ways distinct from other Christian faiths—and certainly very different from faiths outside Christianity.

A Focus on the Trinity

For Catholics—and most other Christian denominations—the cornerstone of faith is the Trinity, the belief that God the Father, Jesus the Son, and the Holy Spirit are one and the same. When we go to God in prayer, we may address Him either as Father, Son, or Spirit, but these are all one being, just with different qualities. We may go to God the Father as our benevolent creator and protector, to Jesus the Son as our compassionate redeemer and shepherd, and to the Holy Spirit as our sanctifier and ever-present guide.

Even every prayer we say begins and ends with this belief in the Trinity, as demonstrated when we bless ourselves with the Sign of the Cross, something I discuss further in Chapter 4. The Trinity and the cross mark us as Catholic and bookend all our prayers.

Fueled by Sacraments

Certain spiritual milestones, or *sacraments,* mark the life of a Catholic:

- Baptism
- Eucharist
- Confirmation
- Reconciliation (also known as penance or confession)
- Anointing of the sick
- Matrimony (marriage)
- Holy orders (ordination)

These seven sacraments provide spiritual graces that strengthen our lives as believers. All the sacraments are important, but those that can be received again and again—Eucharist and reconciliation—provide ongoing spiritual nourishment.

Definition

The term ***sacrament*** refers to outward "instruments of grace" that help a believer grow deeper in faith and closer to God.

Eucharist is the most important, the sacrament of sacraments, because it's when we receive the Body and Blood of Jesus Christ. The Catholic belief in the "real presence"—that the bread and wine truly become Jesus and are not merely symbols of Jesus—is central to our faith and critical to our prayer life. Receiving the Eucharist strengthens our soul just as earthly food strengthens our body. We need the Eucharist not only to move forward but to survive spiritually. Without it, our soul would whither.

Every Mass and every celebration of the Eucharist is another opportunity to gain grace and courage for the difficult work of living out the Gospel. We take a closer look at Eucharist in Chapter 5 and again in Part 4.

Heavenly Helpers

One aspect of prayer life that's probably most widely recognized as specifically Catholic is our friendship with Mary and the saints through prayers and devotions. Catholics believe we have companions along the spiritual path to help us achieve closeness with God. We turn to the Blessed Virgin Mary, the saints, and angels for assistance along our way.

It makes perfect sense, really. When I'm in a bad place or in need of a favor or even just a little extra kindness, I call a family member or friend. The feeling of support I get from that connection does so much to set things right in my life. It works the same way in our spiritual lives. We can call on Mary, the saints, and angels for comfort, support, or a favor. They are our heavenly friends, always willing to come to our aid.

All of us, whether we're here on Earth or already in heaven or somewhere in between, are part of the "communion of saints." We belong to one family of faith, a family that cannot be divided by time or space or even death. So those of us on Earth can look to those who've reached the goal of heaven as our partners in prayer. We pray to Mary and the saints to ask them to pray for us.

We look at these heavenly helpers and the prayers associated with them more in Part 3.

Misc.

Praying to Mary

Catholics do not worship Mary, the Mother of God. Worship is for God alone. We admire Mary with a special kind of affection and see her as our spiritual mother. So when we pray to Mary, we are asking her to help us grow closer to her Son.

Pleading, Thanking, and Exalting

When Catholics go to God in prayer, we often have one of a few basic things in mind. We're either asking for something, saying we're sorry for something, saying thank you for something, or praising God just for being God. These are the bare-bones basics of our prayer life.

Prayers of Petition and Intercession

When we go to God to ask for something, that's known as a prayer of petition. These are the prayers we send up to God when we need something, be it a desperate plea for something we want or a cry for forgiveness for something we've done.

Of course, prayer is not like a dime-store gumball machine. We don't pop in a prayer and then put out our hands to wait for our reward. Catholics believe that we take our petitions to God, and we can ask for whatever we want, but we'd better be ready to take whatever *he thinks we need.* The two might not be the same. So we offer a prayer of petition, hoping for what we want but praying for the strength or grace to accept God's will.

Saying a prayer of petition on behalf of another person is known as a prayer of intercession. That means we're asking God to help someone else, be it a family member, a friend, or even an enemy. Jesus prayed for others, even those who put him to death. We Catholics follow his lead and pray for others as well.

Prayers of Gratitude

Prayers of thanksgiving are, as the name implies, those times when we go to God to say thank you for something good in our lives. It might be for something specific we were praying for or just general thanks for all God has given us.

As with all prayers, a prayer of thanksgiving may be as simple as saying, "Thank you, God." It doesn't necessarily have to be elaborate or eloquent, just heartfelt.

Prayers of Praise and Adoration

When we take that prayer of thanksgiving a step further, it can become a prayer of praise. In this case, we're not looking for anything. We're praising God simply because he deserves to be praised.

Prayers of adoration take our praise to an even higher level. We're not only praising God for being God, we are exalting him. Many Catholics attend what's called Adoration of the Blessed Sacrament, which is the ultimate version of this type of prayer. (We look at this in more detail in Chapter 5.)

Prayer Practice

Don't get too caught up in the kinds of prayer you're saying. Most likely your prayers reflect what's going on in your life and where you need God's extra-loving touch. Just start praying and remember that any prayer is a good prayer.

A Primer on Devotions

We tend to lump together prayer and devotions, but some things set devotions apart from prayers. Devotions *are* prayers, but usually they're particular prayers with a specific focus. Probably the most popular and well-known Catholic devotion is the Rosary.

Devotions are separate from the prayers included in the Church's official liturgical books, which are kind of like Catholic playbooks laying out the rules and regulations of worship. Official liturgical prayers include the Mass, sacraments, and blessings—things that tend to be part of the greater life of the Church. Devotions, on the other hand, tend to be more private.

They're prayers people say on their own or in groups with other Catholics who share their love of a particular devotion.

Whether we say popular devotions or liturgical prayers, or opt to spend time with God in silence, our hearts open more and more with each moment we spend in conversation with our Creator. Little by little, our daily prayers begin to reshape the way we think, the way we act, and the way we live until our spirits are always resting calmly in God, even when life around us is spinning at top speed.

wisdom for the journey

For me prayer is an upward leap of the heart, an untroubled glance toward heaven, a cry of gratitude and love which I utter from the depths of sorrow as well as from the heights of joy.

—Saint Thérèse of Lisieux, nineteenth century

Essential Takeaways

- Prayer is a way to connect with God through words, songs, or even silence.
- Jesus provides a framework for a life of prayer, giving us not only the words to say but also the way to pray.
- Our prayers often fall into one of several categories, including petitions, thanksgiving, praise, and adoration.
- Catholic prayer includes certain key elements: a focus on the Trinity; a reliance on the sacraments, in particular the Eucharist; and a friendship with Mary and the saints.

chapter 2

Where to Begin?

Developing a friendship with God

The importance of the Spirit in a life of prayer

Practical aids to smooth the spiritual path

Setting your day to the rhythm of prayer

Once we decide we want to spend some time in prayer, we face the next big question: where do we go from here? Even if we can rattle off childhood prayers from memory, we may not know how to progress from simply reciting those familiar words to allowing them to transform our hearts and, eventually, our lives.

For starters, we can remember that prayer should never be one more task we have to check off our daily to-do list, another stress in our already-stressful lives. Prayer should be an oasis, a place where we can step outside the chaos for a few minutes of much-needed peace.

When we decide to pray—even the briefest or simplest prayer—we open the door to our own hearts and take the first tentative steps on an inward journey. Day by day, prayer by prayer, we begin to clear out a little space within our deepest selves and allow God to enter.

Learning to See God as Friend

The point of prayer is to connect with God, so perhaps the best place to begin a new life of prayer is with a closer look at our relationship with our Creator. How do we see God? Do we imagine him as a stern taskmaster, a disciplinarian waiting to catch us doing something wrong so he can punish us? Or do we see him as a patient and loving parent, with arms always open? If you nodded your head in agreement to that first description, the stern taskmaster, it's time to pack away that image once and for all.

With all the plagues and floods and general mayhem in the Old Testament, it's easy to see God as having quite the temper. And yet God describes Himself to Moses as "a merciful and gracious God, slow to anger and rich in kindness and fidelity, continuing his kindness for a thousand generations." (Exodus 34:6–7)

When I read those words, "slow to anger and rich in kindness," I feel comforted, hopeful. This doesn't make God sound vengeful at all, but rather how I imagine my best friends will react when I go to them with a problem.

Through prayer, we begin to recognize God as our ultimate best friend, one who has a limitless supply of unconditional love. He is our Creator, so he knows us better than we know ourselves. Yes, we're going to make mistakes—maybe lots of them—but God continues to love and forgive us. He calls to us and then waits for us to come to him in prayer.

Catholic prayer is about turning to face a God who is already facing us, already expecting us. We don't have to worry that we don't have the "right" words to say. There are no "right" words. We can just begin talking to God one on one, the way we'd talk to a close friend, and we're praying. Starting is that simple.

wisdom for the journey

You don't know how to pray? Put yourself in the presence of God, and as soon as you have said, "Lord, I don't know how to pray!" you can be sure you've already begun.

—St. Josemaria Escriva, twentieth-century Spanish priest and founder of *Opus Dei*

Guided by the Spirit

If you were to set off on a hike down a long and winding path through deep and strange woods, you'd probably look for a trail guide, someone to keep you on the right path and continually lead you in a safe direction. When it comes to prayer, the Holy Spirit is your trail guide.

The Spirit is God's presence and loving action here on Earth. We can't see or hear the Spirit, but we can sometimes feel the Spirit, especially as we begin to enter into prayer more deeply. We may have felt the Spirit at work in our life already, at one of those times when we sensed God's presence in a very real way or when we just knew what we had to do in a difficult situation despite the confusion all around us.

During the Last Supper, Jesus told his apostles they would get "another Advocate" (John 14), someone who would help them after he had gone back to his Father. In John 16, this Advocate is called the "Spirit of truth." That same Spirit is with us today, bringing our faith to life and helping us move closer to God.

When we pray, the Spirit leads us through the sometimes dark and strange landscape of our spiritual life to a place where we can see clearly and bask in God's light, just as that trail guide, if we trust and have faith, will lead us out of those deep woods and to our destination. So when we pray, we direct our prayers toward God, praying in union with Jesus and always seeking direction from the Spirit.

Prayer Aids

Despite the fact that we have the Holy Spirit to guide us, it's nice to have some concrete prayer aids to help us set a course and stick with our plan. That doesn't mean we have to sign up for classes or join a prayer group, although those may be things to consider at some point. We can find basic prayer aids right where we are at this moment.

wisdom for the journey

It is not possible, I say not possible, ever to exhaust the mind of the Scriptures. It is a well which has no bottom.

—St. John Chrysostom, fourth-century bishop and early Church Father

Starting with Scripture

The Word of God is always a good place to start when it's time to pray, so having a Bible on hand is critical. We may decide to start each day with a short Scripture reading, or maybe we'd like to read the next Sunday's Gospel and pray on that throughout the week in preparation for Sunday Mass.

Or maybe we just open the Bible to a random page and see what it has to say to us that day.

Whether we read the Old Testament, focus on a familiar Psalm, or turn to a favorite teaching of Jesus from the New Testament, we can't go wrong if we're using the Bible as a prayer guide. (I talk about using Scripture to pray in much more detail in Chapter 8.)

Creating a Sacred Space

When we think of prayer, many of us, especially Catholics, probably conjure up an image of a quiet church with sunlight streaming through stained-glass windows or candles flickering in the darkness. Although you absolutely do not have to be in a church to pray, it helps your prayer life if you can set aside a place specifically for prayer and fill it with elements of the sacred. You don't need a big space. A corner of a bedroom or living room will do. But creating a "prayer space" or "sacred space" within your home gives you a place where you can retreat to.

My own prayer space consists of two shelves of a bookcase, but when I take out a little footstool I've renamed my "prayer bench" and place it in front of my prayer space, the world melts away. It doesn't matter that this space is bookended by a treadmill and a foosball table. It's my space, and it's filled with religious articles family and friends have given to me, along with spiritual books and other items that put me in a prayerful state of mind.

A Catholic prayer space has as its focal point a cross, a reminder of Jesus' suffering and resurrection. You can have a Bible there, perhaps Rosary beads if that's something you like to pray, and maybe a statue or image of Mary or a favorite saint. But you don't have to stick to purely religious elements. You can include anything that brings you peace: a delicate seashell you picked up at the beach, a plant that brings a piece of God's creation inside, or a photo of someone who has died but who's never far from your thoughts and prayers.

prayer practice

It's good to let everyone in your home know why your sacred space is special and that when you're there, quietly reading, listening to sacred music, or sitting with your eyes closed, you are not to be disturbed with questions about what's for dinner or anything else. This is your space, your place, and your time to connect with God.

If you enjoy the outdoors, you can even take your prayer space outside. You can set a chair or bench in a quiet spot that gives you room to breathe deep and enter into God's presence. You can take a walk down a nature trail, praying as you go. Or you can create a garden with prayer in mind. "Mary gardens" are a beautiful way to combine nature and prayer. I have a small Mary garden in my own backyard, with a statue of Our Lady of Guadalupe at its center and plants linked to Mary's name all around it. Marigolds, or "Mary's gold," are one flower you can plant, but the options are endless when it comes to prayer gardens. (Check Appendix C for more information.)

And for those times when you're away from home, you can create a portable sacred space. A Bible; small cross, icon, or statue; and a little battery-powered candle are all you need to create a prayer space that goes wherever you go—vacation, business trips, retreats, etc.

Candles, Incense, Holy Water, and More

What Catholic prayer space would be complete without candles, incense, and other sacramentals that help give you a taste of heaven on earth? We Catholics are known for our love of statues, stained glass, incense, and holy water. To people from other Christian traditions, these might seem superfluous or, worse, maybe even superstitious. But we know they're not. They're aids to prayer—reminders of holy people, of God, and of all things sacred—that can give us a little boost toward heaven when we need it.

Misc.

Beware of Superstitions

Superstition has no place in prayer. Sacramentals and other such things are not meant to ward off evil. They're meant to remind us of Jesus Christ and encourage us on our journey toward God. They're nice, even beautiful, but they do not take the place of the sacraments or of prayer. They are add-ons.

We use candles in church and in our private prayer spaces because they symbolize Jesus Christ, who is the "light of the world." (John 8:12) Candles remind us of God's presence among us today. When we light a candle in church, we see it as a physical sign of the prayer we've offered to God.

Incense is also symbolic of prayer. Although it's used most often at Mass, it's not uncommon to find Catholics burning incense in private prayer spaces. When we light incense, the perfumed smoke rises and swirls toward the sky, just as we hope our prayers rise up to God in heaven. In Psalm 141, we read: "Lord, I call to you; come quickly to help me; listen to my plea when I call. Let my prayer be incense before you …."

Holy water is perhaps the most common sacramental. Blessed by a priest or deacon, this water is a reminder of our baptism. We bless ourselves with holy water as we enter a church not only to remind us of our baptism but also as a way to signify that we are leaving behind the secular world and entering into the sacred.

You might want to add a dish of holy water to your prayer space so you can bless yourself at the beginning of prayer, or even at your front door so you can bless yourself as you go out for the day.

Statues and stained-glass windows are standard in most Catholic churches. But no matter how beautiful or bountiful the statues and stained glass may be, for Catholics there's no image more important than that of Jesus Christ. So why all the images of saints and angels and Mary? Because these heavenly friends help draw us closer to Jesus. We can look at their lives as examples of faith. It's sort of like looking at a big picture album of our Catholic family. We can glance up at our spiritual relatives and, by seeing where they've been, get a better handle on where we're going.

Those are just a few common *sacramentals.* We use many others at home or in church, and I discuss them as they come up throughout this book.

Definition

A **sacramental** is a prayer or object that makes you more open to God's grace. It is not an "instrument of grace," as a sacrament is, but rather a "sacred sign." Holy water, the Sign of the Cross, religious medals, and prayers of blessing are all examples of sacramentals.

Stained-glass windows help believers move deeper into the story of their faith—through depictions of Jesus' life and through the lives of Mary and the saints.
Photo courtesy of Mary DeTurris Poust

Living to the Rhythm of Prayer

With all this talk of sacred spaces and sacramentals, it would be easy to think prayer is something that has to be reserved for church or for one little corner of our home at only certain times of the day or week. Nothing could be further from the truth! Our prayer life and our active life are not opposing forces competing for our time and attention. Prayer can actually give a spiritual rhythm to our days if we see it as something that complements our busy lives rather than something that exists only in that quiet sacred space when we stop and be in that moment.

Prayer is something we can weave into daily life—an idea I'll address throughout this book and in detail in Chapter 23. The best way to start is to begin our day with a prayer. It doesn't have to be a long prayer or even an "official" prayer or Scripture reading. It can be as simple as thanking God for the new day as we open our eyes and asking him to be with us as we go about whatever we'll confront in the hours ahead. We could put a prayer on our nightstand or tape one to the bathroom mirror as a daily reminder. By starting every morning with prayer (see Chapter 6 for specific prayers), we can set the tone for our day.

As we become more adept at prayer, we'll find easy ways to say brief prayers here and there throughout our day to help us stay in sync with God. We can look for unexpected opportunities for prayer, even if it's just a whispered one-line prayer as we wait at the bank's drive-thru window.

And we can find other ways to work prayer into our days, perhaps by listening to a Catholic or Christian radio station or by loading our MP3 player with favorite sacred music. When we get to Chapter 7 and discuss the Liturgy of the Hours, we'll see how monks of old and many Catholics of today mark the hours of every day with regular prayer.

Any time we stop for a moment to send up a message to God is prayer. The beauty of prayer is that it doesn't need to be contained to a certain time or place. It can spill over into the details of our days until our entire life becomes a prayer.

wisdom for the journey

Prayer pervades every aspect of our lives. It is the unceasing recognition that God is wherever we are, always inviting us to come closer and celebrate the divine gift of being alive.

—Henri J. M. Nouwen, twentieth-century priest and spiritual writer

Essential Takeaways

- God is kind and merciful, calling to us and waiting for us to come to him in prayer.
- The Holy Spirit guides us along our prayer path and breathes life into our spiritual journey.
- We can find concrete prayer aids in Scripture, sacred spaces, and sacramentals.
- Prayer does not have to be separate from our active life but can, instead, give a spiritual rhythm to our days.

chapter 3

Unlimited Prayer Options

Praying in community and praying alone

The beauty of both vocal and silent prayer

Developing a daily prayer routine

Getting past the distractions

When it comes to Catholic prayer, there really is something for everyone. Whether you're an introvert or extrovert, champion talker or earnest listener, music lover or nature enthusiast, there's a prayer style to suit your personality, needs, and schedule.

Some of us find it easier to pray when we're in church, as part of a larger group speaking out loud as one. Others of us would rather find a secluded spot in a garden where we can talk to God surrounded by the wonder of his creation. And still others might find prayer most powerful when it's sung.

Catholic prayer offers all those options and more, although it's really recommended that prayer life be a blend of all styles. Even if you really love to pray all alone in your sacred space at home, God calls us to join our prayers with the prayers of others on a somewhat regular basis, at least every week at Sunday Mass.

So how can you find the right mix? It's good to try different prayer styles and see what feels right. If one method doesn't feel right today, you can come back and try it again at some other point. Just as one style of clothes wouldn't suit you for an entire lifetime, one style of prayer isn't likely to satisfy you year after year.

You've already opened yourself to God's invitation to pray. Now all you need to do is follow where the Spirit leads. Prayer is a wonderful journey, with lots of twists and bends along the way. You never know what you're going to find when you turn the next spiritual corner. If you're willing and eager to meet God in a variety of places and ways and times, you're halfway there.

Communal Versus Private Prayer

Prayer is something highly personal, no doubt about it. When you go to God in prayer, it's often with worries or questions you hold deep in your heart, things you wouldn't want to share with another soul. It would be easy to fall into the trap of thinking that because prayer is personal, it must remain strictly private.

Yes, private prayer is critical. We see that by looking at the prayer life of Jesus—his time praying alone in the desert, his prayers in the Garden of Gethsemane before his crucifixion, even his prayers on the cross. But Jesus also taught us that it's equally important to gather with others and pray together, putting our collective needs before God, praising him as a community, and finding spiritual strength in our common bonds. The key is to find a balance between the two styles of prayer.

wisdom for the journey

Private prayer is like straw scattered here and there: If you set it on fire it makes a lot of little flames. But gather these straws into a bundle and light them, and you get a mighty fire, rising like a column into the sky; public prayer is like that.

—Saint John Vianney, nineteenth-century French priest known as the *Curé d'Ars*

A Closer Look at Communal Prayer

In the Acts of the Apostles, we get a glimpse of the earliest Christian communities and how communal life and prayer life were fully integrated:

> They devoted themselves to the teaching of the apostles and to the communal life, to the breaking of the bread and to the prayers. … All who believed were together and had all things in common; they would sell their property and possessions and divide them among all according to each one's need. Every day they devoted themselves to meeting together in the temple area and to breaking the bread in their homes. (Acts 2:42–46)

Obviously the Catholic Church of today is much bigger than in those early days. We cannot all live together and share everything, but we can try to apply those ideals to our lives as they are right now. How can we do that? By making communal prayer part of our faith lives. We can go to Mass on Sundays and during the week. We can attend prayer services or Scripture groups. We can gather for Morning Prayer or pray the Rosary together. Even within the category of communal prayer, endless options are available.

The Mass as Communal Prayer

Catholic communal prayer centers on the Mass, which is the high point of prayer. Mass brings together Catholics from all walks of life and allows us to join our prayers day after day, year after year, in a celebration focused on Jesus in the Eucharist. The beauty of the Catholic Mass is that when a community of believers, say, in New York, is praying together at Mass, other communities of believers all over the United States and around the world are saying the exact same prayers. The languages and cultures may vary, but the prayers are identical and the Scripture readings the same, making communal Catholic prayer something that has a worldwide reach.

I have been at Masses where I didn't speak the language but knew what everyone was saying anyway. It's a powerful experience to sit in a church and hear words rushing by and know them in your heart even if you don't understand them in your head. For me, that's a perfect example of why communal prayer is so critical. It binds us together, gives us a common starting point, and leads us down the same path and toward the same goal. (I discuss the Mass and all of its parts in full detail in Part 4.)

Prayer Practice

If you're not familiar with a particular kind of communal prayer—a novena, for example—you might be nervous about venturing into a church to give it a try. You just have to remember that Catholics who gather at church to pray are thrilled to have new people join them. You can quietly observe the first time you join or until you get the hang of it. Your presence alone will be appreciated.

Communal prayer is not limited to the Mass. We can choose to pray together on a daily basis through a variety of liturgical prayers and popular devotions offered at Catholic parishes. Stop in at any given church on any given day, and you might find people praying the Rosary or the Stations of the Cross, novenas or the Liturgy of the Hours (all things we'll get to in later chapters).

A Closer Look at Private Prayer

Although it's vitally important to be part of a prayer community, it's also important to have a little one-on-one time with God every day. Some days you might have time for a good, long chat with God or maybe a particular devotion. At other times, your prayer may be as short and sweet as a hurried "thank you" uttered as you dress for work or make breakfast.

Private prayer is an important touchstone in the life of a Catholic. It's a way for you to be in constant contact with God. Over time, prayer can become the first thing you turn to when you are happy, sad, worried, or grateful. Your very life can become a prayer.

To Speak or Not to Speak?

Often when we think of prayer, we think of words. Maybe they're the words of a prayer we learned when we were young. Maybe they're the words to a religious song that speaks to us. Maybe they're the words to a favorite Scripture verse that always brings us back to our spiritual center. All those things are good and beneficial to our prayer lives.

Finding Your Voice in Vocal Prayer

"Vocal" prayer can give us the words we need to begin to make a connection with God. So often, especially when we're in the early stages of developing a prayer life, we may find ourselves speechless, wondering what exactly we're supposed to say to God. By using written prayers we know by heart or can read from a book, we have the words at our fingertips. And those words—beautiful words composed by saints or taken from Scripture—help lift our hearts and minds to God, either alone or in community.

Seeking God in the Silence

But sometimes we need to put aside our desire to be the ones doing all the talking. Prayer should sometimes mean an absence of words. In silent prayer, our hearts can speak to God without us ever uttering a sound. In silent prayer, our hearts can listen for the whisper of God's Spirit.

In the Old Testament First Book of Kings, we find the prophet Elijah on a mountain, waiting for the Lord to pass by. After expecting God in wind, earthquake, and fire, Elijah finally recognizes the Lord in "a tiny whispering sound." (1 Kings 19:12–13)

By praying in silence, waiting like Elijah for the Lord to make himself known, we can be ready for the tiny whisper of God in our own lives. Of course, when I talk about God whispering to us, I'm not talking about an actual voice. I'm talking about a message we feel deep in our hearts, something that moves us or inspires us or soothes us, something that is clearly God at work in our lives.

Recognizing God's Hand at Work

When I was younger, I used to think I'd missed out on something big because God had never made himself known to me in some dramatic way. I wondered if perhaps my faith wasn't true enough because I hadn't experienced the spiritual equivalent of a lightning bolt. But over time, I've come to realize that God has, in fact, made his presence known to me through the small, brilliant flashes of light all along my life's journey, from the day I held my mother's hand as she took her last breath, to the moments when I gave birth to my three children, to the seemingly less-significant events that were touched by God in a special way and only recognizable in hindsight.

Prayer Practice

Reflect on your life for a few minutes and see if you can spot moments when you felt God's touch in a palpable way. What did it feel like? Did you know it at the time or only recognize it days, months, or years later? Oftentimes God's presence is hard to recognize in the moment because we may be in crisis or caught up in joy. It's when we reflect that we see his hand at work.

By praying through a combination of speaking and listening, we open a real give-and-take with God and begin to notice his presence in our lives more easily. We stop going to him with a laundry list of things we want or need and start seeing him as someone who wants a real relationship with us, a relationship based on trust and communication and deep love. Prayer paves the way for that deeper relationship.

Praying Through Song

Music can be a powerful instrument in prayer life. Even if you're not particularly musical, music has probably played a role in your life at some point, almost like a personal soundtrack. You probably have favorite songs that remind you of certain events in your life or particular lyrics that feel like they were written just for you. Sacred music can do the same for your spiritual life. Whether it's the haunting sound of monks chanting in Latin, a pipe organ playing a classic church hymn, or a guitar strumming a folk song, sacred music is one more stepping-stone on the pathway of prayer.

St. Augustine is credited with saying, "He who sings prays twice." This is a poetic way of reminding us that singing our prayers to God is a special part of our spiritual lives. At most Sunday Masses and even some daily Masses, music is a critical element of the liturgy, giving us a way to join our voices in praising God. Depending on the season, music can evoke strong spiritual feelings, from the anticipation of Advent, to the sorrow of Lent, to the joy of Easter. (I talk more specifically about singing together at Mass in Chapter 15.)

What about using music in private prayer? It's not necessary, but it certainly is helpful. Music can be a valuable companion when you settle down to pray or when you're on the go and want to make a "chore" more prayerful. You can pop some sacred music into your car's CD player or load up your MP3 player with a spiritual podcast or album and then walk or drive or clean bathrooms while focusing your attention on God. That doesn't mean you don't also stop for "real" prayer that day; just consider this a bonus. Time you'd otherwise use listening to morning radio or thinking about work becomes one more opportunity to bring God into your life and your world.

And of course, when you do sit down in your sacred space to pray, you can play sacred music to add to the atmosphere. Whether it provides background music to put you in the right mind-set or is part of your actual prayer, sacred music can add another layer to your ongoing conversation with God.

wisdom for the journey

Let the word of Christ dwell in you richly; teach and admonish one another in all wisdom; and with gratitude in your hearts sing psalms, hymns, and spiritual songs to God.

—Colossians 3:16

Developing a Prayer Routine

How do you take all the different styles and methods of prayer and turn them into a regular routine? Start small. If you expect to sit in silence for 30 minutes the very first time you pray, you might get discouraged. The best way to reach God is by taking baby steps. Even the smallest effort can add up to huge gains when it comes to your spiritual life.

Start Small

It works best if prayer is not something you leave to chance, thinking you'll fit it in at some point during the day when you have downtime. Chances are, the downtime will never be there. Like an exercise plan, if you don't commit to something specific, even make an "appointment" for it, it's too easy to skip.

Look at your schedule and find a small block of doable time. If you're an early riser, you can set aside five minutes for prayer each morning. If you're a night owl, you can make the time just before bed. If your schedule and location allow you to stop at a church on the way to or from work or during lunch, you can add that into your schedule. Perhaps you can get to one daily Mass each week, or maybe you can manage Evening Prayer at the end of the workday.

Don't Overschedule

You can't plan too much right off the bat because then it's too easy to feel overwhelmed and give up on the whole thing. Just about everyone can find 5 minutes in a 24-hour day for prayer. Even that much time will make a difference, and you're likely to find that the more you pray, the more you want to pray. You can begin to extend your prayer time as you get more used to your routine or find what works best for your schedule.

I'm always ready with an excuse when it comes time to pray. I have too much work. I should play with the kids. I haven't folded the laundry. Prayer often seems like something selfish, something I should do only when every other responsibility is handled. But the truth is, there's always something else on my to-do list. So if I want to have a meaningful prayer life, I need to realize that putting prayer first is not selfish. In fact, it's the most unselfish thing I can do because when I pray, I'm more patient and less stressed. When I'm in tune with God, I'm in tune with life.

wisdom for the journey

Never be in a hurry; do everything quietly and in a calm spirit. Do not lose your inner peace for anything whatsoever, even if your whole world seems upset.

—St. Francis de Sales, seventeenth-century bishop and spiritual writer

Distractions Are Normal

One of the most likely "side effects" you'll experience during prayer is a constant parade of distractions. I'm not just talking about telephones, e-mail, or other people. I'm talking about those internal distractions that start racing through your mind every time you sit down to pray. They're not always easy to deal with, but they are absolutely normal, so don't get discouraged.

When you first start spending time in prayer—especially silent prayer—you're likely to find that your mind comes up with an endless array of thoughts and worries. They flash by like someone switching channels on a TV. You remember something you should have done last week. You visualize someone you wronged 20 years ago. You think about the vacation you have planned and how you haven't packed yet. It's amazing how many things you'll think about during prayer that have nothing to do with God.

It's okay, though. It's all part of the process. The Buddhists call this problem "monkey mind." The thoughts are like monkeys jumping from tree to tree and giving you no peace. You just have to try to let the thoughts go. You can't let the distractions frustrate or annoy you, or take you away from the task at hand—connecting with God. You just have to watch the thoughts come and go, like a leaf floating on the surface of a river. It's there. It's gone. Along comes another leaf.

So far we've covered the basic background to beginning a life of prayer. In the chapters to come, we focus on specific Catholic prayers and how to weave them into everyday life, from liturgical prayers and popular devotions to the Mass, ancient traditions, and more.

wisdom for the journey

Pray inwardly, even if you do not enjoy it. It does good, though you feel nothing; yes, even though you think you are doing nothing.

—Julian of Norwich, fourteenth-century mystic

Essential Takeaways

- Your prayer life should be a blend of private prayer and communal prayer, silent prayer and spoken prayer.
- Music can be a pathway to deeper prayer, whether that's singing at Mass, music played as background to create a prayerful atmosphere at home, or music played as the focus of a reflection.
- Start small with a prayer routine, knowing that even little efforts add up to big spiritual gains.
- Don't be scared off by internal distractions. They're normal. Just let them float by as you continue to pray.

Part 2

The Way to God

Making a decision to commit to regular prayer is the first step on the pathway to a deeper relationship with God. But it helps if you have some specific guidelines and initial instructions to give you a starting point and keep you moving in the right direction.

Catholics have some prayers that are so basic to prayer life they're considered essentials. I'm talking about those like the Our Father, Hail Mary, and Glory Be. Once you move beyond these basics, however, there's a whole world of prayer styles and specific devotions to explore and experience.

Prayer can be as varied or as simple as you want it to be. If you're comfortable saying familiar prayers in the morning and evening, if that's what centers you and connects you to God, then that's a perfectly fine routine. If you want to broaden your prayer possibilities, you can venture into more diverse styles such as meditation or sacred reading.

In Part 2, I cover the Catholic essentials, including family prayer, which allows us to center our home life on God. We also explore an array of other important options that can take our prayer life to the next level: Eucharistic adoration, the Liturgy of the Hours, sacred reading, meditation, and contemplation.

chapter 4

The Cornerstones of Catholic Prayer

- A closer look at basic Catholic prayers
- Making the Sign of the Cross
- Praying the Our Father and Hail Mary
- Understanding and praying the Apostles' Creed
- How and why to say the Act of Contrition

Certain Catholic prayers are so ingrained in our hearts and minds that saying them is as familiar as saying our own name or as breathing. These are the prayers we learn as very young children, before we're old enough even to understand the significance of prayer in our lives, before we learn how to read, before we know our right from our left.

And these essentials—things like the Sign of the Cross, Our Father, and Hail Mary—stay with us for the rest of our lives. Even those raised Catholic but no longer practicing the faith have probably found themselves, on occasion, slipping into the comfortable rhythm of a classic Catholic prayer during a time of crisis. We hit some nasty turbulence during a flight or have a near miss as we're driving down the highway, and suddenly from out of nowhere, the words of the Hail Mary roll off our tongue.

No matter how far a Catholic progresses down the pathway of prayer, these essentials remain at the fore. They serve as a sturdy foundation, providing sure footing as we begin to climb to new spiritual heights. These are the prayers we fall back on when we want to talk to God but aren't sure what to say. These are the words we whisper when we want to enter into deeper prayer and need something familiar to prepare our souls for new spiritual territory. These are the words that give voice to our most basic Catholic beliefs.

The danger is that these prayers are so familiar, we can take them for granted. We've heard them or said them so many times we might not even focus on the meaning of the words anymore. In this chapter, we reflect on these essentials one by one, looking at each prayer's role in leading us closer to God.

In the Name of the Father

The Sign of the Cross is the most basic of the essential Catholic prayers. With these words, we sum up the central belief of our faith, that God is three in one—Father, Son, and Spirit.

Sign of the Cross

In the name of the Father,
and of the Son,
and of the Holy Spirit.

Amen.

This short prayer filled with deep theology marks the beginning and end of every Catholic prayer. It's also the first prayer most Catholics learn as children. It's so basic and so common, it's often overlooked as a prayer in its own right, but it is absolutely a stand-alone prayer.

Making the Sign of the Cross

The Sign of the Cross is accompanied by the following hand gestures:

1. We take our right hand and put it to our forehead when we say "In the name of the Father."
2. Then we move our hand to our heart when we say "and of the Son."

3. Our hand goes to our left shoulder and then right shoulder while saying "and of the Holy Spirit." (With these moves, we make a cross over our body.)
4. Our hands come together in prayer position when we say "Amen," which is a Hebrew word meaning "So be it."

It's not uncommon to see Catholics make the Sign of the Cross—or bless ourselves—when we are preparing to travel, are facing a major challenge, hear news of a terrible tragedy, or walk into a church. We've all probably seen more than one major league baseball player bless himself as he stepped up to the plate. That simple gesture, even when unaccompanied by any other words, is a powerful prayer by itself and a clear sign a person is Catholic.

wisdom for the journey

We make the Sign of the Cross before prayer in order to recollect and compose ourselves spiritually, and to focus our thoughts, heart and will upon God. We make it after prayer so that God's gifts might remain in us.

—Romano Guardini, twentieth-century priest and author

Glory Be to the Father

Another brief prayer centered on the Trinity but in a slightly expanded version is the Glory Be.

Glory Be

Glory be to the Father,
and to the Son,
and to the Holy Spirit,
as it was in the beginning,
is now and ever shall be,
world without end.

Amen.

This short prayer of praise is also said at the end of each decade of the Rosary (which we look at in detail in Chapter 10).

The Glory Be is also prayed—in a slightly modified form—during each of the hours of the Divine Office, or the Liturgy of the Hours (which we explore in detail in Chapter 7). When it is prayed as part of the Divine Office, this is how the Glory Be is said:

> Glory be to the Father,
> and to the Son,
> and to the Holy Spirit,
> as it was in the beginning,
> is now and will be forever.
>
> Amen.

Although we don't know the author of the Glory Be or exactly when it became part of regular Catholic prayer practice, its origin—and Trinitarian theology—can be traced back to Scripture:

> Go, therefore, and make disciples of all nations, baptizing them in the name of the Father, and of the Son, and of the Holy Spirit. (Matthew 28:19)

It is generally assumed that this prayer as we know it today, also known as the "minor doxology" or the Gloria Patri, was part of Catholic liturgy by about the sixth century.

Lord, Teach Us to Pray

In Catholic life—in all Christian life, in fact—no prayer is considered more perfect than the Our Father, or the Lord's Prayer, as it's sometimes known.

> **Our Father (Lord's Prayer)**
>
> Our Father, who art in heaven,
> hallowed be thy name;
> thy kingdom come;
> thy will be done
> on earth as it is in heaven.
> Give us this day our daily bread,
> and forgive us our trespasses,
> as we forgive those who trespass against us;

and lead us not into temptation,
but deliver us from evil.

Amen.

When we speak these words, we repeat what Jesus taught his own disciples when they asked, "Lord, teach us to pray." (Luke 11:1) Even Jesus' disciples had trouble figuring out how to pray! So when we find ourselves struggling with prayer, as we undoubtedly will from time to time, it's good to remember that even the people who had the benefit of hearing and seeing Jesus face to face needed ongoing direction. Like those first disciples, we can return to the words of the Our Father whenever our own words fail us.

This staple says so much in so few lines. And although the words might vary slightly from one Christian denomination to another, the meaning remains the same, making this the central prayer of all Christianity.

A Closer Look at the Our Father

In the words of the Our Father, we get what amounts to a summary of all the Gospel teachings. We pray about our God, about following God's will, about spiritual nourishment, about feeding others, about forgiveness, and about the evil that tempts us away from God.

For Catholics, this prayer is integral not only to our private prayer lives but to our communal prayer as well. It's part of the sacraments, the Liturgy of the Hours, and every Mass. Because this prayer is so critical to our lives as Catholics, let's examine it line by line:

Our Father, who art in heaven When we pray as Jesus taught us, we pray to a God who is approachable and beloved; someone we can call by name. He is "our" Father, Abba, not a distant God.

The rest of this prayer includes petitions, where we first adore God and then ask him to help us face the challenges of our own spiritual lives.

Hallowed be thy name This line is our recognition of God's holiness above all else and a prayer of petition that God's name and God himself be revered and accepted by all.

Definition

Hallowed is simply an old English word for "holy." When we say any prayer, we need to put our words into the right framework. By naming God as holy, we enter into this prayer with our focus clearly on God the Father.

Thy kingdom come Our prayer life is meant to lead us toward heaven, toward God's kingdom. This line acknowledges our desire to reach that eternal kingdom but also our challenge to bring God's kingdom into our daily lives through our thoughts, words, and actions.

Thy will be done on Earth as it is in heaven In this line, we take a big spiritual leap, telling God we will accept his will in our earthly lives, even if we don't necessarily like it. In this short line, we display our total trust in God.

Give us this day our daily bread When we say this line, we may reflexively think of actual food that keeps us alive physically, and that is part of the message. But the heart of this line is about our need for spiritual nourishment as well, the bread that will feed us for all eternity, and the fact that we ask for bread for only "this day," not worrying about tomorrow. The Catechism of the Catholic Church explains that this line also addresses our need to provide for our neighbors' nourishment, which is why we say "our bread" and not "my bread."

Misc.

Catechism of the Catholic Church

All the core teachings of the Catholic faith are contained in one large volume known as *The Catechism of the Catholic Church.* It's a "universal" catechism, meaning it guides the worldwide Church, no matter what language you speak or what country you live in. It takes every Catholic teaching and puts it into context, with references from Scripture, tradition, and numerous Church documents to back it up.

And forgive us our trespasses, as we forgive those who trespass against us Here we ask God for his forgiveness for what we've done wrong, but we go a step further. We tie the forgiveness of our own sins to our willingness to forgive those people who have hurt us through their sins.

And lead us not into temptation This seems like an odd line on the surface. Why would God lead us into temptation? Actually, in Matthew 6:13, the line reads: "and do not subject us to the final test." So any awkwardness is purely in the translation. We're asking God to give us the strength to avoid temptation, but if temptation should find us anyway, to please help us turn away from it. Each of us, over the course of our life, will face difficult and defining moments. This line is a plea that God will keep us from succumbing not only to the individual temptations that creep up but also to the larger "tests"—hopelessness, despair, loss of faith.

But deliver us from evil In this final line of the Our Father, the "evil" refers to Satan. This isn't a petition for help against any old evil but the Evil One and the wickedness that accompanies him.

MISC.

The Final Doxology

For Catholics, the Our Father ends with the line "deliver us from evil." During Mass, however, the priest will say a prayer to expand on that line. The people then say the final doxology: "For the kingdom, the power, and the glory are yours now and forever." (Protestants recite a version of the doxology as part of the Our Father, immediately following "deliver us from evil.")

The Essential Prayer

For Catholics young and old, the Our Father is like a signature, one of those things we say together almost every time we pray as a community, not only at Mass but to start or end meetings or classes or any other event where we might be.

During the elementary-level faith formation class I teach, my students and I stand together around our prayer table to say the Our Father to start our class and the Hail Mary to end it. We've tried other types of prayer—silent prayer, the Rosary, Stations of the Cross—but the essentials remain the things we return to again and again.

In the Arms of Mary

Mary, the Mother of God, has a special place in Catholic prayer life, so much so that non-Catholics often confuse our devotion with worship. But we don't worship Mary; we honor her, love her, and pray to her. Mary is a mother to all of us. We turn to her in prayer the way we turn to our earthly mothers when we need advice or comfort or someone to listen to our worries. For Catholics, Mary is that ever-present mother, always ready to enfold us in her arms and listen.

And Mary deserves that place of prominence in our prayer lives because of her critical role in the redemption of the world. She gave birth to the Son of God. Without her "yes" to God's ultimate call, her *fiat,* God would not have entered the world in the person of Jesus Christ. Mary's very life is a model of what we aspire to—total trust in and openness to God and his plan.

Hail Mary

Hail Mary, full of grace,
the Lord is with thee.
Blessed art thou among women,
and blessed is the fruit of thy womb, Jesus.
Holy Mary, Mother of God,
pray for us sinners,
now and at the hour of our death.

Amen.

The Ultimate Marian Prayer

The most common and beloved of the many Marian prayers in the Catholic prayer repertoire is the Hail Mary, or the *Ave Maria,* which begins with a version of the greeting the Angel Gabriel spoke when he came to Mary to tell her that God had chosen her to bear his Son: "Hail, favored one! The Lord is with you." (Luke 1:28) The second line echoes the words of Elizabeth, who was pregnant with John the Baptist when her cousin Mary came to visit her: "Most blessed are you among women, and blessed is the fruit of your womb." (Luke 1:42)

In this prayer to Mary, we not only acknowledge that she's "blessed among women," but we also ask her to "pray for us sinners." We don't think Mary can answer our prayers; only God can do that. But we do think Mary can pray on our behalf; the Blessed Mother can go to her own Son and place our needs before him.

Perfection in Prayer?

When I was about 12 years old, my maternal grandfather gave me something that explained how if I could say just one "perfect" Hail Mary, it would be worth more than 100 said thoughtlessly. I would lie in bed at night and try to concentrate on each line, working hard to figure out how to make it "perfect."

Can we ever pray a prayer perfectly? I'm not sure, but I've come to learn that in our desire to be in a place of prayer, our efforts—no matter how humble or distracted—have value, even if our prayer isn't textbook-perfect. When I think of Mary as a gentle mother, waiting to walk with me on my journey or hold me in prayer, I cannot imagine her ever turning away from me because my words did not meet a human definition of "perfection." So we pray the best we can and believe that if we give our best to prayer, that is enough.

wisdom for the journey

The Virgin is the one who continues to listen, always ready to do the Lord's will; she is an example for the believer who lives in search of God.

—Pope Benedict XVI, twenty-first-century pope, theologian, writer

Professing Our Faith

Although the Apostles' Creed is the summation of the Catholic faith in prayer form and a foundational prayer, we don't really say this one very often. Most Catholics are more familiar with the very similar Nicene Creed, the profession of faith typically said at Sunday Mass (see Chapter 16).

I've been at events where even the most stalwart Catholics have had to resort to reading the Apostles' Creed from a book because it's so easy to slip into the natural rhythm of the more familiar Nicene version of this prayer. What's the difference? The two prayers teach the same basic doctrine, but the Apostles' Creed is more ancient and shorter.

Apostles' Creed

I believe in God,
the Father almighty,
Creator of heaven and earth,

and in Jesus Christ, his only Son, our Lord,
who was conceived by the Holy Spirit,
born of the Virgin Mary,
suffered under Pontius Pilate,
was crucified, died and was buried;
he descended into hell;
on the third day he rose again from the dead;
he ascended into heaven,
and is seated at the right hand of God the Father
almighty;
from there he will come to judge the living and
the dead.
I believe in the Holy Spirit,
the holy catholic Church,
the communion of saints,
the forgiveness of sins,
the resurrection of the body,
and life everlasting. Amen.

In the Apostles' Creed, we get a clear outline of the Catholic faith. Line by line, as we say this prayer, we are literally professing the basics of our Catholic belief. The first half of the prayer focuses on God; the second half, on God's works.

When we pray the Apostles' Creed, we profess our belief in the Trinity—God, the "Father Almighty"; Jesus Christ, "his only Son, our Lord"; and the Holy Spirit. Woven into this prayer is the story of Jesus, God incarnate—how he was born, how he suffered and died, how he rose from the dead, and how he will come again.

The second part of the Apostles' Creed focuses on God working among us—through the Spirit, through the Church, through the communion of saints. And it reminds us of the most important things God will do for us if we believe and ask for his mercy and love—forgive us, raise us from the dead, give us eternal life. Saying this prayer is like making our baptismal commitment all over again.

prayer practice

The Apostles' Creed was updated with the new translation of the Mass. The revised prayer is only a slight variation on what we've been used to praying. But with the new Order of the Mass, which will be discussed at length in Part 4, the Apostles' Creed can be used on Sundays during Lent and Easter, finally giving Catholics the chance to say this important prayer with more frequency.

I Am Heartily Sorry

Any time we turn to God and tell him we are truly sorry for something we've done wrong, we are making an act of contrition, even if the words aren't part of an "official" prayer.

The particular words we say when making an act of contrition don't matter as much as our attitude. It's not enough to simply say the words; we have to be sincerely sorry in our hearts with no intention of repeating our mistakes. Of course, we're human, so chances are we will repeat some mistakes. When we go before God to express sorrow for our sins, it must be with a contrite heart.

Acts of Contrition

Many Catholics say the Act of Contrition before bed each night as part of a reflection on how our day measured up before God. We may also perform an Examination of Conscience along with it (see Appendix B). This is a way of taking inventory of our actions and seeing where we may have fallen short of God's expectations.

Traditional Act of Contrition

O my God, I am heartily sorry
for having offended Thee,
and I detest all of my sins
because of thy just punishments,
but most of all because they offend Thee,
my God, who art all good
and deserving of all my love.
I firmly resolve with the help of Thy grace
to sin no more and
to avoid the near occasion of sin.

Amen.

Alternate Act of Contrition

O my God, I am sorry for my sins
with all my heart.
In choosing to wrong
and failing to do good,
I have sinned against you
whom I should love above all things.
I firmly intend, with your help,
to do penance,
to sin no more
and to avoid whatever leads me to sin.

Amen.

Some of us know a slightly different version, or a completely different version of the Act of Contrition. Catholics of different ages speak different languages when it comes to this prayer. That's okay. This isn't about some complicated legalistic formula but about a deep, interior conversion of heart.

Confession

Both the Examination of Conscience and Act of Contrition are also part of the preparation for and reception of the Sacrament of Reconciliation/Penance, also known as confession, when we privately confess our sins to a priest.

In decades past, Catholics might have gone to confession once a week. Catholics today use confession with less frequency, but that doesn't mean there's not a need for or benefit to this often-underused sacrament. Confession wipes the slate of sin clean and allows us to start over. Those who continue to go to confession regularly will attest that this sacrament can provide a great sense of peace, renewal, and hope.

wisdom for the journey

... for in confession you do not only receive absolution for your venial sins, but you also receive great strength to help you in avoiding them henceforth, clearer light to discover your failings, and abundant grace to make up whatever loss you have incurred through those faults. You exercise the graces of humility, obedience, simplicity, and love, and by this one act of confession you practice more virtue than any other.

—St. Frances de Sales, seventeenth-century bishop

To go to confession, we simply begin by doing an Examination of Conscience, either at home or at church while waiting to meet with the priest. We can choose to go to confession kneeling in a confessional or behind a small screen hidden from view, or sitting face to face in a more informal and conversational setting.

Confession starts with the Sign of the Cross. Then we begin by saying these or similar words: "Bless me, father, for I have sinned. It has been [*however long*] since my last confession. These are my sins." We then proceed to tell the priest the serious sins we know in our hearts have hurt God or others. And the priest, under the "seal" of the confessional, is not allowed to share anything we have said with anyone else or to use the information learned for any purpose.

After we're finished confessing our sins, the priest may talk to us about what we've said and offer some counsel. Then he will give us our "penance," which are the prayers we will say or actions we will do to make up for our sins. Penance is not punishment. It's really a way to reorient our lives toward God, to refocus our attention in the right direction. After we're given our penance, the priest may ask us to recite the Act of Contrition. Finally, the priest will give us absolution, at which point he will pray over us and forgive our sins in Jesus' name.

All of confession—the preparation, the actual sacrament, the penance we do later—is important to our prayer life. In confession, our hearts are renewed and our spiritual lives reordered so we can see more clearly the path of prayer before us. The more we go to confession and receive Communion (something we'll look at in the coming chapters), the more we are strengthened to continue to move forward on our journey toward the heart of God.

Essential Takeaways

- Certain prayers, like the Sign of the Cross, Our Father, and Hail Mary, are essential to Catholic prayer life.
- The essential prayers form a foundation for all that's to come and remain part of our prayer life no matter how far we progress on the path.
- Catholic beliefs are summed up in prayer form in the words of the Apostles' Creed.
- Expressing our sorrow to God in prayer is an act of contrition, regardless of what words we say or what form we use. This daily prayer is also an important part of confession.

chapter 5

The Heart of Jesus

- Understanding our relationship with Jesus in prayer
- The power and beauty of Eucharistic devotions
- Praying to the Sacred Heart
- A devotion to the Divine Mercy Jesus offers

If we were to strip away all the niceties that often go hand in hand with prayer—the beautiful churches, the statues and incense, even our own sacred spaces and favorite private devotions—the central piece of our prayer life would remain: Jesus Christ, who is God incarnate, at once fully divine and fully human.

We may find various prayer methods that work for us personally or words that most suit our changing moods, but the reality is that Jesus *is* our path of prayer. He is "the way," the constant in an ever-changing world. And no matter how we choose to venture down that path, he walks with us; leading us to his Father; entering into our hearts, if we let him; and transforming us with his mercy, love, and compassion.

Rather than a distant God who is far away from us and foreign to us, our God lived on Earth as one of us. He experienced the joys and fears, celebrations and heartaches that come with being flesh and blood. Jesus showed us through his words and actions what it means to live our faith, to converse with the Father, to trust that the path God has chosen for us is the only one that matters.

And so we pray with Jesus. We pray *to* Jesus. We pray *through* Jesus. And with every prayer, Jesus draws us closer to him, closer to his Father, and closer to heaven.

Turning Toward the Son

Growing up in a traditional Irish Italian Catholic household, I accepted Jesus as a normal and important part of daily life. It wasn't that we talked about Jesus all the time. We didn't, which made us very much like most other Catholics. We aren't really into spontaneous sharing when it comes to our personal relationship with our Savior. It's just that at our house, we knew Jesus was *supposed* to be at the center of our days, our lives, and so it was an ever-present reality, at least for me.

We went to church on Sundays and holy days and attended parish missions and special devotions. My mother went to church as often as possible, and her father went to Mass every day. We had crucifixes hanging in our bedrooms and a big picture of the Sacred Heart in the family room that seemed to watch us no matter where we moved.

prayer practice

Sometimes you don't have time to step outside your routine to pray, but you might have time for one-line prayers, or aspirations, said on an inhale or an exhale. I remember my grandmother would always say "Jesus, Mary, and Joseph, I love you. Save souls." Even a prayer this short and simple is a powerful thing and can bring God into your day on an almost-constant basis. In Chapter 21, we spend time talking about one of the most famous short prayers, the ancient "Jesus Prayer," so closely identified with the Eastern Church.

Through all the rituals and routines, however, I learned to see Jesus as a friend, someone who would always be there for me, no matter what I did or didn't do. I never saw God as someone to fear, despite the strict religious rules and expectations in our home. He was someone to seek out, someone to follow, someone who came here and died so I might live forever. Even as a child, that registers pretty profoundly on a person.

No matter how we were raised to view God, we Catholics are very much in tune with the fact that our Lord walked on this Earth, that he had a human heart that beat for each one of us, a heart that continues to reach out to us today. Jesus pours out his love and mercy like water in never-ending streams that wash over us and give us new life. Jesus is the heart of our prayer life.

Eucharistic Devotions

Before he suffered and died for us, Jesus left us an everlasting gift. At the Last Supper, he took bread and wine and transformed them into his body and blood, commanding his apostles to continue this practice "in memory of me." Jesus did not just come to Earth, do his work, and then leave us orphans. He gave us himself in the Eucharist, a gift that allows us to unite ourselves with God in the most spiritually intimate way every day, or as often as we can get to Mass.

Catholics recognize early on that the greatest way to make a connection with Jesus is to receive him in the Eucharist or even to simply be present before him in the Eucharist. The Mass, which centers on the celebration of the Eucharist, is the summit of prayer life for Catholics. It's the most common and important way we can honor Jesus in the Eucharist and be nourished for our spiritual journey. (I cover the Eucharist prayer by prayer in Part 4.)

Eucharistic devotions outside Mass also allow us to make the Eucharist, or the Blessed Sacrament, the center of our prayer. Jesus remains present in any consecrated bread, even if it's not consumed at Mass and is kept in a *tabernacle.* This offers us an opportunity to pray in Jesus' presence even when we are not at Mass.

Definition

The **tabernacle,** which is Hebrew for "dwelling place," is a box-type receptacle. usually made of metal, stone, or wood, where the reserved Eucharist is kept in a church. When the Blessed Sacrament is present within the tabernacle, a candle is burning near it so visitors know to show proper reverence.

To many modern Catholics, Eucharistic devotions may seem to be the product of an earlier time. Perhaps we've heard some of the terms but don't really know what they all mean. It's true that these practices were more common in the era before the Second Vatican Council (1963–1965), but they're still practiced at most parishes around the world today. And they still have abundant graces to offer Catholics of any age here in the twenty-first century.

Eucharistic Adoration

When I stop and think about Eucharistic Adoration, I can't help but hear in my head the words of a traditional hymn written in 1854 but sung so often during my own childhood at Eucharistic devotions:

Jesus, My Lord, My God, My All

Jesus, my Lord, my God, my all,
How can I love Thee as I ought?
And how revere this wondrous gift,
So far surpassing hope or thought.
Sweet Sacrament, we Thee adore.
O make us love Thee more and more!
O make us love Thee more and more!

The words of that hymn, even in their old-fashioned prose, spell out how believing Catholics feel as they approach the Eucharist. This is Jesus actually present before us, not a symbol of Jesus, not simply a piece of bread, but *Jesus*. How can we possibly be reverent or worthy enough to receive such a tremendous gift?

Adoration allows us to pray before Jesus in the Eucharist in a special way, to ponder the mystery of God being present there with us. Typically during Adoration, a large host (the bread that has been consecrated at Mass to become Jesus) is put in a special holder called a monstrance and placed on the altar.

Sometimes liturgical services, such as Exposition and Benediction, that include Scripture readings take place; other times hymns and prayers of adoration are said together as a community. Sometimes churches may offer quiet Adoration on a particular day, for example, on the first Friday of every month; through the night, which is known as nocturnal Adoration; or on a 24/7 basis, which is called perpetual Adoration. In these instances, Catholics sign up to sit and keep vigil, staying with the Blessed Sacrament in prayer for a certain amount of time.

wisdom for the journey

God dwells in our midst, in the Blessed Sacrament of the altar.

—St. Maximilian Kolbe, twentieth-century priest and martyr killed by the Nazis at Auschwitz

Holy Hours

The idea of spending a "holy hour" before the Blessed Sacrament has its roots in Scripture. After the Last Supper, Jesus went to the Garden of Gethsemane, asking some of his disciples to sit with him while he prayed. "Remain here and stay awake," he said. (Mark 14:34) When Jesus came back from praying, he found his disciples asleep and said: "You could not stay awake for even an hour?" (Mark 14:37) And so in parishes today, Catholics continue to sit with Jesus and remain awake—spiritually and physically—for an hour.

We might make a holy hour in a group during a specified time of Adoration, or we might simply make a solitary vigil in front of the tabernacle. What do we do while sitting before the Blessed Sacrament for an hour? We pray. Just how we do so, however, can vary. We might pray without words, simply sitting before Jesus and letting his presence fill our hearts and souls. We might read a Scripture reflection and meditate on that. We might say the Rosary or the Liturgy of the Hours. We might say prayers specifically written to be prayed before the Blessed Sacrament.

Prayer Before the Blessed Sacrament

Here,
O good and gentle Jesus,
I kneel before you,
and with all the fervor of my soul
I pray that you engrave within my heart
lively sentiments of faith, hope, and love,
true repentance for my sins,
and a firm purpose of amendment.
While I see and I ponder your five wounds
with great affection and sorrow in my soul,
I have before my eyes those words of yours
that David prophesied about you:

"They have pierced my hands and feet;
I can count all my bones." (Psalms 22:17)

Amen.

Making a Visit

Perhaps we don't have time to make holy hours on a regular basis but we like the idea of praying before Jesus in the Blessed Sacrament. In that case, we can "make a visit," which means we stop in at a church and pray before the Blessed Sacrament, even if it's only for 5 or 10 minutes.

With my busy work schedule and home life, I typically can't do a holy hour, but I am often at my parish church for meetings or faith formation classes or waiting to pick up my son from Catholic school. Every once in a while, I will stop in the chapel and head to the kneelers placed before the tabernacle. Sometimes I just sit before God. Other times I pick up one of the prayer books left there for visitors and read something to start me thinking and praying. And still other times I have my 5-year-old daughter with me and spend most of my visit trying to explain how Jesus could be inside the gold box with the candle next to it. Already she knows that the lighted candle means Jesus is there. And that—combined with attendance at Mass and lessons from home—is how Catholics grow up understanding that the Eucharist is the most important part of anything we do at church.

wisdom for the journey

The Holy Hour becomes like an oxygen tank to revive the breath of the Holy Spirit in the midst of the foul and fetid atmosphere of the world.

—Servant of God Archbishop Fulton J. Sheen,
twentieth-century bishop and preacher

Devotion to the Sacred Heart

The image of the Sacred Heart can be off-putting. We see a gentle-faced Jesus with his human heart exposed, surrounded by a crown of thorns. A bright fire burns above it, and light emanates from around it, with a cross at the top.

Even the most devout Catholics may not get what this image or devotion is about. Are we praying to a heart? Not at all. The image of Jesus' physical heart is intended as a symbolic reminder of his divine love for us. The wound and thorns remind us of his suffering and death. The fire represents the power of his love to transform us.

Like so many things in the Catholic faith, this image is meant as a visual aid to our prayer life, to help our human minds come to terms with our redeemer's infinite love and mercy.

Praying to the Sacred Heart

Early devotion to the divine love of Jesus as represented by his heart began back in monastic communities in the eleventh and twelfth centuries, but it wasn't until the second half of the seventeenth century that we got a popular devotion to the Sacred Heart of Jesus.

At that time, St. Margaret Mary Alacoque, a French Visitation nun, is said to have had a series of visions in which Jesus revealed the importance of devotion to his Sacred Heart, which represents the all-encompassing love he has for all humanity. This devotion was once so popular that Catholics *consecrated* their families to the Sacred Heart and hung large framed pictures of Jesus and his Sacred Heart in their living rooms.

Definition

Consecrate and **consecration** can have different meanings in the Catholic faith. Most Catholics first associate these words with the Eucharist. During Mass, when the priest prays over the bread and wine to make it the body and blood of Jesus, it's called the *consecration.* However, people can also *consecrate* themselves to something, meaning they devote or dedicate themselves to some particular purpose.

Today, although not as common throughout the mainstream Church in general, this devotion still has a large following. It includes numerous prayers—consecrations, litanies, novenas, and more. (Check Appendix C for links to websites with prayers.) The month of June is a time of special devotion to the Sacred Heart and includes the Feast of the Sacred Heart, which falls 19 days after Pentecost, always on a Friday in June. There's also a Mass of the Sacred Heart, which can be celebrated throughout the year.

Novena to the Sacred Heart

O my Jesus, you have said: "Truly I say to you, ask and it will be given you, seek and you will find, knock and it will be opened to you." Behold, I knock, I seek and ask for the grace of *(mention your special intention here).*

Recite an Our Father, Hail Mary, Glory Be.

Sacred Heart of Jesus I place all my trust in you.

O my Jesus, you have said: "Truly I say to you, if you ask anything of the Father in my name, he will give it to you." Behold, in your name, I ask the Father for the grace of *(mention your special intention here).*

Recite an Our Father, Hail Mary, Glory Be.

Sacred Heart of Jesus I place all my trust in you.

O my Jesus, you have said: "Truly I say to you, heaven and Earth will pass away but my words will not pass away." Encouraged by your infallible words I now ask for the grace of *(mention your special intention here).*

Recite an Our Father, Hail Mary, Glory Be.

Sacred Heart of Jesus I place all my trust in you.

O Sacred Heart of Jesus, for whom it is impossible not to have compassion on the afflicted, have pity on us miserable sinners and grant us the grace which we ask of you, through the sorrowful and Immaculate Heart of Mary, your tender mother and ours.

Pray the Hail, Holy Queen (see Appendix B).

Close with the words: "St. Joseph, foster father of Jesus pray for us."

Saint Pio of Pietrelcina, whom I discuss in Chapter 12, recited this novena prayer every day. You don't have to know or recite this particular novena to pray to the Sacred Heart, however; you can say something as simple as this:

Sacred Heart of Jesus, I place my trust in you.

First Friday Masses

If you went to Catholic school, you may remember going to First Friday Mass. This tradition grew out of devotion to the Sacred Heart. It's said that Jesus made 12 promises to St. Margaret Mary, one of which had to do with granting *final repentance* and *assured refuge* to those who attend Mass and received Communion on nine consecutive first Fridays of every month. And so the First Friday tradition developed. It continues in many places to this day, even though most modern Catholics don't know the reasons behind it.

wisdom for the journey

There is in the Sacred Heart the symbol and express image of the infinite love of Jesus Christ which moves us to love in return.

—Pope Leo XIII, late nineteenth and early twentieth centuries

Divine Mercy

In more recent years, a devotion to what's known as the Divine Mercy has gained popularity. Although this devotion grew out of the reported 1930s visions of St. Maria Faustina Kowalska, a Polish nun, the central messages echo the main teachings of the Catholic faith: we are not only given Jesus' mercy in abundance but are expected, in turn, to show mercy toward others, and we are called to put our complete trust in God.

Much of the imagery and prayers associated with Divine Mercy have the same feel as the imagery and devotions associated with the Sacred Heart. The one-line prayer that always accompanies the Divine Mercy image is this:

Jesus, I trust in you.

However, just as with the Sacred Heart, numerous prayers are connected to this devotion, including a *chaplet* that uses ordinary Rosary beads to recite the prayers of Divine Mercy. (See Appendix C for more information.)

Divine Mercy Chaplet

Optional Opening Prayer:

You expired, Jesus but the source of life gushed forth for souls, and the ocean of mercy opened up for the whole world. O Fount of Life, unfathomable Divine Mercy, envelop the whole world and empty yourself out upon us.

O Blood and Water, which gushed forth from the heart of Jesus as a fountain of mercy for us, I trust in you!

Begin with the Our Father, the Hail Mary and the Apostles' Creed.

On the large bead before each decade, say:

Eternal Father,
I offer you the Body and Blood,
Soul and Divinity,
of your dearly beloved Son,
our Lord, Jesus Christ,
in atonement for our sins
and those of the whole world.

On the ten small beads of each decade, say:

For the sake of his sorrowful Passion,
have mercy on us and on the whole world.

Conclude by saying the following three times:

Holy God,
Holy Mighty One,
Holy Immortal One,
have mercy on us
and on the whole world.

Optional Closing Prayer:

Eternal God, in whom mercy is endless and the treasury of compassion inexhaustible, look kindly upon us and increase your mercy in us, that in difficult moments we might not despair nor become despondent, but with great confidence submit ourselves to your holy will, which is love and mercy itself.

Prayer Practice

Many devotions, such as those to the Sacred Heart or Divine Mercy, include novenas, which literally mean "nine." So when we pray a novena, we say special devotional prayers every day for nine consecutive days. Why nine days? According to tradition, it comes from Jesus' instruction to his disciples and his mother to wait for the fulfillment of his Father's promises and "stay in the city until you are clothed in the power from on high." (Luke 24:48–49) They waited in the upper room, praying, and on the ninth day, the Holy Spirit descended upon them.

Catholics who have a special devotion to the Divine Mercy try to pray every day at 3 P.M., the time of day that commemorates Jesus' death on the cross. Many pray the chaplet at that time. Some pray the Stations of the Cross or make a visit to the Blessed Sacrament. Others, busy at work or home, simply pause to focus on Jesus for a brief moment. Divine Mercy Sunday, a day dedicated to this devotion, is celebrated by the worldwide Church on the Sunday after Easter each year.

It's important to remember that although many devotional prayers and practices are related to different aspects of Jesus' love for us, the one thing they all have in common is Jesus Christ, who is God. We can never lose sight of Jesus as the path to our heavenly Father.

Jesus said, "I am the way, the truth, and the life; no one comes to the Father but through me." (John 14:6) As long as we keep that always in the forefront of our mind as we pray—no matter what words or images we use to do it—we will be headed in the right direction.

Essential Takeaways

- Jesus is our path to prayer. He is “the way” that leads us to God.
- The most powerful way to make a connection to Jesus is through the Eucharist, either at Mass or through devotions such as Adoration.
- No matter what devotions, images, or words we use, if we pray to Jesus, with Jesus, and through Jesus, we will be on the right track.
- Devotions to the Sacred Heart, Divine Mercy, and other aspects of God’s all-encompassing love are designed to lead us ever closer to the heart of Jesus.

chapter 6

The Domestic Church

Your home as a little church

Starting children on the path of prayer

Family prayers to anchor your days

Allowing prayer to connect you to others

In the earliest days of Christianity, when the first disciples were forging the path of what it meant to be "church," they met in each other's homes, prayed together, and shared meals and possessions. In other words, they did what most of us do in our homes today.

That ancient tradition serves as a model of what today's modern family can be, the "domestic church." In every Catholic home, the awesome opportunity exists to create a small version of church right where we live, a place where people already held together by familial bonds build spiritual bonds that connect us to each other and to the communion of saints for all eternity.

It's something many of us are already doing without even knowing it. To be a domestic church is to create a Christ-centered home wherein Catholic prayers and Christian values pervade everyday life, from the dinner table to the bedside to the bus stop. And although prayer is an important part of life as a domestic church, it's by no means the only part. Anything that mirrors God's love for us and provides a genuine Christian witness is critical, from the support we give each other during times of crisis to the laughter we share when we're simply enjoying each other's company.

Whether we live alone, as part of a married couple, or as part of a larger family with children, our home is meant to be a place where our faith is a vital part of our daily routine.

Praying as a Family

For many of us, home is where faith begins—at the feet of our parents, our first teachers, who show us through their words and actions what it means to be Catholic.

When it comes to family prayer, varying degrees of devotion exist, to be sure. For some of us, it might mean saying a simple grace before dinner. For others, it might be a whole Rosary prayed together before a statue of Mary each night. Being a domestic church isn't about following a set of rules; it's about creating an atmosphere of love and service within the home, an atmosphere wherein God takes root and begins to affect how we think, how we speak, and how we act.

wisdom for the journey

Parents are the first evangelizers of children, a precious gift from the Creator, and begin by teaching them to say their first prayers. In this way a moral universe is built up, rooted in the will of God, where the child grows in the human and Christian values that give life its full meaning.

—Pope Benedict XVI, twentieth/twenty-first-century pope, theologian, author

Helping Children Understand Prayer

A prayer life starts simply for most of us. Saying nightly prayers is one of the strongest memories I have from my very young childhood. My mother would kneel with us at our bedside each night and give us the words to the prayers that would become the backbone of our faith. We began with a simple blessing for all our loved ones, rattling off the names of siblings, grandparents, aunts, uncles, and cousins. From there we stretched, year by year, into the essentials until we could say the prayers on our own. The Our Father, Hail Mary, Angel of God—these prayers echoed in my head each night as I drifted off to sleep as a child.

Of course, it's not simply a matter of getting the words down pat but understanding and eventually living out the meaning behind the words, which can sometimes feel like it takes a lifetime. As is so often the case with matters of faith and spiritual growth, we can begin with baby steps, teaching our children to string one word after another until the prayers become so much a part of our family life that not saying them makes our day feel incomplete.

At first, children may not fully understand the purpose of prayer, but we begin with the basics anyway, much the same way we teach them their letters long before they're ready to read. If we do our job, by the time they've progressed to the next level, they'll have the necessary building blocks in place.

Over time, in a home where prayer is woven into the fabric of everyday life, children will begin to turn to God on their own, not because Mom or Dad said so but because that's where they've learned to go for the spiritual strength they need to get them through the ups and downs of growing up.

Morning and Evening Prayers

If we want to start our day off right, there's really no better way than to begin with a greeting of gratitude to God for another new day and with a prayer that we'll do the right thing until we close our eyes again at night. If we're praying as a family, we might want to take a more "formal" approach so we can say a morning prayer out loud together. We could pray something like the Traditional Morning Offering or even the Our Father before we go about the details of our day. Or we can each say a morning prayer quietly to ourselves. The same holds true for evening prayers.

Traditional Morning Offering

O Jesus,
through the Immaculate Heart of Mary,
I offer you my prayers, works,
joys, and sufferings of this day
in union with the holy sacrifice
of the Mass throughout the world.
I offer them for all the intentions
of your Sacred Heart: the salvation
of souls, reparation for sin,

the reunion of all Christians.
I offer them for the intentions
of our bishops and of all
the apostles of prayer,
and in particular for those recommended
by our Holy Father this month.

Amen.

An Evening Family Prayer

Lord, behold our family here assembled.
We thank you for this place
in which we dwell,
for the love that unites us,
for the peace accorded to us this day,
for the hope with which
we expect the morrow;
for the health, the work,
the food and the bright skies
that make our lives delightful;
for our friends
in all parts of the earth.

Amen.

—Robert Louis Stevenson

The idea behind morning and evening prayers is to mark our days with an awareness of God's presence in our lives. The Traditional Morning Offering gives us a good template, even if we don't use the exact words. We want to offer to Jesus our day and all that we will do and experience. That's the key part of any morning prayer—to put ourselves in God's hands for the next 24 hours.

Evening prayer provides an opportunity to reflect on our day. It's a time to be grateful for our blessings, to be sorry for our mistakes, and to pray for the grace to do better the next day. Evening prayer lets us end our day as we began—in God's presence. Sometimes we may be too tired to do much more than make the Sign of the Cross and simply say, "thanks," and that's okay. But if we can remember to do even that much, we will drift off to sleep with an awareness that our days and nights, months, and years are intimately connected to our Creator.

You and your family can explore different kinds of morning and evening prayers together and find something that feels right for your family. Your prayer habits are likely to change with the seasons or with life and family situations. As children grow or spouses retire, prayer routines can be adapted. Maybe you simply want to gather around the breakfast table to offer a one-line prayer of thanks and a blessing for the day as children rush off to school. Maybe, as children get older, you can begin to explore the Morning and Evening Prayer of the Liturgy of the Hours (see Chapter 7). Maybe you have to say your prayers on the run—literally—praying an Our Father as you race to the bus stop with the kids. Or perhaps there's a particular saint whose words inspire you, and you can add them to your regular prayer routine.

Taped to my bathroom mirror is the following prayer written by St. Francis de Sales, a seventeenth-century bishop. For me, it's a good way to start the day.

Be at Peace

Do not look forward in fear
to the changes of life;
rather, look to them
with full hope that as they arise,
God, whose very own you are,
will lead you safely through all things;
and when you cannot stand it,
God will carry you in His arms.
Do not fear what may happen tomorrow;
the same everlasting Father
who cares for you today
will take care of you then and every day.
He will either shield you from suffering,
or will give you unfailing
strength to bear it.

> Be at peace, and put aside
> all anxious thoughts and imagination.
>
> —St. Francis de Sales

Whatever prayers you choose to say, the key is consistency. Eventually, if you stick with your practice and encourage your children to pray with you and on their own, daily prayer will become as natural as setting the table for dinner or brushing your teeth before bed. Rather than something you do when you have extra time to fit it in, prayer becomes something you do every day, without fail. That's not always easy with today's hectic schedules, but it's the first step to building your domestic church.

Guardian Angels

Catholics believe every soul that enters the world has a guardian angel, an angel for lifelong protection and guidance.

> **Angel of God**
>
> Angel of God,
> my guardian dear,
> to whom God's love
> commits me here,
> ever this day (night),
> be at my side
> to light and guard,
> to rule and guide.
>
> Amen.

Angels seem to be everywhere these days. You can find chubby little winged cherubs peeking out from flower gardens, worn on necklaces, hanging from rear-view mirrors, and so many other places. But angels aren't some modern-day fad. They're mentioned at key moments in Old Testament Scripture, at the resurrection of Jesus in the New Testament, and elsewhere in Scripture.

Angels are messengers and guardians. Here an angel looks out over the Tiber River from Ponte Sant'Angelo in Rome.

Photo courtesy of Mary DeTurris Poust

wisdom for the journey

We cannot pass our guardian angel's bounds, resigned or sullen, he will hear our sighs.

—St. Augustine

Angels are not to be confused with the souls of those who have died. Angels are spiritual beings who have never had earthly bodies. They're God's unseen creations, his messengers who are often called on to bring his news to people on Earth. Remember the angel Gabriel coming to Mary with news that she was chosen to bear God's son, or the angels who alerted the shepherds in the field that the Savior had been born?

Angels in Scripture

Several Scriptural references speak indirectly of personal angels. When talking about children, Jesus says, "See that you never despise one of these little ones. I assure you, their angels in heaven constantly behold my heavenly Father's face." (Matthew 18:10) In the Garden of Gethsemane, when Jesus prays that God might take the cup of suffering away from him, Luke's Gospel says, "An angel then appeared to him from heaven to strengthen him." (Luke 22:43) Later, in Hebrews 1:14, in reference to angels, we are told, "Are they not all ministering spirits, sent to serve those who are to inherit salvation?" So when we say the Angel of God prayer, we are calling on the spiritual being sent by God to minister directly to us.

Angels in Prayer

Catholics tend to teach the Angel of God prayer to their children. The sing-song nature of it makes it a natural fit for kids. But guardian angels are by no means child's play. Adults also pray to their guardian angels and to the guardian angels of their children or loved ones, asking them for protection.

For a long time, I thought I had outgrown angels. They seemed like something too much associated with my childhood, and the pop-culture angel fad didn't help. It's only been in recent years that I've found myself turning back to the angels, comforted by the belief that I have an angel watching over me and that my children have that same protection. As I check on my children at night and say a quick prayer before closing their doors, I often ask their guardian angels to stand watch over them until morning and to guide them on right paths when they go out into the world.

Angels at Home

Children can easily identify with and cling to the idea of a guardian angel. It's a child-friendly belief, something that's easy for little ones to embrace. After all, children are used to inventing imaginary friends, so how wonderful is it when they learn that they have a real but unseen friend with them all the time, a being whose job it is to look out for them?

This is an area of domestic church where we can learn from our children's enthusiasm and wonder. We're likely to see in them a total trust in the concept of a guardian angel and a willingness to turn to their angel in prayer in many different types of circumstances. Of course, they may also try to let their angel take the rap when milk is spilled or clothes are strewn about their room, but that only adds to the joy of this belief. It's good when our children learn to see their faith as part of everyday life—even to have fun with a particular aspect of faith while still remaining reverent.

We can teach our children—through nightly prayer, daily example, and occasional conversations—to turn to their angel when they're afraid or need guidance. We're not asking the angel to answer a prayer but to go to God with our prayer and surround us with love.

The hard part comes when someone gets sick or an accident occurs and a child wonders why their guardian angel didn't do its job. That's a tough situation even for adults to face. Our best approach is to remind our children that angels aren't magic. They are there to be with us, but they cannot act for us or for others, and so sometimes our angel's job is to give us strength and comfort when something bad does happen. Of course, we typically aren't aware of our angel's presence or participation in our life. It remains unseen in the background.

Prayer Practice

Whenever our family is headed out on a long car ride, I make the Sign of the Cross and pray that our guardian angels will watch over us as we travel. It's something I do silently, but many people I know make praying on car trips a family affair. We can say an Our Father together before we fire up the DVD players or turn on the radio, or call on our guardian angels as we pull out of the driveway.

Giving Thanks at Mealtime

At our house, grace before dinner can be a noisy affair. With forks held in mid-air, sometimes with little one's mouths already chewing, we set about saying grace every night. It doesn't necessarily sound like a prayer you'd hear in a grand cathedral or quiet monastery, but it's our family's prayer style.

Grace Before Meals

Bless us, O Lord,
and these thy gifts
which we are about to receive
from thy bounty
through Christ Our Lord.

Amen.

I have friends who joke that they say Grace *During* Meals because half the time they forget to say the prayer until everyone has already started eating. And there is, for all those procrastinators in the crowd, an official grace for after we've finished eating.

Grace After Meals

We give thee thanks,
for all thy benefits,
almighty God,
who lives and reigns forever.

Amen.

Praying a blessing at mealtimes reminds us to be thankful for what we have and perhaps to be mindful of those who have nothing to eat. It sets the tone for a meal where, even in the noisiest of houses, God has a place at the table.

The beauty of getting your family into the habit of saying grace is how quickly this short prayer takes hold. It is often my children who remind us that we need to pray if one of the adults forgets. When we're out at a restaurant, they will make the Sign of the Cross and say grace, even if it's silent and to themselves, before they dig in. In the realm of domestic church, that awareness of God and of the need to pray is the first rung on the spiritual ladder.

Baptismal "Birthdays"

In most families, birthdays are a big deal. We bake cakes, buy presents, and invite friends over to share in the celebration because birthdays are important milestones in our lives. Well, Catholics have two birthdays, in a sense—the one that marks the day we came into the world, and the one that marks the day we came into the faith. Celebrating baptismal "birthdays" is a great way to recognize the importance of that sacrament in our lives, then and now.

A baptismal birthday celebration can be very much like a regular birthday celebration. We can make a cake or have a special dinner, but, as an added bonus, say a special prayer together, look at pictures from the baptism, and, if possible, invite the godparents over. We can even create our own prayer service to celebrate the event.

Prayer Practice

For a baptism birthday celebration, set the table with a baptism photo, a bowl of holy water, and a candle. (Water and light are two of the symbols of baptism.) Ask the guest of honor to light the candle and then read from Galatians 3:26–28: "For through faith you are all children of God in Christ Jesus. For all of you who were baptized into Christ have clothed yourselves with Christ." After the reading, join hands around the table and say the Our Father together. Each person can then trace the Sign of the Cross on the guest of honor's forehead. To close, everyone can dip their fingers in the holy water and bless themselves.

No Occasion Too Small

When it comes to family life, almost any event can be marked with prayer. To everything there is a season, and that goes for prayer as well. From the first day of school or times of illness to college graduation or the loss of a job, prayer can bring the presence of God to joyful or sorrowful situations at home. We can pray spontaneously, speaking to God from our hearts, or we can use traditional prayers written for just about every occasion.

We can begin to look for opportunities to add prayer into our family's life. If a child is going off to summer camp, we can say a blessing over her. If our spouse is starting a new job, we can gather everyone together for words of support and prayer. If a little one is seriously ill, we can pray together for healing and for God's grace to accept whatever is ahead. If our spouse is given a promotion at work, we can say a prayer of thanksgiving as a family.

Prayer is not something we are meant to turn to only in times of crisis. In the domestic church, it's like a spiritual metronome that gives a steady rhythm to the concert of our lives.

An Abundance of Blessings

In addition to traditional or spontaneous prayers, Catholic family life can and should include blessings—lots of them. Blessings are "sacramentals" because they help open us to God and the grace we receive through the sacraments.

Although Catholics are more accustomed to seeing priests or bishops giving blessings, the *Catechism of the Catholic Church* (CCC) teaches that every baptized person is called to "be a 'blessing' and to bless." (*CCC*, 1669) Parents especially, because of their "priestly" or teaching role as head of their family, can bless their children and certain elements of home life.

It's important to remember that a blessing is not a gesture—the Sign of the Cross a priest makes during a blessing, for example. A blessing is a prayer sent up to God, giving him praise and asking him to send down his protection to us.

We can also offer prayers of blessing over certain objects, such as a new home, a Christmas tree, or a vegetable garden getting ready for harvest. Certain seasons also get specific blessings (see Chapter 20).

Another helpful sacramental that can aid daily prayer life at home is holy water. Holy water reminds us of our baptism, that we belong to God, that we're children of God. Like lighting a candle or burning incense, holy water also is a physical expression of our interior prayers. I installed a small holy water *font* near our front door at home. The kids love to dip their fingers and bless themselves as they head out to school in the morning or up to bed at night. It's one more way to bring a prayerful presence into our home and instill in our children an understanding that even in the most "normal" events of the day, God is present and available to them.

Definition

A **font** is a receptacle that holds holy water. They come in various shapes, sizes, and designs and are found both in private homes and parish churches. In churches, holy water fonts are at the entrances so people can bless themselves as they come in. Sometimes the fonts are small and hanging near a door; sometimes a large font, also used for baptisms, serves as the holy water font for daily or weekly use. At home, you can hang a holy water font near your front door, bedroom door, or anywhere your family can have regular access to it. You can get holy water from your parish church.

Seeing Prayer as a Connector

The domestic church of our home is where faith is first planted, but it's by no means where it remains, fixed. It's meant to grow first around the family and then spread like vines out into the world. Prayer links Catholics to one another, even when we live on different continents or speak different languages.

wisdom for the journey

It is possible to offer fervent prayer even while walking in public, while buying or selling, or even while cooking.

—St. John Chrysostom, fifth century, early church father

It's through those earliest prayers said at home—the blessings each night for far-off family members, the petitions whispered around the table when someone we love is sick, the prayers of thanksgiving before meals—that we begin to understand that our faith is not meant to be kept locked inside our church, our home, or even our heart. It's meant to reach ever outward, uniting us to untold thousands; to those who have gone before us; to the saints in heaven; and ultimately to God the Father, Son, and Spirit.

Essential Takeaways

- It's in the comfort and safety of our family home, our own little church, that faith takes root and begins to grow.
- The everyday routines of family life can be marked with prayers, from morning offerings to grace before a meal, to special blessings for people, events, or objects.
- Children and adults alike can call on guardian angels for protection and guidance each day.
- Prayer connects us to Catholics in our extended family, our parish community, our worldwide church, and to those already with God.

chapter 7

The Liturgy of the Hours

The roots of the Liturgy of the Hours

The general flow of prayers, Psalms, and canticles in the "hours"

Adapting the hours to modern life

Support and encouragement from outside resources

I admit right off the bat that I have a love-hate relationship with the Liturgy of the Hours, which is also called the Divine Office or the Breviary. Why? Because it's one of the few areas of Catholic life that feels so incredibly foreign to me. Most Catholics aren't taught to pray the Liturgy of the Hours, even though it's called the "Prayer of the Church." At first glance, and maybe even second or third glance, it can seem complicated and somewhat intimidating.

One night a few years ago, I walked into 5 P.M. Evening Prayer at my parish church. As I stepped inside the chapel, I picked up a copy of *Christian Prayer: The Liturgy of the Hours* from the shelf and sat down with three other people who were preparing to pray. Before I knew it, they were flipping back and forth to pages in all different sections of the book. I never caught up. I spent the 15 minutes or so it took to complete Evening Prayer in a state of confusion, never sure what they were doing, how they knew where to turn, or why no one had ever taught me how to do this. I left frustrated—but determined to figure out this prayer that is truly a beautiful way to give the entire day and even the night a God-centered rhythm all grounded in Scripture.

In this chapter, we explore the basics of the Liturgy of the Hours so you have what you need to get started, either on your own or in a group.

The Prayer of the Church

The Liturgy of the Hours is basically what it sounds like—a prayer that marks the hours of the day. Catholic priests and many communities of religious brothers and sisters are required to say the Divine Office every day, but more and more lay people are taking up the practice, praying at home on their own or with small groups at their local churches.

There's something really powerful about this prayer. With roots in Jewish tradition, it was developed by the earliest monastic communities and clergy serving in cathedrals, and it continues to mark the hours of the day for so many Catholics around the world. Right now, somewhere, people are praying one of the hours of the Divine Office.

wisdom for the journey

Creation itself was a daily process—each day, God spoke more and more into being … our bodies, and our lives, still reflect these basic rhythms of creation, which are also captured in the Church's tradition of daily prayer, also known as the Liturgy of the Hours.

—Kathleen Norris, author and Benedictine Oblate

The Liturgy of the Hours finds its beginnings in the prayer practices of Judaism. In Exodus 29:38–39, God commands the Israelites to offer animal sacrifices in the morning and evening. Eventually, those rituals evolved into sacrifices of prayer rather than animals, with Scripture readings, psalms, and hymns. This grew into a practice of praying at specific hours—namely, morning and evening as well as the third (9 A.M.), sixth (noon), and ninth (3 P.M.) hours of the day. The earliest Christians, who were Jews, continued these prayer practices.

Both the Old and New Testaments contain references to the idea that we should pray not once a day or even twice a day but over and over all day. The psalmist wrote: "Seven times a day I praise you." (Psalm 199:164) St. Paul urged early Christians to "pray without ceasing." (1 Thessalonians 5:17)

This regular, almost constant prayer was eventually molded into what we have today in the Liturgy of the Hours. It's meant to be a prayer said in community and out loud—a liturgy. How did it go from informal tradition of the whole Christian people to official Prayer of the Church? We can thank the early Church Fathers, the earliest monks, known as the Desert Fathers, and later Western monastics like St. Benedict for making this prayer what it is today.

From Monasticism to Modern Times

Although early Christians continued to pray the hours according to Jewish custom, eventually the Desert Fathers and Western monks, in an effort to truly "pray without ceasing," began to expand the prayer—in some cases praying all of the 150 psalms every day. Similarly, priests assigned to cathedrals and large parishes gathered together to pray throughout the day. Obviously lay people, with jobs and families and responsibilities, could not pray this version of the Divine Office, so praying the hours became a monastic tradition, no longer a household practice for everyday Christians.

Prayer Practice

In the early Church, many people couldn't pray the Liturgy of the Hours because they were illiterate. People began to say Hail Marys instead, one for every psalm. Sometimes they would knot a chord to keep track, producing the first unofficial version of the Rosary.

With the Second Vatican Council in the 1960s, things began to change. A shift in attitude, from clerical to more inclusive, and a change in language, from Latin to the vernacular, opened the door for lay people interested in praying the Liturgy of the Hours.

"Now that the prayer of the Holy Church has been renewed and entirely revised in accordance with its very ancient tradition and in the light of the needs of our day, it is supremely to be hoped that the Liturgy of the Hours may pervade and penetrate the whole of Christian prayer, giving it life, direction and expression and effectively nourishing the spiritual life of the people of God," wrote Pope Paul VI in 1970, expressing "confidence" that the unceasing prayer would "take on new life."

Despite that enthusiasm, the practice did not catch on like wildfire. Instead, it's been a bit of a slow burn, with more growth occurring in the last couple of decades. Increasing numbers of Catholics are seeking out the Liturgy of the Hours as a way to sanctify the day, by offering regular prayers of praise and thanksgiving.

If you want to pray the full Liturgy of the Hours in the monastic tradition, you'd have to devote quite a bit of time to it. Here's how the complete Liturgy of the Hours breaks down:

Office of Readings (also known as Matins or Vigils, major hour)

Morning Prayer (Lauds, major hour)

Mid-Morning Prayer (Terce)

Midday Prayer (Sext)

Mid-Afternoon Prayer (None)

Evening Prayer (Vespers, major hour)

Night Prayer (Compline)

The Latin words terce, sext, and none refer to the "third," "sixth," and "ninth" hours of the day in monastic life and are based on the ancient Jewish prayer schedule. It's clear from looking at the schedule that it would be very difficult for average lay Catholics to say the entire Liturgy of the Hours every day. And so the Church has recommended two major hours—Morning Prayer and Evening Prayer—for those who want to say this prayer on a regular basis.

Making the Hours Work for You

True to its Jewish roots, the Liturgy of the Hours revolves around Scripture, especially the psalms and canticles, with hymns, other Scripture readings, prayers of intercession, and the Our Father rounding out the practice. It would be impossible to outline every hour of prayer in its entirety because so many different options exist for various seasons, feast days, and specific hours. (The Liturgy of the Hours prayer books, which I discuss later in this chapter, provide the essentials to say this prayer.)

The most important thing to understand is the general structure, especially of the two major hours you're most likely to pray when you begin this practice.

An "Hour," Up Close

For the most part, praying Morning or Evening Prayer on your own or with a small group at church would go something like this:

Invitatory, which is a psalm said before whichever "hour" (e.g., Morning or Evening Prayer) you choose to begin the Divine Office, but not necessary if you want to use a shorter form.

Introductory prayer: "God, come to my assistance. Lord, make haste to help me. Glory to the Father and to the Son and to the Holy Spirit, as it was in the beginning now, is now, and will be forever. Amen." (This is a slightly different version of the Glory Be, as covered in Chapter 4.)

A hymn. (You may opt to skip this if you're praying alone.)

Psalms and Old and New Testament *canticles,* which are kinds of biblical songs, and *antiphons,* which are responses said before and after the psalms and canticles.

Definition

Canticles are "hymns" taken from Scripture, excluding the psalms. The Gospel canticles used during the Liturgy of the Hours include the Canticle of Zechariah, said during Morning Prayer; the Canticle of Mary, said during Evening Prayer; and the Canticle of Simeon, said during Night Prayer. **Antiphons,** used throughout all the hours, are simply responses taken from the psalms.

Reading from Scripture.

Responsory.

One of the Gospel canticles (or songs), either the *Magnificat* (Canticle of Mary) or the *Benedictus* (Canticle of Zechariah).

Prayers of intercession.

Our Father.

Concluding prayer and verse.

It seems simple enough, doesn't it? And yet, when I first started to explore the Liturgy of the Hours on my own, I was completely overwhelmed by how to find the right reading for the day, what to do on special feast days when we move out of the regular cycle of readings and prayers, and how to adjust to a liturgical way of praying despite the fact that I was alone in my private prayer space.

wisdom for the journey

There is no aspect of the interior life, no kind of religious experience, no spiritual need of man that is not depicted and lived out in the psalms. But we cannot lay hands on these riches unless we are willing to work for them.

—Thomas Merton, Trappist monk and writer, twentieth century

The Hinges of the Day

In my own practice, the key to feeling comfortable with the Liturgy of the Hours was to start small—with Morning Prayer only. I focused on that one hour, which doesn't take anywhere close to an hour—15 minutes, at most. I stuck with basic Morning Prayer, with no special feasts at first because I knew that might throw me off the path if things got too complicated. I just moved through the main four-week cycle one day at a time. Essentially, you pray the same psalms over and over in a repeating cycle. If you were to pray the full Liturgy of the Hours every day for 4 weeks, you'd cover all 150 psalms.

I found it helpful to pray out loud, even though I was alone. Hearing the psalms and canticles as I spoke them, rather than simply letting my eyes glide over them, made them more real to me and helped me pull meaning from them, which wasn't always easy. (I discuss the psalms in particular in just a bit.)

Morning and Evening Prayer are known as the "hinges of the day." These two hours stand apart as the most critical in the Liturgy of the Hours. Prayers of praise offered at sunrise and prayers of thanksgiving offered at sunset give the day a basic framework of prayer. The structure of these prayer hours is identical. The Gospel canticles for morning and evening alternate: the Canticle of Zechariah is said in the morning, and the Canticle of Mary in the evening.

Morning Prayer is said upon waking, so you can fit it into even the busiest schedule if you get up just a few minutes earlier than usual. Evening Prayer, however, is prayed around dinnertime, which makes it a bit of a challenge for people working all day, commuting home, or cooking for a family. Most churches or monasteries offer Evening Prayer fairly early, say around 5 P.M.

If you want to pray the Liturgy of the Hours later in the day but can't fit in Evening Prayer, Night Prayer might turn out to be a good option. It's the shortest of the hours, and you can say it just before going to bed, or perhaps with your spouse or family if you have older children.

The important thing to remember here is what the Liturgy of the Hours is meant to give you—an awareness of God's presence during the regular events of your days and the opportunity to praise and thank God every day in union with the rest of the Church. You can't get caught up in doing every hour or even two particular hours every day if your life is filled to overflowing with work and family responsibilities. You have to give yourself permission to adapt this monastic-style prayer to your modern life in a way that, rather than frustrate you, leads you deeper into the heart of God.

Learning to Love the Psalms

Catholics are no strangers to the psalms. Every Sunday at Mass, every day if we can get there, a psalm is sung or read as part of the normal cycle of readings. Some are probably so familiar that we can almost quote them from memory. "The Lord is my shepherd, there is nothing I shall want." (Psalm 23) The Liturgy of the Hours, however, takes the psalms to a whole new level. As we begin to pray the various hours of the day, we may find ourselves saying psalms that are not only unfamiliar but violent, depressing, and vengeful. And we may start to wonder why saying these ancient prayers is so important to our daily spiritual lives here and now.

This was an issue for me when I began saying Morning Prayer. Sitting in my sacred space with my prayer book, some days the words of the psalms seemed written just for me, so profound and moving. Other days I'd read the same psalm several times, trying to make sense of it. Images of God striking down enemies or of ancient tribes exacting torture on one another felt so out of sync with my understanding of a loving God and my day-to-day life. How could I reconcile the words of Hebrew Scripture with the realities of modern life?

A priest who is a close friend of mine suggested I look at the psalms from a new perspective: perhaps the words don't relate to my life on any given day, but somewhere someone *is* struggling with war, famine, terrible suffering, or amazing joy.

The Liturgy of the Hours is meant to link us to the entire Church, a Church filled with people on every continent, of every background, of every circumstance. A particular psalm might not speak to us directly, but it certainly speaks to one of our brothers and sisters in Christ somewhere in the world. Through our prayers, we unite ourselves to them, and their sorrow and joy, difficulties and accomplishments. We are one, which is at the heart of the Liturgy of the Hours. One prayer for one people.

wisdom for the journey

My strength returns to me with my cup of coffee and the reading of the psalms.

—Dorothy Day, founder of the Catholic Worker Movement, twentieth century

Outside Assistance

If you're going to dive into the Liturgy of the Hours, it's imperative to seek support from other outside resources—books, websites, and most important, parishes or religious congregations where you can join in communal prayer and learn the rhythm of the hours from those with experience.

First off, to pray the Liturgy of the Hours, you need a book or set of books. For the ultimate version of the Divine Office, there's a four-volume set. Unless you're taking up permanent residence in a monastery, this probably isn't the place to start. The one-volume *Christian Prayer: The Liturgy of the Hours* is the book more commonly used by individuals and parishes. For an even more abbreviated version containing only Morning and Evening Prayers, try the *Shorter Christian Prayer.*

There are even simpler ways to pray the Liturgy of the Hours. *Magnificat* is a subscription monthly that provides not only the daily Mass readings but also the Liturgy of the Hours in extremely shortened form with necessary canticles conveniently printed on the back cover so you never have to search for them. In addition, technology has greatly expanded access to the Liturgy on the Hours on a day-by-day basis. You can sign up for e-mails, podcasts, iPod applications, and other devices that provide the exact readings and prayers needed for just that day. It's the perfect way to get started. (See Appendix C for links to websites and other helpful prayer aids.)

Better than any of these printed or high-tech versions, however, is the "live" version of the Liturgy of the Hours. Check with your local parish or another Catholic church near your home or office to see if they offer Morning and Evening Prayer. If not, try a community of religious sisters, priests, or brothers who allow the public to join their communal prayers. By praying with a community and feeling the full force of hymns sung together and psalms prayed in alternating patterns between opposite sides of a chapel, the rhythm of the Liturgy of the Hours will take root in you.

Essential Takeaways

- The Liturgy of the Hours, also known as the Divine Office, is meant to sanctify the day and night through regular periods of prayer.
- Rooted in Jewish tradition, early Christianity, and monasticism, this prayer is based in Scripture, specifically the psalms and the canticles of the Old and New Testaments.
- Morning and Evening Prayer are considered the essential hours, known as the "hinges of the day."
- Outside assistance is critical when first learning the Liturgy of the Hours; seek support through books, websites, and local church communities.

chapter 8

Entering the Silence

How to practice *Lectio Divina,* or sacred reading

Learning the fine art of Christian meditation

Silencing our minds to listen for God

The deep, inner prayer of contemplation

So often when we pray to God, we spend a lot of time talking *at* him. We have worries, fears, and other things we need God to handle for us. We feel like someone should be saying *something*. But prayer is meant to be a two-way street—talking to God and then being quiet so God can have his say. Once we let go of our need to fill all the empty spaces of our prayer time with words, we often find that our deepest conversations with God actually happen in the silence.

Although the old adage says that silence is "golden," our society doesn't really treat it that way. We seem to equate being quiet with being unproductive. And so we spin our yarns, filling up every minute with activity and noise. Even when we stop talking, we're usually still being bombarded by noises that disrupt our thoughts—the ding of an e-mail coming in, the TV blaring in another room, or the neighbor's lawnmower buzzing outside our window. It can be a real challenge to shut out the rest of the world—as well as our own urge to talk—and simply listen. Silence is somewhat foreign territory.

Several prayer methods can help you get to a place where you're not only comfortable in silence but revel in it, crave it, and sink into it on a daily basis. This is where God waits for you.

Learning to Listen

Why would you need to learn to listen? You've been listening to various sounds and voices, music, and speeches all your life. You should have this skill down, right? Maybe on a practical, earthly level you do, but when it comes to deep, silent prayer, that's a very different kind of listening.

St. Benedict, the father of Western monasticism, told his monks to "listen with the ear of your heart." In other words, you have to try to strip away what the world has trained you to hear—the noises buzzing past your ears, the thoughts that bounce around your head, making a silent kind of clatter—and let your heart, the deepest part of your being, do the listening.

Once you get the hang of this, what you're likely to hear is very different from what you're used to. Instead of the clear sound of a spoken word, you may "hear" murmurings of the Spirit—not words, but rather feelings instead. It's in these silent murmurings that you begin to understand God talking to you, calling to you, guiding you.

wisdom for the journey

You must speak to Jesus not only with your lips but with your heart; in fact on certain occasions you should speak to Him only with your heart.

—Saint Pio of Pietrelcina, twentieth-century Capuchin Franciscan friar known as "Padre Pio"

To enter into this kind of listening, a few things are necessary. You need to turn off or close out any unnecessary noise you can control. Remember the dinging e-mail mentioned earlier? Turn down the computer's volume. Shut off the cell phone. Silence the TV or any other electronic "voices" that are likely to distract you. What about the noises you can't control—the neighbor's lawnmower, a plane flying overhead, a fly buzzing around the room? Those are sounds you have to learn to accept as the white noise in the background of your silent prayer. They may prove to be an added challenge at first, but nothing is insurmountable. And if all else fails, try a set of earplugs to get you started.

You also need to be in the right environment for silent prayer. You can go to your private sacred space, a church, or any quiet spot away from other people. Settle into a comfortable position—sitting in a straight-backed chair, sitting on a meditation cushion, kneeling on a prayer bench, or whatever makes you more inclined to stay put for a while.

Finally, you have to enter this kind of listening with a gentle heart. You can't fight every sound you hear, every scratch that wants to be itched, every thought that pulls you away from your center. You just have to be ready to let those things come and go without any resistance.

When you begin any silent prayer, it's good to start with a prayer to the Holy Spirit for guidance. Even in total silence, your heart and mind should always be set on God, and the Spirit helps lead you in that direction.

Prayer to the Holy Spirit

Come, Holy Spirit,
fill the hearts of your faithful
and enkindle in them the fire of your love.
Send forth your Spirit,
and they shall be created.
And you shall renew the face of the earth.
Let us pray.
O God, who has taught the hearts
of the faithful by the light
of the Holy Spirit,
grant that by the gift of the same Spirit
we may be always truly wise
and ever rejoice in his consolation,
through Christ our Lord.

Amen.

Lectio Divina, Sacred Reading

A good place to start, if you want to begin to explore silent prayer but aren't quite ready to go off the high dive of deep contemplation, is with *Lectio Divina*, literally "divine reading." Through this ancient monastic prayer practice, you use Scripture as a guide into a deeper relationship with God. This is different from Bible study or reading for basic understanding. In *Lectio Divina,* you don't simply read a Scripture passage; you allow the passage to speak to you.

Lectio Divina has four main stages:

1. Reading a passage (*lectio*)
2. Meditating on it (*meditatio*)
3. Praying or responding to God (*oratio*)
4. Contemplating or listening for God to respond (*contemplatio*)

Let's take a closer look at each.

wisdom for the journey

Anyone who has been in love or had a close friendship will understand. I look forward every day to meeting the Lord in *lectio.*

—Father Basil Pennington, twentieth-century Trappist monk and spiritual writer

Step by Step

To practice *Lectio Divina,* you start by making the Sign of the Cross and saying a prayer to the Holy Spirit. Then you read a Scripture passage. You could choose one of the readings for that day's Mass, select a certain book of the Bible and take one passage each day, or simply start with some of your favorite Scripture passages and work your way through them one day at a time.

In the first stage, you read your chosen Scripture passage slowly. *Lectio Divina* is a process of entering into the passage in a sense, and allowing it to touch your heart rather than your mind. As you read, take notice of any word or sentence that seems to ring especially true, something that calls out to you.

In stage two, you reflect on the line or word that spoke to you. Read it again or repeat it. Let it become part of you. Allow your feelings and thoughts to come and go, honoring them as something God is inviting you to ponder.

In stage three, you offer a spontaneous prayer to God, whatever comes to mind, using words or images or both. Tell God what you're thinking and feeling, or offer prayers of praise, thanksgiving, or petition.

Finally, in stage four, you sit in silence with God, "resting" in Him. Now is the time to let your heart speak to God without words or thoughts or feelings, and to wait patiently and silently for God to speak to you. This last stage is where contemplative prayer begins. Remember that God speaks louder at some times than other times, and sometimes it might seem that he has chosen not speak at all. Or you might hear his message after you get up from your *lectio* and are involved in the other activities of your day.

What Was Old Is New Again

Like the Liturgy of the Hours, *Lectio Divina* was for many centuries something practiced only in monastic communities. But after the Second Vatican Council, more lay people began to explore this prayer practice. And like the Liturgy of the Hours, *Lectio Divina* springs from an ancient Hebrew practice of interpreting Scripture, known as *haggadah,* that was practiced during the time of Jesus.

More and more, these ancient prayer traditions are finding their way into the lives of today's Catholics hungry for a friendship with Jesus Christ.

wisdom for the journey

Transformation is completely God's work. We can't do anything to make it happen. We can only prevent it from happening.

—Father Thomas Keating, twentieth/twenty-first century, Trappist monk and a founder of the Centering Prayer movement

Meditation: Is That Catholic?

Many people hear the word *meditation* and immediately think of Eastern spiritual practices. But Catholics have long used meditation as a way of directing their thoughts and prayers, in union with Jesus Christ, toward God the Father. Unlike Eastern meditation, which aims to clear the mind of all thought and enter into a kind of nothingness, Catholic meditation is just the opposite. Catholic meditation is active. Rather than empty your mind, in Catholic meditation you focus your mind on a specific Scripture passage, spiritual scene, or image that will lead you further and further down the path of Christ.

You may choose to meditate on a Gospel scene, one of the Stations of the Cross, or a mystery of the Rosary. Or you may meditate in front of the cross and concentrate on Christ's Passion. You can focus your meditation in endless ways, but the critical thing is not to allow your meditation to morph into a "negative" experience of prayer—an emptying out—but rather a positive or active experience of prayer—filling up.

In Catholic meditation, you work through four basic steps:

1. Placing yourself in the presence of God
2. Asking for God's help
3. Meditating
4. Giving thanks to God

Before beginning meditation, choose your focus. Then, as with *Lectio Divina* and most other forms of prayer, find an appropriate place to meditate, someplace quiet and without outside distractions. Then begin.

First, make the Sign of the Cross, say a prayer to the Holy Spirit for guidance, and settle down into the silence to become aware that you're not alone, that God is with you.

Next, ask God to help you in your prayer, knowing you cannot do it without him. Pray, in your own words, that he will lead you in the right direction and guide your thoughts. You can also call on Mary and the saints to walk with you on this inward journey.

Now actively meditate, which means you focus on the story or scene you've chosen. Try to enter into it by imagining yourself as part of it, making it as vivid as you can. If you're meditating on the Gospel reading where Jesus multiplies the loaves and fishes and feeds the crowd of 5,000, for example, try to smell the smells and see the hillside. How does it feel to be hungry and not know where you'll get food? What do you think when suddenly baskets filled to overflowing seemingly appear from nowhere? Reflect on the meaning of this for the people then and for you now, allowing the passage to give you a deeper understanding of this particular piece of your faith story.

Remember that this process of meditation is guided by the Spirit; it's not just mental work on your part. And you have to leave space for God to speak; it's not just your agenda. Sometimes God will surprise you.

Finally, thank God for his assistance during your meditation and make the Sign of the Cross to end your prayer.

The *Catechism of the Catholic Church* calls meditation a "quest" through which we better understand our lives as Christians, emphasizing that, for Catholics, meditation must always go forward with the Spirit and toward Jesus Christ. (*CCC*, 2705–2708)

Misc.

Eastern Christian Meditation

Eastern meditation, as referred to in this book, is non-Christian meditation, such as that practiced by Buddhists. However, Eastern Christian meditation has long been a part of Catholic spirituality, dating to at least 400 A.D. It was a vital part of St. Benedict's monastic spirituality, in fact.

State of Transcendence

Once you feel comfortable with silent prayer forms such as *Lectio Divina* and meditation, you can begin to explore the more intense form of prayer known as *contemplation*. In this silent, inward prayer, you "rest" in God and allow your spiritual gaze to settle on Jesus Christ, who leads you ever deeper into the silent wellspring of prayer.

It's natural to think that contemplative prayer is something reserved for monks and mystics who have access to and time for long sessions of silence in a totally spiritual setting. But everyday Catholics out in the world can use contemplation to reach a new level of union with Jesus Christ and to bring a Christ-centered attitude to even the most ordinary details of daily life.

Now, you don't just sit down and enter into deep contemplation. It takes practice and a shift in perspective from the other kinds of prayer we've been discussing. Even *Lectio Divina* and meditation give you something hefty as a focus of your silence. In contemplation, you're going to go to a place with few of the typical spiritual road markers you used to find your way until now.

Centering Prayer

Some people find they can work their way toward deep contemplative prayer by practicing what's known as *centering prayer*. This style of silent prayer comes out of general Christian contemplative prayer methods and *Lectio Divina*. Its focus is always on Jesus Christ, and its goal is always the eventual "indwelling" of the Holy Trinity within you. You want to reach a place where you're resting in God, completely open to his presence in your heart and your life and to whatever message or plan he has for you.

Centering prayer grew out of the anonymous writings in the fourteenth-century Christian classic *The Cloud of Unknowing,* a work on Christian mysticism that guides students of prayer to seek God not through words or ideas but through prayers of pure love from the heart. Trappist monks William Meninger, Basil Pennington, and Thomas Keating developed the centering prayer method in the 1970s.

Centering prayer begins with the repetition—in thought only—of a "sacred word," something that will call you back to God whenever your mind starts to wander. And your mind will wander—a lot. The sacred word could be something like *Jesus, Abba, Father, Savior, Creator,* or *Holy Spirit*. Or it could be something like *love, peace, faith, hope,* or *mercy*. Once you choose a word, however, stick with that word throughout your entire prayer session.

In centering prayer, as with all silent prayer, you first want to find a quiet place where you won't be disturbed. Sit comfortably in a straight-backed chair or on a meditation bench or cushion. The goal here is to be comfortable enough that you're not distracted by aches and pains in your body but not so comfortable that you fall asleep!

Begin with the Sign of the Cross and a prayer to the Holy Spirit to guide your thoughts. Close your eyes and sink into the silence, thinking of your sacred word as a way to feel God's presence there with you. You don't have to repeat the word over and over without end. The method really involves using your sacred word to call you back to God every time your thoughts or memories rush in and pull you away.

You need to try to let your thoughts and memories pass by without offering resistance or reacting emotionally. Simply think of your sacred word and come back to your resting place. Your eventual goal is to reach a place of total mental quiet where you can hear the "still small voice" of God. (1 Kings 19:12)

Adherents recommend you spend 20 minutes in centering prayer twice a day, but the reality is that for most everyday Catholics, 20 minutes of deep silent prayer right off the bat would feel like a lifetime. If you can do even 5 minutes of silence once a day to start, you should pat yourself on the back! Don't attempt anything so overwhelming that it's not a realistic fit for you.

I decided to use centering prayer with my fourth-grade religion class one day. Accustomed to praying the Our Father or Hail Mary together, they didn't know what to make of it when I turned off the lights and told them to close their eyes. After the initial giggling subsided, a rare quiet fell over our classroom. I think that unusual prayer experience had an impact on the children, showing them a whole new way of reaching out to God, something they could do without words or prayer books. Centering prayer can have that same impact in your life, opening the door to a new way of relating to God.

MISC.

Resting in God

More traditional Catholics are skeptical of centering prayer, fearing that it's more akin to Eastern-style meditation than Christian contemplation. Unlike Eastern meditation, however, centering prayer is not focused on creating mental clarity through nothingness. It's focused on Jesus and union with God. It's about being with and resting in God rather than thinking about and speaking to God.

Contemplation

For many of us, the word *contemplation* often brings up images of mystics in ecstasy, great saints, and monks and nuns. We think of St. John of the Cross or St. Teresa of Avila, and we can't imagine the contemplative prayer that's so closely identified with them could be accessible to us. It's true that for most of us, that level of contemplation is something we'll never achieve. But contemplative prayer is something every Catholic can consider and work toward.

Contemplative prayer is not like vocal prayer. You don't decide to do it, kneel down, and start. Contemplation requires being receptive to God's Spirit moving within you. You cannot really reach your so-called "goal" in contemplation if the Spirit has not given you that gift. You can simply prepare yourself to be ready for the Spirit through *Lectio Divina,* centering prayer, and other daily prayer efforts to develop your relationship with God—a.k.a. *active contemplation.*

To do this, you have to have a truly open heart, which means learning not to be so bogged down or distracted by the things of this life. And that's not an easy task for those of us living out in the world on a day-to-day basis. Still, the potential is there if you can begin to strip away those worldly concerns and desires that tend to rule you (known as *purgation*) and turn your heart and mind over to more spiritual thoughts and activities (known as *illumination*) to reach the heart of deep contemplation (known as *union*).

Silent prayer does not require us to retreat to a monastery. It is an inner journey that depends on a change in spiritual attitude, not necessarily a change in physical location.

Photo courtesy of Mary DeTurris Poust

wisdom for the journey

Mental prayer is nothing else than an intimate friendship, a frequent heart-to-heart conversation with Him by whom we know ourselves to be loved.

—Saint Teresa of Avila, sixteenth-century Carmelite nun and mystic

Essential Takeaways

- Silence is a critical element of prayer life.
- Learning to listen with your heart paves the way for meditation, *Lectio Divina,* and contemplative prayer, creating a space for God to speak.
- Begin all your silent prayers with a petition to the Holy Spirit to guide your thoughts.
- Christian meditation and contemplation focus on Jesus Christ and have as their ultimate goal union with God.

Part 3

Mary and the Saints

In Mary and the saints, Catholics find friends who have walked the road of faith before them, believers who have experienced the ups and downs of a spiritual life that's not always easy. They serve as examples, role models, partners on our path.

We can look at the lives of Mary and other saints and see faith lived out in a very real way, on a day-to-day basis, sometimes against incredible odds. These heroic men and women of God show us how to live, how to pray, and how to embrace God's plan for us.

Mary and the saints can't do the work for us, and they can't answer prayers, but they can partner with us, serving as companions for the journey.

In Part 3, we explore Mary's role in our prayer life and specific devotions to Mary, with special attention to the Rosary. We also spend time with some of the most popular Catholic saints, learning their stories and sharing their prayers.

chapter 9

Turning to the Blessed Mother

- Understanding Mary's role in the history of salvation
- Mary, first disciple and role model
- Seeing Mary as mother to us all
- Going to the Blessed Mother in prayer

Catholics have a special reverence and affection for the Blessed Virgin Mary. She holds a place of honor in our hearts and our prayer lives, and with good reason. Mary's "yes" to God—her fiat—allowed Jesus to enter the world, making Mary a collaborator with God's plan.

In Mary, we find everything we could hope for in a spiritual mother. She is tender and tough, a mother who has known both joy and heartache on monumental levels. She is quiet and strong, a woman who willingly accepted God's plan in the face of the unknown and, even worse, the inevitable suffering ahead. She is ordinary and yet oh-so-extraordinary, a human being entrusted with the birth and care of the Messiah. She is the Mother of God. How could we not have an enduring and deep love for her?

The Blessed Mother is intimately intertwined in our prayer lives as Catholics because she is intimately intertwined in our salvation story. Jesus enters the world, and Mary is there. Jesus leaves the world, and Mary is there. Jesus' Church takes root and grows, and Mary is there. Although some people question the depth of Catholic devotion to Mary, what would be more unusual would be a *lack* of devotion toward the woman who played such a critical role in our redemption.

The First Disciple, a Role Model

Mary is not only a source of comfort and a companion to us on our spiritual journey; she is also a role model who shows us how to live out the Gospel and how to pray. Although we don't have a tremendous amount of information about the details of Mary's life, Scripture reveals key moments that offer glimpses of who she was and how deeply she believed. She is the first disciple of Jesus, the first one to follow him even as she brought him into the world.

wisdom for the journey

As mariners are guided into port by the shining of a star, so Christians are guided to heaven by Mary.

—Saint Thomas Aquinas, thirteenth century

When I was a young woman, I had issues with Mary. Her seemingly supporting role in Scripture didn't speak to me. I wanted more. I wanted to go right to Jesus, and no detours to his mother seemed necessary. It wasn't until I was older that I began to fully appreciate the great gift of Mary in my spiritual life and in the life of the greater Church.

How could I have seen it any other way? She is far from a supporting character in this story. She is at its heart, bearing the child who would redeem the world. I think it was giving birth to three children that eventually made me appreciate Mary's importance then, and now. She became the role model I was searching for in my spiritual life—a strong woman, a devoted mother, a committed Christian, and a spiritual seeker who never stopped moving forward, even when the path proved threatening.

Mary's "Yes" to God

Let's go back to the moment that changed everything. The Angel Gabriel appears to Mary, a young Jewish woman—a girl really—and says, "Hail, favored one! The Lord is with you." (Luke 1:28) Mary is told that she has been chosen to bear a son, conceived by the Holy Spirit. This child, who should be called Jesus, is the Son of God.

And there, in her home in Nazareth, this scared girl, knowing what awaits her if she ends up pregnant and unmarried, freely chooses to say "yes" to God. "I am the handmaid of the Lord. May it be done to me according to your word," she answers. (Luke 1:38) In her prayer of abandonment to God's will, we see total and complete trust. Her own plans come second to what God has chosen for her. Without knowing all the reasons or what the eventual outcome will be, she agrees.

When we go to God in prayer, we can look to Mary as our model. We may ask for things we need or want, but in the end, the truest prayer is one in which we tell the Lord we will accept whatever he wills. "May it be done to me according to your word."

For those of us who like to be at the controls in life—or who like to *think* we're at the controls—this kind of abandonment can be difficult, almost impossible. To put ourselves into God's hands so completely can make us feel vulnerable, childlike. And yet this is what God asks of us, to come to him full of trust and acceptance, like a little child, knowing that our Father knows exactly what we need.

The *Magnificat*

Mary, already facing her own difficult road as an unwed mother in a world where exile or even death by stoning were real possibilities, puts her own concerns aside to go to her cousin Elizabeth, who is pregnant with John the Baptist. Imagine this pregnant young woman traveling far away to be with her pregnant older cousin—two unlikely women given two unlikely missions: one to bear a prophet, the other a King.

When Mary arrives at Elizabeth's home, her cousin greets her: "Most blessed are you among women, and blessed is the fruit of your womb. And how does this happen that the mother of my Lord should come to me?" (Luke 1:42–43)

And Mary's response to Elizabeth is what we Catholics now pray as the *Magnificat,* Mary's joyous song to God. The *Magnificat* is a well-known and beloved prayer among Catholics and part of Evening Prayer of the Liturgy of the Hours. The *Catechism of the Catholic Church* says the *Magnificat* is the song of both the Mother of God and the entire Church (*CCC,* 2619).

The Magnificat

My soul proclaims the greatness of the Lord,
my spirit rejoices in God my Savior,
for he has looked with favor on his lowly servant.
From this day all generations will call me blessed.
The Mighty One has done great things for me and
holy is his name.
He has mercy on those who fear him in every generation.
He has shown might with His arm;
he has scattered the proud in their conceit.
He has cast down the mighty from their thrones,
and has lifted up the lowly.
He has filled the hungry with good things,
and the rich he has sent away empty.
He has come to the help of his servant Israel
for he has remembered his promise of mercy,
the promise he made to our fathers,
to Abraham and his children forever. (Luke 1:46–55)

prayer practice

Many Catholics have statues of Mary in their homes or yards. I can't remember a time when I didn't have a statue of Mary on my bedroom dresser. Having a Mary statue isn't "idolatry," but rather a sacred reminder of what God has done for each one of us through Mary's willing acceptance of his divine plan. With Mary statues or images, as with prayer, we look to the Blessed Mother to help us move closer to Jesus.

The Miracle at Cana

The wedding feast at Cana gives us a chance to see a different side of Mary. Jesus and his disciples are at a wedding, we are told in the Gospel of John, when the wine runs short. Mary says to Jesus: "They have no wine." To which Jesus replies: "Woman, how does your concern affect me? My hour has not come." (John 2:3–4)

This is my favorite Mary story from Scripture. Our Blessed Mother, at this moment in the Gospel, seems like any other mother. She's asking her son to do something for her, and it appears he clearly isn't interested. And then, like any ordinary mother might do, she ignores his protestations and says to the servants, "Do whatever he tells you." (John 2:4) And Jesus has them fill six large jars with water and produces the best wine of the night.

Here, in this snippet from a day in the life of Jesus and Mary, we get so much more than a mother and son going back and forth about how things need to go. We see Mary interceding on behalf of someone else. She goes to Jesus to ask him to help the wedding hosts. And she doesn't do so tentatively, as if there were some chance Jesus might not listen. She makes her request confident in the knowledge that he will listen to whatever she asks of him.

For Catholics, this is Mary's role in our prayer life on an ongoing basis. We are like that bridegroom, worried about where we'll get more wine, so we go to Mary with our concerns and ask her if she'll put in a good word for us with her Son. We go to her with confidence, knowing she'll never turn away from us and her Son will never turn away from her. This is intercessory prayer at its finest.

At the Foot of the Cross

We don't see much else of Mary as we move through the Gospel accounts of Jesus' preaching years. But as his Passion nears, Mary moves to the fore. She doesn't give us words to live by but rather actions, as she remains a steadfast and faith-filled presence even as her Son suffers in agony on the cross.

It's hard to imagine what it must have been like for Mary to stand by silently, watching as her Son was tortured and killed. Even in her silence, she surely was calling out to God, longing to run to her child and comfort him. But she stood by, quiet and strong, knowing God's plan was unfolding as it should. The image of the Pieta, with Mary cradling the body of her dead Son, speaks volumes as we ponder what she went through and wonder what she was thinking and feeling.

In our own lives, when we're dealing with particularly difficult circumstances, we often go to God and cry out, "Why?" Maybe Mary asked "Why?" too, but if she did, she never lost hope, always trusting that God's way was the only way. She knew from Jesus' earliest days that this role she'd accepted wasn't going to be easy. When Jesus was just a baby and Mary and Joseph presented him at the temple, Mary was told, "and you yourself a sword will pierce." (Luke 2:35) There, at the foot of the cross, that prophecy was fulfilled. Mary knew suffering, and so she knows our suffering. Mary prays with us even when we cry out, "Why?" She stays with us when we otherwise feel alone. She takes our pleas to Jesus and asks him to help her children still on Earth.

The Universal Mother

Most of Jesus' disciples had gone into hiding by the time Jesus was being nailed to the cross. They feared for their lives. Even Peter, the "rock," denied even knowing Jesus on three separate occasions just hours earlier. But Mary is there at the cross, accompanied by her sister, Mary the wife of Clopas, and Mary Magdalene. One disciple—often assumed to be John but recorded in Scripture only as the disciple whom Jesus loved—stood with them.

> When Jesus saw his mother and the disciple there whom he loved, he said to his mother, "Woman, behold your son." Then he said to the disciple, "Behold, your mother." And from that hour the disciple took her into his home. (John 19:26–27)

Catholics believe that in this moment, Jesus gave his mother to all of us. He was not just providing for his own mother's physical needs for the rest of her earthly life. He was providing for our spiritual needs for all time, giving us a spiritual mother who would never abandon us, just as she never abandoned Jesus. And like that beloved disciple, we gladly become her sons and daughters, happy to rest in the arms of our heavenly mother.

Mary becomes the "new Eve," a spiritual mother to all people just as Eve was a physical mother. But unlike Eve, whose "gift" to us was original sin, Mary gives us the gifts of intercession and prayer, the gifts of spiritual comfort and companionship.

wisdom for the journey

We never give more honor to Jesus than when we honor his Mother, and we honor her simply and solely to honor him all the more perfectly. We go to her only as a way leading to the goal we seek—Jesus, her Son.

—Saint Louis Marie de Montfort, seventeenth-century French priest and spiritual writer

The Beginning of the Church

Although Scripture doesn't directly tell us Mary was present at the Ascension and at Pentecost, we can make some assumptions based on the fact that other Scripture accounts place her in the upper room, praying with the disciples.

We are told that the apostles, when they returned to Jerusalem after Jesus' ascension to heaven, went to the upper room. "All these devoted themselves with one accord to prayer, together with some women and Mary the mother of Jesus, and his brothers." (Acts 1:14)

So Mary, who was there at the beginning of Jesus' life, who is present throughout his ministry, and who witnesses his death, is also there at the beginning of his Church. Along with the other disciples, it appears that this first disciple receives the Holy Spirit at Pentecost in the upper room and goes about continuing her Son's mission.

Mary's role has come full circle, from the Spirit who came upon her at the annunciation, to the Spirit who came upon all the disciples at Pentecost. In her we find not only the first disciple, but the one disciple who was physically present for all the key moments of God's plan for salvation. She is the common thread running through all of it. When we weave Mary into the fabric of our own spiritual journey, we enter into her story in a way that helps shape our own story.

To Jesus Through Mary

It's not uncommon to hear the phrase "to Jesus through Mary." This sums up succinctly what our prayers to Mary are meant to do. Jesus is the "way" to the Father, and Mary is a guidepost leading us to Jesus. She cannot be the way. She cannot answer our prayers. She can only join her prayers to ours and bring our prayers—and us—to Jesus.

No matter what prayers we say to Mary, no matter how focused on the Blessed Mother our words may seem, our hearts and minds always need to be set on Jesus.

"Sometimes anxiety is expressed that devotion to Mary may detract from the position of Jesus, our one Lord and Mediator. Such fear is unfounded," the U.S. bishops wrote in a 1973 pastoral letter. "The more we know and love Mary, the more surely will we know and love Jesus and understand his mission in the world. It's also true that the more we know Jesus and love him, the better we will appreciate his mother's place in God's plan for man's redemption."

God chose Mary to bring the Messiah into the world. It seems only natural we would choose Mary to bring the Messiah into our everyday lives.

Over the years, countless devotions to Mary—most notably the Rosary—have become part of everyday Catholic prayer life. We look at those prayers and devotions in the next two chapters. The important thing to remember as we explore these devotions to Mary is that our end goal always is to move closer to Jesus Christ and ultimately to be united with our Father in heaven.

wisdom for the journey

So far, every prayer addressed to the Holy Mother has been answered. … But I do want to point out, the reason I think she intercedes so well for us, is because she too is a human being.

—Jack Kerouac, letter to Bob Giroux, February 1963

Essential Takeaways

- Mary, the Mother of God, was Jesus' first disciple and serves as a model of prayer for all of us.
- In Mary, the "new Eve," we have been given a spiritual mother, someone to whom we can turn for help and comfort.
- Although we may pray to Mary, she cannot answer our prayers. She can only lead us to Jesus and intercede for us.

chapter 10

The Rosary

- The origins of the Rosary
- The reasons for the Rosary
- How it's prayed
- A look at the mysteries

The Rosary is probably the most universally recognized Catholic devotion—even if it's not universally understood—by people both inside and outside the Catholic faith. The Rosary seems to be everywhere: a strand of crystal beads dangling from the hands of an old woman kneeling in a darkened church, wooden beads swinging from the rearview mirror of a minivan as it speeds down a highway, a pop star with Rosary beads hanging irreverently around her neck. There's no doubt that this devotion has a pull on people.

It's surprising sometimes to learn just how many people continue to pray this ancient prayer in modern times. We pray it while jogging, while driving, while waiting for Mass to start, while kneeling with our family at home, while drifting off to sleep at night. Moving the beads through our fingers, unaware of how many Hail Marys we've said, we go deeper and deeper into prayer.

The repetition of the familiar prayers—Our Father, Hail Mary, and Glory Be—becomes a jumping-off point for a meditation on Jesus Christ. As we say the words either silently or aloud, we reflect on Jesus' life through sets of "mysteries."

Although the Rosary is the most popular of all Marian devotions, the end goal, as with all prayers to Mary, is always a deeper relationship with Jesus.

The Roots and Reasons Behind the Rosary

The term *Rosary* refers to two things: the actual set of beads used to say the prayers and the devotion itself. It's said that the Rosary developed as a substitute of sorts for the Liturgy of the Hours among Catholics who could not read.

These ancient Christians replaced the psalms of the Liturgy of the Hours with the Our Father and the Hail Mary. Saying these Scripture-based prayers over and over, often while counting them on knots in a cord, gave worshippers a way to reflect on the central teachings of the faith without reading. Later on, when I review the "mysteries," you'll see an even deeper scriptural connection in the meditations on key moments in Jesus' life.

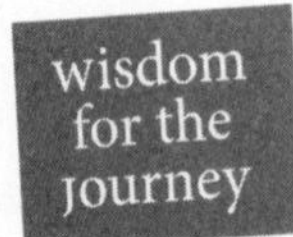

For Christians, the first of books is the Gospel, and the Rosary is actually the abridgement of the Gospel.

—Jean-Baptiste Henri Lacordaire,
nineteenth-century French priest and writer

The Rosary, in the form as we know it today, dates to medieval times. Some connect it to St. Dominic, who founded the Order of Preachers, known as the Dominicans, in the early thirteenth century. It's said that St. Dominic had a vision of the Blessed Mother that inspired him to pray and promote the Rosary during a time when the Church was plagued by heresy. Others refute that story, saying the Rosary developed more gradually over the centuries. Regardless of its specific origins, the Rosary has remained unchanged in the form we recognize today since about the sixteenth century. It has been a favorite devotion of saints, popes, and people in the pews for hundreds of years.

Pilgrims to the Shrine of the North American Martyrs in upstate New York hang Rosary beads near a statue of Mary as an outward sign of their hope that their prayers will be answered.

Photo courtesy of Mary DeTurris Poust

Praying the Rosary

Rosary beads come in all colors, sizes, and materials, from gemstones to wood to plastic. Every set of Rosary beads has a crucifix at the end of a small, straight strand of beads, followed by a circle of beads. The circle is made up of 5 "decades," or sets of 10 beads, separated by single beads. Of course, we don't need Rosary beads to say the Rosary. We can just keep track on our fingers or in our head, but the beads free us from the work of counting so we can focus on prayer. They also give us a physical connection to the spiritual prayers we're sending up to God.

To pray the Rosary, it's best if you can be in a place—physically and mentally—where you can concentrate on saying the words and reflecting on the mysteries. Your sacred space, a church, a quiet room, or a spot outside are all good places to go for prayer.

Some people, however, like to pray the Rosary while on the move. It can be the perfect prayer to say while taking a meditative morning walk or going for a long solo car ride. It can be prayed privately or in a group, with a leader saying the first half of each prayer and the community joining in to finish. The Rosary is also a great devotion for family prayer time because children usually know its basic prayers and can take turns leading the decades.

Generally, this is how the Rosary is prayed:

1. Holding the cross on the Rosary beads, make the Sign of the Cross and recite the Apostles' Creed.
2. On the first separate bead, say the Our Father.
3. On each of the next three beads, say a Hail Mary.
4. On the next separate bead (or medal, depending on your Rosary beads), announce the first mystery and say an Our Father. (I discuss each of the mysteries in the next section.)
5. On each of the next 10 beads, say a Hail Mary. End the decade with a Glory Be.
6. Repeat the process: announce a mystery and say an Our Father, 10 Hail Marys, and a Glory Be for each of the next 4 decades until you go around the entire set of beads.
7. Conclude with the Hail, Holy Queen:

    Hail, Holy Queen

    Hail, Holy Queen,
    Mother of Mercy,
    our life, our sweetness, and our hope.
    To thee do we cry,
    poor banished children of Eve.
    To thee do we send up our sighs,
    mourning and weeping in this valley of tears.
    Turn then, most gracious advocate,
    thine eyes of mercy toward us,
    and after this our exile

show unto us the blessed fruit of thy womb,
Jesus.
O clement, O loving, O sweet Virgin Mary.
Pray for us, O holy Mother of God.
That we may be made worthy of the promises
of Christ.

Amen.

Prayer Practice Rosary recordings may prove to be a help as you begin to practice this devotion. Although the styles vary widely, it's possible to download or purchase recordings or podcasts that include the prayers, reflections on the mysteries, and meditative music to help you develop your prayer routine.

Decoding the Mysteries

While you're saying the words of the Our Father and Hail Mary, you're supposed to focus your heart and mind on Jesus' life as outlined in the joyful, luminous, sorrowful, and glorious mysteries. I haven't always found that easy to do, however. Although I'm a champion multitasker, I sometimes struggle with this one, caught between wanting to focus completely on the words I'm saying and knowing I should be focusing on the subject of a particular mystery.

Some Catholics can move through the Rosary without a misstep, but others of us stumble along, constantly having to pull our attention back to the subject at hand or, more typically in my case, trying to stay awake. When I was younger, I would take my Rosary beads to bed and lie there saying the prayers I knew so well. I never made it very far. I'd drift off to sleep and find the beads tangled in the sheets in the morning, making me feel like a failure at this popular prayer.

My attitude changed when my mother was battling cancer. She prayed the Rosary each night in hopes it would put her to sleep. Drifting off to the rhythm of the Hail Mary was the answer to her prayers in those difficult days of dying. Her approach turned my perspective on its head, making me realize that it's okay if I fall asleep. What could be better than drifting off with the words of my faith wrapped around me like a blanket?

It's okay if you can't always figure out how to say the words of one thing and meditate on something else. If you're praying and setting your heart on Jesus, you're moving forward. It's okay if your mind wanders and you have to keep starting over. That's all part of your journey through prayer, your journey to the heart of God.

For most of its history, the Rosary had three sets of mysteries: joyful, sorrowful, and glorious. But in 2002, Pope John Paul II added a fourth set of mysteries, the luminous mysteries, that focus on key moments in Christ's ministry. He said in his apostolic letter, "On the Most Holy Rosary," that the addition would make the rosary "more fully a compendium of the Gospel" and said he hoped it would give the Rosary "fresh life" and renew interest in the prayer as a "true doorway to the depths of Christ."

Typically, Catholics meditate on certain sets of mysteries on specific days, as you'll see in the following breakdown.

The Joyful Mysteries

The joyful mysteries, recited on Mondays and Saturdays, focus on the happy moments in Jesus' and Mary's life, from the moment of his conception by the Holy Spirit to the last scriptural story from Jesus' childhood.

Annunciation: The angel Gabriel tells Mary she has been chosen to bear the Son of God, and Mary readily agrees. (Luke 1:26–38)

Visitation: Mary visits her cousin Elizabeth, who greets her with words now found in the Hail Mary. Mary responds with the *Magnificat.* (Luke 1:39–56)

Nativity: Jesus is born in a manger in Bethlehem. Shepherds and magi alike follow a star to pay homage to him. (Luke 2:1–14)

Presentation in the Temple: Mary and Joseph bring Jesus to the Temple, as was Jewish custom, to present him to the Lord. (Luke 2:22–38)

Finding of the Child Jesus: During an annual pilgrimage to Jerusalem, Mary and Joseph unknowingly leave Jesus behind and find him three days later in the Temple surrounded by teachers. Jesus says to them, "Why were you looking for me? Did you not know that I must be in my Father's house?"(Luke 2:41–52)

The Luminous Mysteries

The luminous mysteries, or mysteries of "light," recited on Thursdays, focus on moments of revelation—key points in Jesus' life of ministry that have particular importance for Catholics.

Baptism in the Jordan: Jesus approaches his cousin John the Baptist to be baptized, even though he doesn't need to be cleansed of any sin. God speaks from heaven and says, "This is my beloved Son, with whom I am well pleased." (Matthew 3:13–17)

Wedding at Cana: Jesus' first recorded public miracle occurs at a wedding feast, where both his mother and disciples are in attendance. When the wine runs out, Mary approaches her Son and asks him to do something. "Do whatever he tells you," she tells the servants. The miracle of turning water into wine makes true believers of many of Jesus' disciples. (John 2:1–12)

Proclamation of the Kingdom of God: This mystery doesn't focus on one particular Scripture passage but on certain truths Jesus preached that challenged people to a conversion of heart. "This is the time of fulfillment. The kingdom of God is at hand. Repent, and believe in the Gospel." (Mark 1:14–15)

Transfiguration: Jesus goes up a mountain with the apostles Peter, James, and John, and there is transfigured, with Elijah and Moses on either side of him. God says from above, "This is my beloved Son. Listen to him." (Mark 9:2–8)

Eucharist: At the last supper, Jesus took bread and wine and transformed it into his own body and blood, saying, "Do this in remembrance of me." (Luke 22:14–20)

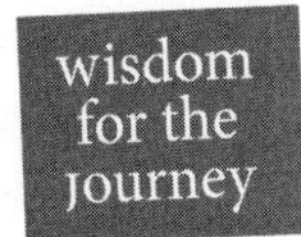

Without [the Rosary's] contemplative dimension, it would lose its meaning. ... Without contemplation, the Rosary is a body without a soul. ...

—Venerable Pope John Paul II, twentieth century

The Sorrowful Mysteries

The sorrowful mysteries, recited on Tuesdays and Fridays, turn our attention toward Christ's suffering and Passion. One by one, we move through the final moments of his life, moments that set a course for the salvation of humankind.

Agony in the Garden: After the last supper, Jesus went to the Garden of Gethsemane to pray. There he begged his Father to spare him the cup of suffering he knew was coming, but then, deferring always to his Father's plan, said, "Yet not as I will, but as you will." (Matthew 26:36–46)

Scourging at the pillar: Jesus goes before Pilate, who does not quite know what to make of this man or why he is so feared. Pilate sends Jesus to be brutally whipped by his soldiers. (John 19:1–5)

Crowning with thorns: The Roman soldiers who scourge Jesus, taunt him, saying that if he is a king, he should be dressed like a king. They put a purple cloak on him and push a crown of thorns into his head. (Mark 15:16–20)

Carrying of the cross: Beaten almost to death, Jesus is then forced to carry his own cross to the place of crucifixion. He is helped by a stranger and greeted by Jewish women as he walks the road to Calvary. (Luke 23:26–31)

Crucifixion: Jesus is nailed to a cross between two common criminals. He forgives the "good thief" who expresses remorse, forgives those who are crucifying him, gives his mother to the care of his beloved disciple, and cries out to his Father before bowing his head and dying. (Luke 23:33–46)

The Glorious Mysteries

The glorious mysteries, recited on Wednesdays and Sundays, are reflections on Christ's victory over death and his promise of eternal life for us all.

Resurrection: On the third day after he died, Jesus rose from the dead. In the Gospel, a group of Jewish women go to the tomb to anoint Jesus' body according to their custom—something they had not been able to do immediately after his death because it was the start of the Sabbath—and they are met by two men in "dazzling garments" who say, "Why do you seek the living one among the dead? He is not here but has been raised." (Luke 24:1–12)

Ascension of our Lord: After remaining with his disciples for 40 days after his resurrection, Jesus returns to his Father in heaven. (Acts 1:8–11)

Descent of the Holy Spirit: Fifty days after Easter, on Pentecost, the advocate or helper Jesus had promised before his ascension descends on the disciples gathered in the upper room and gives them the courage and strength they need to begin to spread the Gospel. (Acts 2:1–4)

Assumption of Mary into Heaven: Catholics believe Mary was assumed bodily into heaven. (There is no direct scriptural reference to Mary's assumption.)

Crowning of Mary: Mary is considered queen of heaven and all the saints. Again, there is no direct scriptural reference, but Catholics often point to this image of Israel from the Book of Revelation as a fitting image of Mary's heavenly glory: "A great sign appeared in the sky, a woman clothed with the sun, with the moon under her feet, and on her head a crown of twelve stars." (Revelation 12:1)

wisdom for the journey

Just as two friends, frequently in each other's company, tend to develop similar habits, so too, by holding familiar conversations with Jesus and the Blessed Virgin, by meditating on the mysteries of the Rosary and by living the same life in holy Communion, we can become, to the extent of our lowliness, similar to them and can learn from these supreme models a life of humility, poverty, hiddenness, patience and perfection.

—Blessed Bartolo Longo, nineteenth- and twentieth-century lay Dominican

Essential Takeaways

- Praying the Rosary venerates Mary, the Mother of God, but always remains focused on the life and works of her Son, Jesus Christ.
- The Rosary is a scriptural devotion, with prayers and mysteries grounded in Gospel stories.
- You can pray the Rosary in private or with a group, out loud or in silence, with beads or without.
- The joyful, luminous, sorrowful, and glorious mysteries provide meditations designed to lead you closer to Jesus Christ.

chapter 11

Other Devotions to Mary

- Popular and traditional prayers to Mary
- An explanation of the "miraculous medal" and prayers that go with it
- A look at Our Lady of Guadalupe, patroness of the Americas
- Getting to know Mary's many different titles

Mary is a saint, the queen of all saints. After all, she is the Mother of God, so she's elevated to a special status among all the holy men and women of history. Most commonly she's known as the Virgin Mary, the Blessed Mother, or Our Lady, but Mary has a long list of titles that represent what she's meant to different people in different times, and what she still means to people today.

As a child named after the Blessed Mother, I was somewhat frustrated by Mary's many titles. In religion class, we would often be told to write something about our patron saint. In my young mind, I felt a bit cheated. I didn't have a nice, neat, "normal" saint—like St. Anthony, St. Francis, or St. Bernadette. I had a saint with so many names and titles I wasn't sure which one to choose. Mary didn't seem like a "saint" to me back then. She was in a class by herself, which just made life complicated for a 9-year-old doing a fourth-grade religion assignment.

Turns out I wasn't really so far off. Mary isn't a saint in the typical sense because there's nothing typical about her. She brought the Son of God into the world, bearing in her heart and in her body the child who would save the world. One title, one name simply isn't enough to convey all that, and so over the centuries, Catholics have poured their own hearts out to Mary, creating devotions in an attempt to honor her for her great sacrifice and trust.

Mary is at once a motherly protector and defender to all those who come to her in prayer. She is a womanly caregiver and comforter to all those who are in need. She is a spiritual role model and companion to all those struggling along the path of life. She is, truly, the queen of all the saints.

Mary's Immaculate Heart

Sometimes, when I want to try to understand Mary better, I remember the fact that, while she was a saint and called in a special way by God, she was also a very real mother to a very real child. I know the depth of my connection to my children, a love that goes beyond anything else in my life. My heart aches when they're hurting. My heart is filled with joy when they're happy. My heart is forever connected to their hearts—first as a physical lifeline that provided all they needed before they were born, and now as a spiritual tie that will remain intact long after I leave this earth.

Imagine, then, how much more powerful was Mary's heart-to-heart connection to her Son, the child who entered the world to save it through his suffering. Imagine, as she nourished him with her own body throughout her pregnancy, the deep connection that was forged as she wondered what this miraculous event would mean for her—the fear that had to be there, but also the joy in knowing God had chosen her for this monumental role in salvation. Imagine, after Jesus' birth, as shepherds and kings came to visit her newborn, how she loved him and protected him and, as Scripture tells us, "kept all these things, reflecting on them in her heart." (Luke 2:19)

It's no surprise, then, that a devotion to Mary's heart would develop over the course of time, connected to devotion to Jesus' sacred heart. Mary's heart is said to be a mirror of Christ's heart. Just as Jesus' heart overflows with love for all humankind despite our failings and sinfulness, Mary's heart overflows with love for the Son and the Father and, in turn, all humankind—her spiritual children on Earth. Both hearts symbolize compassion, mercy, and love beyond measure.

Devotion to Mary's heart began early in the Church and was grounded in Scripture, such as the earlier writing from Luke, the *Magnificat,* and the prophecy of Simeon at the time of Jesus' presentation in the temple:

> Behold, this child is destined for the fall and rise of many in Israel, and to be a sign that will be contradicted, and you yourself a sword will pierce so that the thoughts of many hearts will be revealed. (Luke 2:34–35)

Early Christians recognized in Mary's heart a special way to move closer to Jesus Christ. It was not until the twelfth and thirteenth centuries that a more systematic type of devotion to Mary's heart started to develop, thanks to the efforts of St. Bernard of Clairvaux and, later, sister saints Mechtilde and Gertrude. It was in the fifteenth century, however, that the devotion as we know it today began to take form. Consecration to the Immaculate Heart of Mary was popularized by St. Louis de Montfort in the seventeenth century; the appearance of the Blessed Mother to St. Bernadette at Lourdes, France, in the nineteenth century, and the apparitions of the Blessed Mother to three peasant children in Fatima, Portugal, in the twentieth century, when the Blessed Mother is reported to have said: "God wishes to establish in the world devotion to my Immaculate Heart" to save souls from hell and bring about world peace.

The image of the Immaculate Heart of Mary is that of a heart surrounded by a crown of flowers (as Christ's sacred heart is surrounded by a crown of thorns) and pierced by a sword. A flame burns at the top of the heart, and light emanates from around the heart. Devotion to the Immaculate Heart of Mary and the Sacred Heart of Jesus are linked because Jesus and Mary are forever connected by both their physical and spiritual bonds.

Novena to the Immaculate Heart of Mary

O most Blessed mother, heart of love,
heart of mercy ever listening,
caring, consoling hear our prayer.
As your children, we implore your intercession
with Jesus your Son.
Receive with understanding and

compassion the petitions we place
before you today, especially (special intention).

We are comforted in knowing your heart
is ever open to those who ask for your prayer.
We trust to your gentle care and intercession,
those whom we love and who are sick
or lonely or hurting. Help all of us,
Holy Mother, to bear our burdens in this life
until we may share eternal life and
peace with God forever.

Amen.

wisdom for the journey

Only after the last judgment will Mary get any rest; from now until then, she is much too busy with her children.

—St. John Vianney, nineteenth-century priest known as the *Curé d'Ars*

The Miraculous Medal

In 1830, in a chapel in Paris, 24-year-old Catherine Laboure had visions of the Blessed Mother. Mary told Catherine, then a novice with the Daughters of Charity, to have a medal struck in her honor, saying that all who wear the medal will receive special graces. Before Catherine's death in 1867, more than 1 billion medals were distributed around the world. To this day, millions of Catholics and even non-Catholics wear the miraculous medal.

The medal has on its front an image of Mary standing on a globe with her foot crushing the head of a serpent (Genesis 3). Rays of light emanate from her hands, and 12 stars—reminiscent of the woman of the Apocalypse in Revelation 12:1—encircle her head. Around the edge of the medal are the words: "O Mary, conceived without sin, pray for us who have recourse to thee." On the back of the medal, 12 stars ring the outside edge. The Sacred Heart of Jesus and the Immaculate Heart of Mary are side by side, and above them is a cross linked with the letter *M*, representing Mary's role in God's divine plan.

Although you don't need to be wearing or looking at a Miraculous Medal when you pray to Mary under this title, it's likely that those who choose to say the Prayer to Our Lady of the Miraculous Medal on a regular basis would already have her medal hanging from around their neck. Many Catholics who wear the Miraculous Medal every day without fail have probably never even heard of this particular prayer; the devotion has grown far beyond the confines of Catholic prayer life to include anyone who has a deep love for the Blessed Mother.

Prayer to Our Lady of the Miraculous Medal

Virgin Mother of God, Mary Immaculate,
we unite ourselves to you under your
title of Our Lady of the Miraculous Medal.
May this medal be for each one of us a sure sign
of your motherly affection for us and a constant reminder of our filial duties toward you.
While wearing it, may we be blessed by your loving
protection and preserved in the grace of your Son.
Most powerful Virgin, Mother of our Savior, keep
us close to you every moment of our lives so that
like you we may live and act according to the teaching and example of your Son. Obtain for us, your
children, the grace of a happy death so that in union
with you we may enjoy the happiness of heaven forever.

O Mary, conceived without sin,
Pray for us who have recourse to you.

Amen.

The Memorare

One of the most popular Catholic prayers to Mary is the Memorare, which implores Mary's help with an utter and absolute trust and surrender. Its origin is somewhat mysterious. It's often attributed to St. Bernard of Clairvaux, a Cistercian monk in the twelfth century. However, it was popularized by a seventeenth-century French priest, Claude Bernard, who said he learned it from his father. Hence the possible confusion due to the similar names.

The Memorare

Remember, O most loving Virgin Mary,
that never was it known that anyone
who fled to your protection,
implored your help or sought
your intercession was left unaided.
Inspired by this confidence, I fly unto you,
O virgin of virgins, my mother.
to you I come, before you I stand,
sinful and sorrowful.
O Mother of the Word Incarnate,
despise not my petitions,
but in your mercy hear and answer me.

Amen.

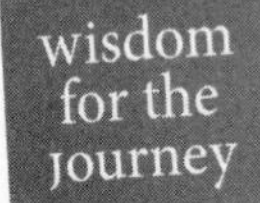

All my own perception of beauty both in majesty and simplicity is founded upon Our Lady.

—J.R.R. Tolkien, twentieth-century writer

The Angelus, Then and Now

Catholics of days gone by could mark the main hours of the day by the *Angelus* bells that rang at 6 A.M., noon, and 6 P.M., calling them to prayer. The *Angelus,* no longer prayed with such regularity, is a celebration of the Incarnation—God becoming human. To this day, despite the decline in popularity, church bells often ring at those hours, reminding us of the need to mark the rhythm of our days with prayer. Some Catholics continue to say this ancient prayer, which originated with the eleventh-century monastic practice of saying three Hail Marys as the evening bell was rung.

When said in a group, the *Angelus* is a sort of call and response of four short verses, punctuated by three Hail Marys and a concluding prayer. If you say the *Angelus* alone, say both parts to yourself. If you want to mark the hour but don't have the prayer in front of you and can't remember it, you can simply pray the Hail Marys.

The name of the prayer comes from its opening line in Latin: *Angelus Domini nuntiavit Maria,* or "The angel of the Lord declared unto Mary."

The *Angelus*

Leader: The angel of the Lord declared to Mary:

Response: And she conceived by the Holy Spirit.

Hail Mary ....

Leader: Behold the handmaid of the Lord.

Response: Be it done to me according to your word.

Hail Mary ....

Leader: And the Word was made flesh:

Response: And dwelt among us.

Hail Mary ....

Leader: Pray for us, O holy mother of God

Response: That we may be worthy of the promises of Christ.

Leader: Let us pray.

Response: Pour forth, we beseech you, O Lord,
your grace into our hearts, that we,
to whom the incarnation of Christ, your Son,
was made known by the message of an angel,
may be brought by his Passion and cross
to the glory of his resurrection,
through the same Christ our Lord.

Amen.

During the Easter season—from Easter Sunday through Pentecost—the *Regina Caeli* replaces the *Angelus*. The *Regina Caeli,* which means "queen of heaven," celebrates resurrection.

Regina Caeli

O Queen of heaven, rejoice! Alleluia.
For he whom you did merit to bear, Alleluia,
Has risen as he said. Alleluia.
Pray for us to God. Alleluia.
Rejoice and be glad, O Virgin Mary, Alleluia.
For the Lord has risen indeed. Alleluia.
Let us pray.
O God, who gave joy to the world through
the resurrection of your Son
our Lord Jesus Christ,
grant that we may obtain,
through his virgin mother, Mary,
the joys of everlasting life.
Through the same Christ our Lord.

Amen.

Our Lady of Guadalupe

Mary is known by many titles, but one of the most popular in the United States is Our Lady of Guadalupe, patroness of the Americas. The image of Our Lady of Guadalupe, also known as the Virgin of Guadalupe, popularized in this country and around the world is a replica of the image that appeared on the *tilma,* or cloak, of Blessed Juan Diego, a Mexican peasant to whom the Blessed Mother appeared in 1531.

The image is of Mary, clothed in traditional Aztec dress. She wears a flowing blue robe covered in gold stars with a pink dress underneath and a sash that signifies she is pregnant. She stands on a crescent moon with its "horns" pointing up. Underneath is an angel holding up her robes. She seems to be blocking out the sun, which shines from behind her. Her face is that of a Mexican peasant, clearly similar to the indigenous people of the country where she appeared. In addition, she spoke to Juan Diego in the language of the indigenous people, making her seem like one of them.

Mary's appearance at Tepeyac outside Mexico City set off a flurry of conversions—9 million Aztecs became Catholic after Juan Diego's vision. And the basilica at that spot is now the most visited Catholic shrine in the world.

As with so many Marian apparitions, Mary comes to those in need, speaking their language, understanding their plight. Like the Mary of Scripture, who in the *Magnificat* speaks of a God who will lift up the lowly, Our Lady of Guadalupe appears as a mother to the disenfranchised, those on the edges of society. She welcomes all to her, making her a comforting and compassionate figure. She is especially popular among Mexican Catholics, but her devotees cut across all cultural, economic, and even religious boundaries. She is not only a religious icon, but a cultural one as well.

When my Irish grandfather was dying, he had a pilgrim image of Our Lady of Guadalupe—a close-up of just her face—hanging near his bed. He prayed to her constantly in those final months, weeks, and days. I was so moved by the image and his faith in Mary's ability to help him during this difficult time that when he died, my aunt gave me that image of the Virgin. I have it in my kitchen today, where I can see her as I cook dinner or wash dishes. There's something about Our Lady of Guadalupe that draws me to her, makes me feel at home near her despite the fact that the imagery is from another culture. She's clearly a mother figure for all people.

Our Lady of Guadalupe, whose feast day is December 12, is not only patroness of the Americas, but also patroness of the unborn and is a favorite among those working on behalf of the pro-life cause.

Prayer to Our Lady of Guadalupe

O Lady of Guadalupe, mystical rose,
intercede for the whole Church,
and especially protect our Holy Father the pope.
Help all of us who invoke you in our needs.
Since you are the ever-virgin Mary,
Mother of God, obtain for us
from your most holy Son the grace
to preserve our faith and our hope
in the midst of bitterness and trials;
help us to live with true charity for all men.

From the Spirit, obtain for us, O Lady of Guadalupe,
the precious gift of perseverance in the faith,
that we may come to the Father.

Amen.

Our Lady of Guadalupe, seen here in a close-up clay reproduction of the image that appeared on Juan Diego's tilma, is a tender mother figure to Catholics and non-Catholics alike.
Photo courtesy of Mary Deturris Poust

A Woman of Many Names

Our Lady of Guadalupe is just one of Mary's many titles. She is known by names that originate from particular Church doctrines, such as Immaculate Conception or Our Lady of the Assumption; from particular apparitions, such as Our Lady of Lourdes or Our Lady of Fatima; or from particular qualities or experiences, such as Our Lady of Sorrows or Our Lady of Perpetual Help. Mary is also known by various titles that express all the things for which she is most honored, loved, and venerated, some springing from Old Testament roots, others from later Church decrees or teachings, such as Mystical Rose, Arc of the Covenant, Queen of the Apostles, and Queen of Peace.

Many of Mary's titles are combined in prayer form in what's known as a *litany*. This type of prayer is a series of petitions, or requests. There are many different litanies to Mary, the most famous being the Litany of Loreto or Litany of Our Lady.

Litany of Our Lady (Litany of Loreto)

Leader:	*Response:*
Lord, have mercy.	*Lord, have mercy.*
Christ, have mercy.	*Christ, have mercy.*
Lord, have mercy.	*Lord, have mercy.*
Christ, hear us.	*Christ, graciously hear us.*
God the Father of heaven,	*have mercy on us.*
God the Son, redeemer of the world,	*have mercy on us.*
God the Holy Spirit,	*have mercy on us.*
Holy Trinity, one God,	*have mercy on us.*
Holy Mary,	*pray for us.*
Holy Mother of God,	*pray for us.*
Holy Virgin of virgins,	*pray for us.*
Mother of Christ,	*pray for us.*
Mother of divine grace,	*pray for us.*
Mother most pure,	*pray for us.*
Mother most chaste,	*pray for us.*
Mother inviolate,	*pray for us.*
Mother undefiled,	*pray for us.*
Mother most lovable,	*pray for us.*
Mother most admirable,	*pray for us.*
Mother of good counsel,	*pray for us.*
Mother of our creator,	*pray for us.*
Mother of our Savior,	*pray for us.*
Virgin most prudent,	*pray for us.*
Virgin most venerable,	*pray for us.*
Virgin most renowned,	*pray for us.*

Virgin most powerful,	*pray for us.*
Virgin most merciful,	*pray for us.*
Virgin most faithful,	*pray for us.*
Mirror of justice,	*pray for us.*
Seat of wisdom,	*pray for us.*
Cause of our joy,	*pray for us.*
Spiritual vessel,	*pray for us.*
Vessel of honor,	*pray for us.*
Singular vessel of devotion,	*pray for us.*
Mystical rose,	*pray for us.*
Tower of David,	*pray for us.*
Tower of Ivory,	*pray for us.*
House of gold,	*pray for us.*
Arc of the covenant,	*pray for us.*
Gate of heaven,	*pray for us.*
Morning star,	*pray for us.*
Health of the sick,	*pray for us.*
Refuge of sinners,	*pray for us.*
Comfort of the afflicted,	*pray for us.*
Help of Christians,	*pray for us.*
Queen of angels,	*pray for us.*
Queen of patriarchs,	*pray for us.*
Queen of prophets,	*pray for us.*
Queen of apostles,	*pray for us.*
Queen of martyrs,	*pray for us.*
Queen of confessors,	*pray for us.*
Queen of virgins,	*pray for us.*
Queen of all saints,	*pray for us.*
Queen conceived without original sin,	*pray for us.*
Queen assumed into heaven,	*pray for us.*
Queen of the most holy Rosary,	*pray for us.*
Queen of peace,	*pray for us.*
Lamb of God, you take away the sins of the world,	*spare us, O Lord.*

Lamb of God, you take away the sins of the world, *graciously hear us, O Lord.*
Lamb of God, you take away the sins of the world, *have mercy on us.*

Leader: Pray for us, O holy mother of God.

Response: That we may be worthy of the promises of Christ.

Leader: Let us pray.

Response: Grant that we your servants, Lord, may enjoy unfailing health of mind and body, and through the prayers of the ever Blessed Virgin Mary in her glory, free us from our sorrows in this world and give us eternal happiness in the next. Through Christ our Lord.

Amen.

So we come to the end of our chapters on Mary, but by no means does that mean she disappears from the picture. She can't, because she's so intimately connected to our prayer lives as Catholics. Regardless of how frequently we pray to Mary or whether we pray these more traditional prayers or something more contemporary, the reality is that Mary, through her relationship to her Son and the Father, serves as a central role model of prayer. In her, we see how we can approach God, how we can turn our lives over to God, and how we can journey with Jesus through any suffering to the eternal glory that lies at the end of this road.

wisdom for the journey

From Mary we learn to surrender to God's will in all things. From Mary we learn to trust even when all hope seems gone. From Mary we learn to love Christ her Son and the Son of God!

—Venerable John Paul II, twentieth-century pope

Essential Takeaways

- Devotion to the Immaculate Heart of Mary is always linked to devotion to the Sacred Heart of Jesus, reminding us of Mary's eternal connection to her Son.
- The miraculous medal and devotions to it remain popular among Catholics of all ages around the world.
- The *Angelus,* once a common prayer used to mark the morning, noon, and evening hours, celebrates the incarnation and is still said by some Catholics privately and in groups.
- Mary is known and venerated under many names based on doctrine, apparitions, and general qualities attributed to Mary. Litanies bring all these titles together in one place.

chapter 12

Help from Holy Men and Women

Finding friends and companions in the saints

Praying with the Church's most popular holy men and women

Relics, medals, and other sacred items to assist prayer life

We all need a few good role models, people we can look up to who can show us how to succeed at whatever it is we're working toward. In that sense, spiritual life is no different, really, from sports or politics or acting. We need to turn to the pros if we want to see how it's done. Thankfully, there are countless holy men and women from every background and age whose real-life experience with prayer can serve as a template for us.

We can find saints who discovered their deepest connection to God in solitude, and those who found it on the streets serving the poor. There are men and women whose lives didn't start out focused on God, but slowly—sometimes kicking and screaming—they developed into saintly examples whose transformations inspire us and propel us forward.

Catholics look to the saints as real friends and companions. To us, they're not some far-off ideal in ivory towers but flesh-and-blood believers who overcame obstacles and setbacks to achieve a kind of spiritual oneness that gives witness to the fact that anyone can be a saint. In fact, each and every one of us is called to be a saint, so it's good to have people who've gone before us to show us the way.

Catholic Roll Call

If you want a quick glimpse at one small slice of Catholic sainthood—although it doesn't feel at all "small" when you're saying it—spend some time with the Litany of the Saints, which is, in effect, a Catholic roll call. Used most commonly at the Easter Vigil Mass, when new Catholics are entering the Church, and during Holy Orders, when men are being ordained, this particular litany is probably the most famous of all the litanies in the Church.

The Litany of the Saints starts first with prayers to God and moves from there to Mary, the angels, apostles, martyrs, and saints of every stripe, from founders of religious orders to hermits. The latter part of the litany focuses on prayers for all people. When said or sung in community, the leader or cantor says the first line, and you say the second part. Or you can say the entire thing on your own.

wisdom for the journey

The saints are the sinners who keep on going.

—Robert Louis Stevenson, nineteenth-century poet and author

There's something absolutely haunting and beautiful when this long litany is sung in church. It's deeply prayerful and hopeful, giving Catholics a reminder of the long list of saints who are praying for us and with us. It's a recap of our history, showing in prayer the wildly diverse group of men and women who make up this communion of saints of which we are all a part.

What follows is a basic Litany of the Saints, as would be sung at Easter Vigil Mass. You may hear variations on it, depending on the occasion or location, with regional saints added into the litany when appropriate.

Litany of the Saints

Leader:	*Response:*
Lord, have mercy on us.	*Lord, have mercy on us.*
Christ, have mercy on us.	*Christ, have mercy on us.*
Lord, have mercy on us.	*Lord, have mercy on us.*
Christ, hear us.	*Christ, graciously hear us.*
Holy Mary, Mother of God,	*pray for us.*
St. Michael,	*pray for us.*
Holy Angels of God,	*pray for us.*
St. John the Baptist,	*pray for us.*
St. Joseph,	*pray for us.*
St. Peter and St. Paul,	*pray for us.*
St. Andrew,	*pray for us.*
St. John,	*pray for us.*
St. Mary Magdalene,	*pray for us.*
St. Stephen,	*pray for us.*
St. Ignatius,	*pray for us.*
St. Lawrence,	*pray for us.*
St. Perpetua and St. Felicity,	*pray for us.*
St. Agnes,	*pray for us.*
St. Gregory,	*pray for us.*
St. Augustine,	*pray for us.*
St. Athanasius,	*pray for us.*
St. Basil,	*pray for us*
St. Martin,	*pray for us.*
St. Benedict,	*pray for us.*
St. Francis and St. Dominic,	*pray for us.*
St. Francis Xavier,	*pray for us.*
St. John Vianney,	*pray for us.*
St. Catherine,	*pray for us.*
St. Teresa,	*pray for us.*
All holy men and women,	*pray for us.*
Lord, be merciful,	*Lord, save your people.*
From all evil,	*Lord, save your people.*
From every sin,	*Lord, save your people.*

From everlasting death,	*Lord, save your people.*
By your coming as man,	*Lord, save your people.*
By your death and rising to new life,	*Lord, save your people.*
By your gift of the Holy Spirit,	*Lord, save your people.*
Be merciful to us sinners,	*Lord, hear our prayer.*
Jesus, Son of the living God,	*Lord, hear our prayer.*
Christ, hear us.	*Christ, hear us.*
Lord Jesus, hear our prayer.	*Lord Jesus, hear our prayer.*

Perennial Favorites

Certain Catholic saints are recognized almost universally by Catholics and non-Catholics alike—Francis, Anthony, Patrick, to name a few. And others are incredibly popular in Catholic circles but the rest of the world probably doesn't even know their names. If you have a particular cause or passion, a particular need or intention, there's a saintly patron to whom you can turn.

Some saints are patrons of specific illnesses, such as cancer, or occupations, such as writers or mariners. Others are patrons of more broad and desperate needs, such as lost causes, or entire countries. And often, a single saint will be a patron of multiple and disparate causes. Take Augustine, for example. He's the patron of brewers, theologians, printers, and people suffering from sore eyes. Quite an eclectic assignment he has!

In the following sections, we look at some of the most popular Catholic saints, dating to the first century all the way up to the present.

Misc.

Separating Saints from Superstitions

Catholics pray to the saints to ask them to pray for us and with us. We do *not* believe if we do certain things, we can guarantee the answer to a prayer. So those house kits that promise you'll sell your home if you bury a statue of St. Joseph or those chain e-mails that say bad things will happen if you don't forward a novena to 12 people before midnight are not in any way part of true Catholic prayer. They're superstition and contrary to true prayer.

St. Joseph

When it comes to popular saints, St. Joseph is at the top of the list. The spouse of the Virgin Mary and the "foster father" of Jesus, this simple carpenter from Nazareth is celebrated and loved for his silent strength, his courage in the face of adversity, and his fatherly care of Jesus.

We don't know much about St. Joseph from Scripture. We *do* know he was a descendant of the royal house of David, the lineage from which the Messiah would come. In the Gospel of Matthew, we're told he was a "righteous man," who was unwilling to expose Mary to shame when she is found to be with child. He plans on quietly divorcing her until an angel appears to him in a dream and tells him not to be afraid, that Mary is pregnant by the Holy Spirit with the child who will "save his people from their sins." (Matthew 1:19–22) The last we see of Joseph in Scripture is during the finding in the temple when Jesus is 12.

St. Joseph is typically depicted holding either a lily or a carpenter's tool. His feast day is March 19. He is patron saint of carpenters, fathers, workers, and more.

From the Novena to St. Joseph

Loving St. Joseph, faithful follower of Jesus Christ, I raise my heart to you to implore your powerful intercession in obtaining from the divine heart of Jesus all the graces necessary for my spiritual and temporal welfare, particularly the grace of a happy death, and the special grace I now implore (special intention).

Guardian of the Word incarnate, I feel confident that your prayers in my behalf will be graciously heard before the throne of God.

Amen.

Misc.

Come to the Feast

Every Catholic saint has a "feast day," a day in the calendar year when the Church celebrates his or her life in prayer and sometimes with special events. For example, the feast of St. Francis of Assisi on October 4 is often celebrated with the Blessing of Animals in church communities because the saint is known for his love of all living things, especially animals. Feast days also mark special events in the lives of Jesus and Mary, such as the Ascension or the Immaculate Conception.

St. Peter

Peter, also known as Simon Peter or *Cephas,* meaning "the rock," isn't celebrated much in popular Catholic piety. That doesn't mean he isn't beloved; he is, as one of the most important saints of early Christianity. It's just that you don't see statues of Peter on front lawns or hear of novenas to Peter prayed at parishes. Peter, "prince" of the apostles, is a saint who tends to stay in the background of everyday Catholic life but is very much front and center of Catholic scriptural and liturgical life.

I'm particularly fond of Peter, a fisherman and brother of Andrew, another apostle, because he is a reminder that even those who make mistakes—big mistakes—can follow Jesus Christ and become a saint. He doubted, he denied, he ran scared, but he was a true believer. He recognized Jesus as the Messiah, saw him transfigured, saw the Risen Christ soon after the resurrection, and after Jesus' ascension, becomes the earthly leader of his followers.

Under all Peter's surface flaws beat the heart of a true disciple, a rock; it reminds us that Jesus chose his disciples—chooses us—not because he wants perfection but because he wants faith, trust, and love.

Peter's successors begin the long, unbroken line of Roman Catholic popes. He was martyred in Rome in 64 A.D. during the reign of Nero—crucified upside down, it's said, because he didn't think he was good enough to die the same way Christ did.

His feast day is June 29. He is often depicted as an elderly man holding keys and a book, or represented by an inverted cross to remind us of his martyrdom, or a rooster to remind us of his denial of Christ. He is patron saint of fisherman, bridge builders, the papacy, and more.

St. Paul

St. Paul is linked with St. Peter because the two great leaders of the early Church evangelized the gentiles and died for their faith in Rome. But Paul entered into his experience with Jesus Christ as a persecutor, not a promoter of the faith.

Paul, previously known as Saul, was a Pharisee, an opponent of Christianity, and was present when St. Stephen, a deacon in the early Church, was stoned to death. (Acts 8:1) While on the road to Damascus to carry out further persecutions, Paul was blinded by a light that he understood to be Jesus Christ and spent three days in darkness. He converted to Christianity and became the "apostle to the gentiles" and the early Church's greatest missionary of the Church. He wrote extensively and is credited with 13 "epistles," or letters, of the New Testament.

His feast day is June 29, shared with St. Peter. The feast of St. Paul's conversion is January 25. He is often portrayed or represented with a sword or a book. He is patron saint of writers, evangelists, tent makers, and more.

St. Mary Magdalene

Mary Magdalene is perhaps one of the most misunderstood and mischaracterized saints of the early Church. Literature and film often cast her as the reformed prostitute of Scripture or, in contradiction to anything written anywhere, as the lover or wife of Jesus. So let's get the facts straight on Mary Magdalene, whose name is derived from the Galilean town of Magdala.

Mary is first referenced in Scripture in Luke 8:2, when Jesus expels seven demons from her and from some other female followers who not only were his disciples but who are believed to have supported his mission financially.

Mary becomes a stalwart disciple and close friend of Jesus. She witnesses the crucifixion and is the first person to whom Jesus appears after his resurrection. At first she doesn't recognize him, but then he calls her by name and she responds, "Rabbouni," which means "teacher" in Hebrew. (John 20:11–18)

Mary Magdalene's feast day is July 22. She is patron saint of penitents and perfumers.

St. Patrick

Despite what's often popularly assumed, St. Patrick, patron saint of Ireland, was not born on the Emerald Isle. He was born in 385 in an unknown location, possibly Wales. He was taken to Ireland and sold into slavery at 16. During six years of slavery, he went through a religious transformation. He escaped to Europe, studied the faith, and became a bishop and missionary, returning to Ireland to bring Christianity to the pagans there. He eventually brought about the conversion of the entire Irish people.

Legend has it he used the shamrock to explain the Trinity. His feast day is March 17. He is the patron saint of Ireland and engineers and is invoked against snakes due to the legend that he drove all the snakes out of Ireland.

From St. Patrick's Breastplate

Christ be with me, Christ before me,
Christ be after me, Christ within me,
Christ beneath me, Christ above me,
Christ at my right hand, Christ at my left,
Christ in quiet, Christ in danger,
Christ in the hearts of all who love me,
Christ in the mouth of friend and stranger,
Christ in every eye that sees me,
Christ in every ear that hears me.

St. Francis of Assisi

Drive through any suburban neighborhood, and you're likely to see at least one statue of St. Francis of Assisi peeking out from a flower garden. This thirteenth-century saint is beloved for so many reasons—his care for all of God's creation, especially animals, his commitment to the poorest of the poor, his dedication to peace, and his total transformation through God. Francis was born to a wealthy silk merchant in Assisi and liked the good life. That all changed when he was captured on his way to battle and spent some time in prison, followed by a period of illness. He had a total conversion, renounced all his worldly possessions, and dedicated his life to preaching the Gospel. He founded the Franciscan Order that to this day remains a powerful force on behalf of the poor around the world. He bore the "stigmata," the wounds of Christ on his own body, and heard Christ tell him, from a cross hanging in the chapel of San Damiano, to "rebuild my church."

Francis, whose feast day is October 4, wrote many prayers and poems, among them the "Canticle of Brother Sun." But the prayer that's most closely associated with Francis is the "peace prayer," written by an unknown author but often attributed to the saint from Assisi. He is patron saint of animals, the environment, merchants, and Italy.

Prayer of St. Francis

Lord, make me an instrument of your peace.
where there is hatred, let me sow love;
where there is injury, pardon;
where there is doubt, faith;
where there is despair, hope;
where there is darkness, light;
and where there is sadness, joy.
O divine Master, grant that I may not so much seek
to be consoled as to console,
to be understood as to understand,
to be loved as to love;
for it is in giving that we receive,
it is in pardoning that we are pardoned;
and it is in dying that we are born
to eternal life.

Amen.

Canticle of Brother Sun

Most High, all-powerful, good Lord,
yours are the praises, the glory, the honor, and all the blessing.
To you alone, Most High, do they belong,
and no man is worthy to mention your name.

Praised be you, my Lord, with all your creatures,
especially Sir Brother Sun,

who is the day through whom you give us light.
And he is beautiful and radiant with great splendor;
and bears a likeness to you, Most High One.

Praised be you, my Lord, through Sister Moon and the stars,
in heaven you formed them clear and precious and beautiful.

Praised be you, my Lord, through Brother Wind, and through the air, cloudy and serene, and every kind of weather through which you give sustenance to your creatures.

Praised be you, my Lord, through Sister Water,
which is very useful and humble and precious and chaste.

Praised be you, my Lord, through Brother Fire,
through whom you light the night and he is beautiful and playful and robust and strong.

Praised be you, my Lord, through our sister Mother Earth,
who sustains and governs us, and who produces varied fruits with colored flowers and herbs.

Praised be you, my Lord, through those who give pardon for your love and bear infirmity and tribulation.

Blessed are those who endure in peace
for by you, Most High, they shall be crowned.

Praised be you, my Lord, through our sister Bodily Death,
from whom no living man can escape.
Woe to those who die in mortal sin.
Blessed are those whom death will find in your most holy will, for the second death shall do them no harm.

Praise and bless my Lord and give him thanks and
serve him with great humility.

—St. Francis of Assisi

St. Anthony of Padua

Known most commonly as the "finder of lost things," St. Anthony is a beloved Catholic saint who today's Catholics call on when searching for keys or eyeglasses or remote controls. But that modern-day view of St. Anthony betrays the depth of this man who walked directly in the footsteps of St. Francis of Assisi. This Franciscan, who served the poor in the thirteenth century, was a powerful preacher and teacher, spreading God's love and mercy to all people.

Anthony is often pictured carrying the child Jesus and holding a white lily in his hand. His feast day is June 13. He is the patron saint of poor people, seekers of lost things, harvests, shipwrecks, sterility, and more.

Prayer to St. Anthony

Holy St. Anthony, gentlest of saints,
your love for God and charity for His creatures,
made you worthy, when on earth,
to possess miraculous powers.
Encouraged by this thought, I implore you
to obtain for me [special intention].
O gentle and loving Saint Anthony,
whose heart was ever full of human sympathy,
whisper my petition into the ears of
the sweet infant Jesus, who loved
to be folded in your arms;
and the gratitude of my heart will ever be yours.

Amen.

St. Therese of Lisieux

St. Therese, a Discalced Carmelite mystic, is popularly known as the "little flower," which tends to denote a sort of meekness and fragility, yet her faith and her spirit were anything but meek. Although she died of tuberculosis at only 24 years old, she left her mark on the Catholic faith through her daily example and her spiritual autobiography, *The Story of a Soul,* which remains among the most popular spiritual books.

St. Therese's approach to spirituality is known as the "little way," which means doing even the most mundane or simple tasks with great love. Her feast day is October 1; she is often represented by flowers, particularly roses. St. Therese is patron saint of foreign missions, those suffering from illness and those who have lost their parents, and is co-patron, along with St. Joan of Arc, of France.

Morning Prayer by St. Therese

O my God! I offer thee all my actions
of this day for the intentions and for
the glory of the Sacred Heart of Jesus.
I desire to sanctify every beat of my heart,
my very thought, my simplest works,
by uniting them to Its infinite merits;
and I wish to make reparation for sins by
casting them into the furnace of Its merciful love.

O my God! I ask of thee for myself
and for those whom I hold dear,
the grace to fulfill perfectly
thy holy will, to accept for love of thee
the joys and sorrows of this passing life,
so that we may one day be united
together in heaven for all eternity.

Amen.

St. Bernadette

Famous for her eighteenth-century visions of the Blessed Virgin Mary at Lourdes, France, St. Bernadette's story was popularized in this country by the 1943 film *Song of Bernadette*. The real-life Bernadette was from an extremely poor family and was out collecting firewood when the Blessed Mother appeared to her in a cave above a riverbank, identifying herself as the Immaculate Conception. A spring began to flow near the cave, with waters seemingly capable of healing the sick. To this day, millions flock to the spring and the shrine at Lourdes hoping for a miracle.

Bernadette's feast day is April 16. She is patron saint of the sick, of shepherds, and of those living in poverty.

Prayer of St. Bernadette

O my God, I beg you, by your loneliness,
not that you may spare me affliction,
but that you may not abandon me in it.
When I encounter affliction, teach me
to see you in it as my sole comforter.
Let affliction strengthen my faith,
fortify my hope, and purify my love.
Grant me the grace to see your hand
in my affliction, and to desire
no other comforter but you.

Amen.

St. Jude Thaddeus

Known popularly today as the saint of impossible or hopeless causes, St. Jude Thaddeus dates to the first century. According to tradition, he was a cousin of Jesus, an apostle, and the author of the Letter of Jude in the New Testament. St. Jude is not to be confused with Judas Iscariot, the apostle who betrayed Jesus.

Jude Thaddeus is said to have preached in Judea; Syria; Samaria, Mesopotamia; and Libya and was martyred in Lebanon. His remains were brought back to Rome and placed in a crypt in St. Peter's Basilica. His feast day is October 28. He is the patron saint of lost causes and desperate situations.

Prayer to St. Jude

St. Jude, glorious apostle, faithful servant
and friend of Jesus, the name of the traitor
has caused you to be forgotten by many.
But the Church honors and invokes you universally
as the patron of difficult and desperate cases.
Make use, I implore you, of that particular privilege
accorded to you to bring visible and speedy help
where help was almost despaired of.
Come to my assistance in this great need
that I may receive the consolation and help of heaven
in all my necessities, tribulations and sufferings,
particularly (special intention), and that I may
praise God with you and all the elect throughout
all eternity.

Amen.

Misc.

Prayer Promises in the Pews

It's not uncommon to find a little slip of paper in a church pew with the following instructions: "The Saint Jude novena must be said nine times, for nine consecutive days, leaving nine copies in church each day. Your prayer request will be answered on or before the ninth day. This novena has never been known to fail!" You may also see "thank you" notes to St. Jude printed in newspapers. This is where prayer morphs into superstition, and it should be avoided. Catholic prayer is not about a magical combination of prayers and days. No prayer is guaranteed, even by the saint of impossible causes.

St. Elizabeth Ann Seton

Elizabeth Ann Seton is one of those saints who has something for everyone. She was a wife, a mother, a widow, an educator, and a religious sister. As if that's not enough, she's the first native-born American to be canonized a saint by the Church. Born into an Episcopal family in New York in 1774, Elizabeth married a wealthy businessman and had five children. After her husband's death, she converted to Catholicism and founded the Sisters of Charity. She established the first Catholic schools in the United States.

Her feast day is January 4. She is patron saint of children who are dying, people who are ridiculed for their faith, and widows, among other causes.

Prayer of St. Elizabeth Ann Seton

O Father, the first rule of
our dear Savior's life was to do your will.
Let his will of the present moment be
the first rule of our daily life and work,
with no other desire but for its most full
and complete accomplishment.
Help us to follow it faithfully, so that doing
what you wish we will be pleasing to you.

Amen.

St. Ignatius of Loyola

Founder of the Society of Jesus, more commonly known as the Jesuits, Ignatius was born in Spain in the fifteenth century. While recovering from a war wound, he experienced a spiritual conversion and dedicated his life to serving Jesus Christ. He wrote his "Spiritual Exercises" (which I discuss in more detail in Chapter 22) after spending time in deep prayer in a cave. He became a priest and formed the Jesuits, with a special focus on education and missionary work.

His feast day is July 31. He is patron saint of the Society of Jesus, retreats, soldiers, and more.

Prayer of St. Ignatius of Loyola

Take, O Lord, and receive my entire liberty,
my memory, my understanding, and my whole will.
All that I am and all that I possess
you have given me: I surrender it all to you
to be disposed of according to your will.
Give me only your love and your grace;
with these I will be rich enough,
and will desire nothing more.

Amen.

Blessed Kateri Tekakwitha

Known as the Lily of the Mohawks, Kateri Tekakwitha will become the first Native American saint when she is canonized. Born in the village of Ossernenon, Auriesville, in upstate New York, in 1656, Kateri was the daughter of a Mohawk chief and an Algonquin Christian woman. She was orphaned during a smallpox epidemic and was left disfigured and partially blind by the disease. She asked to be baptized into the Catholic faith, a decision that brought her abuse from other Mohawks, so much so that she fled to a village for Christian Indians near Montreal, Canada. It's said that Kateri had mystical gifts and that, on her deathbed, her smallpox scars and blemishes disappeared.

She was beatified in 1980 by Pope John Paul II. Her feast day is July 14. Kateri is often represented by a lily or a turtle because she was a member of the Mohawk Turtle Clan. She is the patron of ecologists and exiles.

Misc.

The Road to Sainthood

Holy men and women who are officially recognized by the Church as potential saints go through a long, four-step process that includes a review of their lives and approval of alleged miracles. When a person is first being investigated for possible canonization, he or she is given the title "Servant of God." The next step is to be declared "venerable" for a life of heroic faith and virtue. The third step is "beatification," when a person is declared "blessed," typically after the approval of miracles due to the holy person's intercession. The fourth and final step is "canonization," which means a person is publicly recognized as a saint by the universal Church.

St. Pio of Pietrelcina

Known more commonly as "Padre Pio," this Franciscan Capuchin mystic who died in 1968 had many unusual spiritual gifts. He bore the "stigmata," the wounds of Christ, on his own body; was said to be able to "read" people's hearts, telling them their sins before they confessed; and allegedly was able to bi-locate, levitate, and speak in tongues. But those headline-grabbing characteristics threaten to hide the real gift of Padre Pio, which was his intense and profound devotion to Christ, especially in the Eucharist, and to the Blessed Mother.

Padre Pio was canonized in 2002 by Pope John Paul II, who had met the saint when he was young. Padre Pio's feast day is September 23.

Blessed Mother Teresa of Calcutta

Blessed Mother Teresa of Calcutta, known as the "saint of the gutter," is one of those rare people recognized popularly as a "saint" even before she died. Born in Albania in 1910, Mother Teresa knew, even as a child, that she would dedicate her life to God and service as a religious sister. At age 18, she joined the Sisters of Loreto and went to India as a missionary. In 1946, at age 36, she received a "call within a call" and was convinced that God was pushing her to serve the poor while living among them. She founded the Missionaries of Charity in 1952, and over the ensuing decades, became known worldwide for her work on behalf of the poor and disenfranchised.

Mother Teresa died in 1997, but her legacy lives on. Today the Missionaries of Charity have 5,000 sisters serving in 137 countries. With the publication of Mother Teresa's letters after her death, it became apparent that she suffered a "dark night of the soul" for decades. This was a time when she felt completely cut off from God (a common spiritual problem I discuss in Chapter 22), yet she continued her mission and her ministry right up until her death.

She was beatified in 2003 by Pope John Paul II. Her feast is celebrated on September 5.

Two Missionaries of Charity give food to a homeless man on the streets of Rome.
Photo courtesy of Mary DeTourris Poust

Venerable Pope John Paul II

I remember when Pope John Paul II made his first trip to the United States in 1979. I was there, among the throngs of screaming teens, when he met with young people at Madison Square Garden in New York. From the outset, this pope had a hold on people. When he died in 2005, more than 4 million mourners made their way to Rome to pay their respects to their beloved "papa."

Born in Poland, Pope John Paul II became pope in 1978 and would shape the Church—and the world—for almost 30 years. Considered by Catholics and non-Catholics alike to be one of the most influential leaders of the twentieth century, he was instrumental in the fall of communism in Poland and all of Europe. He visited 129 countries during his papacy and worked to improve relations between the Catholic Church and the Jewish people, Muslims, Anglicans, and Eastern Orthodox. His prolific writings focused on the sanctity of life, social teachings, and the dangers of moral relativism. He was declared venerable by Pope Benedict XVI in 2009.

prayer practice

When you visit a shrine dedicated to a particular saint, it may be possible to have a sacred item touched to that person's grave or to something that belonged to them, making it a "relic." (More on relics coming up.) When I was in Rome, at the grave of Pope John Paul II, I quietly asked a security guard—mostly through pointing and gesturing because talking was forbidden—to place my Rosary beads and religious medals on top of the grave for a moment. He did, and now I have in my possession third-class relics of this first-class pope. It doesn't make the items magical but sacred, giving me a different kind of closeness and connection to this pope who was so much a part of my youth and young adulthood.

Medals, Scapulars, and More

Sometimes, even with all the saints and prayers and rituals, we can still use a little extra help getting our prayer lives moving in the right direction. Earlier I wrote about using sacramentals such as incense and candles and statues to assist you in prayer, but there are also sacramentals you can wear or keep in your home to keep you focused on God.

Crosses and Medals

Many Catholics wear crosses, more typically crucifixes rather than plain crosses, as an outward sign of their faith. And of course, the miraculous medal first popularized back in the mid-1800s remains a popular medal for Catholics today. Truth is, however, many modern Catholics see these sacramentals more as cultural jewelry than spiritual aids.

I have many different crosses and medals, some given to me at my baptism as an infant and some given to me in more recent years. The one I wear most often now was given to me by my husband for Christmas. It's a cross with Greek letters on it—the Alpha and Omega, reminders that God is the beginning and the end, and in the center of them the Chi Ro, the first two letters of Christ in Greek. On the back is a dove, representing the Holy Spirit. When I look down and see this cross, whether I'm cleaning the house or shopping at the market, I get a regular reminder that I'm supposed to be living out what Jesus taught. I don't always live up to it. In fact, more often than not, I don't. But the constant reminder of what I should be doing is a help. Even when it's unseen, under my clothing, I am well aware of its presence and its meaning.

Scapulars

Although this sacramental is not nearly as popular as it once was, some Catholics wear a scapular, which consists of two small rectangular pieces of cloth bearing religious images or words and connected by a band or string. The scapular is worn with one square over the chest and one on the back, with the cords of the band going over the shoulders. It's worn under a shirt so others can't see it. More than a dozen scapulars with connections to various religious orders or lay movements are approved by the Church.

Wearing a cross or medal or scapular is not meant to be a focus of *other people's* attention but a focus of *your* attention. These sacramentals are part of your private devotion, giving you gentle reminders about your goal: Jesus Christ. They're worn not only as an outward sign of faith, but as a reminder of your inward journey.

Relics

Relics are another type of sacramental that can aid your spiritual life. A relic is something connected to a saint. A piece of a saint's bone, for example, would be a "first-class" relic; a piece of their clothing, a second-class relic; and a piece of cloth or Rosary beads or a medal that was touched to their body or grave, a third-class relic. This sacramental can seem a little odd to non-Catholics—and even to some Catholics!—but there are good reasons for relics.

I have some relics of all three classes in my possession, and when I brought them into my fourth-grade religion class one afternoon, I had all eyes on me. There's nothing like the 800-year-old bone of a dead saint to get a 9-year-old's attention, even if it's barely larger than the period at the end of this sentence. But as I explained to them, the relics aren't creepy or magical or weird. They're physical reminders of people we love and look up to. If we love baseball, we'd probably like nothing more than to have Babe Ruth's bat. If we like music, maybe we dream of seeing or touching John Lennon's guitar. Well, if we love the saints, why not have something that belonged to them or was touched by them as an inspiration for our own spiritual lives? It's that simple.

Misc.

Hands Off Relics

You can't buy a relic. That's called *simony* and is against Church law. Despite that fact, relics are for sale on the Internet. Buyer beware. Not only is it wrong, but they're often counterfeit.

For Catholics, being able to learn about or reflect on the lives of the saints is like opening up a spiritual family album. In the pages of their lives, we can find examples of deep faith, overwhelming suffering, great joys—all the things we encounter in our own lives. In the saints, we have companions for the journey, friends who remind us that the path may not always be easy but we are not the first to walk it and we certainly won't be the last. We are not alone.

Essential Takeaways

- You can turn to the saints as examples of how to live your faith in your day-to-day life.
- Saintly men and women come from all walks of life—rich and poor, educated and uneducated, married and unmarried, priests, nuns, bishops, and popes.
- Some of the most popular saints are beloved not only for the lives they lived but for the legacy of prayer and service they left behind.
- Sacramentals such as medals, scapulars, and relics can aid you on your spiritual journey, providing inspiration for the long road ahead.

Part 4

Prayer's High Point: The Mass

When it comes to Catholic prayer life, Mass is the apex. It is at once the foundation, the cornerstone, and the pinnacle of prayer.

Mass gives us an opportunity to pray in community, to receive Jesus in the Eucharist, and to be nourished for the journey ahead. Through the wisdom of Scripture and the words of prayers and songs, we find encouragement and inspiration, motivation and affirmation. In the power and beauty of the Eucharist, we find strength and grace, humility and wonder.

No matter where we go in the world, no matter what language we speak, no matter what our education or background or nationality, the Mass is the Mass. It unites us and reminds us that we are part of one holy, catholic, apostolic Church that spans the globe as well as the annals of history.

In Part 4, we look at the parts of the Mass, including new language that was approved by Pope Benedict XVI in 2010, marking the first major changes to the Mass in more than 40 years.

chapter 13

The Liturgy as Ultimate Prayer

Tracing the Mass back to the Last Supper

The importance of the Sabbath and ways to prepare for it

Understanding the centrality of the Mass

A look at the gestures and postures of prayer

No part of Catholic prayer life is more important than the Mass, our communal celebration of Jesus' Passion, death, and resurrection. Whether we attend Mass weekly or daily, participating in this pivotal public prayer, a prayer focused on the real presence of Jesus in our midst, is central to our spiritual lives. It's the engine that moves us forward.

For most of us, Mass is so familiar that we go through the motions without needing to think about them. In unison, we sit, we stand, we kneel, we respond, we sing. The sights and sounds are so engrained in us, they feel as natural as walking. And as in the old adage about riding a bike, once you've got it down, Mass is something you never forget.

Still, sometimes even those of us who've been doing this for as long as we can remember don't know all the reasons behind the rituals. Sometimes we can take Mass for granted, and become complacent to the fact that this celebration makes Jesus present to us in a very real way. Sometimes we just need to step back and refocus on why the Mass is so special.

Starting with the Last Supper

The night before he died, Jesus gathered with his apostles to celebrate the Passover meal, knowing that his death was imminent. It was during this meal, the Last Supper, that he took bread, broke it, and said, "This is my body that is for you. Do this in remembrance of me." And he took the cup of wine and said, "This cup is the new covenant in my blood. Do this, as often as you drink it, in remembrance of me." (1 Corinthians 11:25, the oldest scriptural version of this event, written in the mid-50s A.D.)

Jesus wanted his followers then—and us today—to have something that would forever connect us to him and to his sacrifice on the cross for us, and so he not only gave us his body and blood but also asked us to remember him this way. The Mass is our remembrance, our opportunity to receive Jesus in the Eucharist just as the apostles did that first time during the Last Supper.

This gift, this spiritual nourishment, is at the heart of Catholic prayer life. It gives us the spiritual strength we need to live out Jesus' often-difficult Gospel challenges: to love others as we love ourselves; to treat our neighbors the way we want to be treated; to care about and pray for everyone, even our enemies.

Although we are expected to be at Mass on Sundays, churches around the world celebrate Mass every day, often at multiple times, so you can participate in this ultimate prayer daily.

prayer practice

The only days in the Church year when Mass is not celebrated are Good Friday and Holy Saturday, when we commemorate the death of Jesus on the cross and wait in the darkness of a spiritual "tomb." Although a Vigil Mass is celebrated on Saturday night, it is no longer Holy Saturday, according to the liturgical calendar, but the start of the Easter season.

Entering into the Sabbath

Catholics are obligated to attend Mass every Sunday, or the Saturday evening "vigil" Mass, but by no means is Mass meant to *feel* like an obligation. It's meant to be a real celebration, a feast, a big family meal. This is our Sabbath, the day of the week we commemorate Christ's resurrection, a day when we rest in the knowledge of God's love for us.

So we center our Sunday on Mass, trying to experience it not as something we have to be done with, but something we enter into. Typically the physical act of getting to Mass isn't a problem. Depending on where we live, there are usually a multitude of Mass times and locations from which to choose. Now, getting ourselves into the right frame of mind for Mass can be a different story. It's not always easy to make that shift from busy work and family life to a quiet interior place where we can focus on God and on the celebration at hand.

With three young children, Sunday morning at our house can be a bit like a circus. Getting little ones dressed, serving breakfast, gathering the "church bag" filled with books and crayons for our preschooler—all of it can add up to a most un-prayerful state of mind. Even the drive to church is usually fraught with last-minute lectures or backseat arguments among siblings. It inevitably leaves me wondering how we can prepare for Sunday Mass in a way that will put all of us in the right spiritual place, a place where we are open to God rather than sitting in our pew with arms folded.

wisdom for the journey

The Mass is the most perfect form of prayer!

—Pope Paul VI, twentieth century

It helps if we can begin to make small preparations that will put us in the right mental and spiritual state of mind *before* we get to church on Sunday. The good news is that preparing for Mass has some positive side effects. When we make the mental and spiritual transition from the world's time to God's time, that shift has the tendency to reverberate throughout our day, making our entire Sunday more peaceful and enjoyable. Sabbath, after all, is not only a day for going to church; it's a day for personal downtime, recreation, and relaxation.

"Sunday is a time for reflection, silence, cultivation of the mind, and meditation, which furthers the growth of the Christian interior life," says the *Catechism of the Catholic Church*. (CCC, 2186)

So we can think of Sunday as a time to refocus our energy—spiritual, mental, and physical. And we can begin by creating a transition from the workweek to our day of rest, even if "rest" means a family picnic or a trip to a museum.

We can say a special prayer together on Sunday morning, or we can read the Gospel for Sunday Mass as a family ahead of time and talk about it. Our transition time doesn't have to revolve only around prayer. We can do something decidedly less "churchy" but still special—like a breakfast ritual that signals our Sunday has begun, or even a Saturday evening family routine that sets the tone for the rest of the weekend. Anything we can do to mark Sunday as special helps us enter into the Sabbath in a more focused way.

If we live alone, it's no different. Special rituals, spiritual reading, maybe simply playing sacred music as we clean up the dinner dishes can help center us and prepare us to enter into the Sabbath in the right frame of mind.

Meeting Jesus at Mass

Being at church and participating in Mass is a real boost to prayer life. There, with our brothers and sisters in faith surrounding us, we can join our voices and experience prayer in a way that's impossible to replicate at home in our little sacred space. At Mass we feel the spiritual power of communal prayer. We let the words of Scripture wash over us. We raise our voices and lift up our hearts. We meet Jesus in the Eucharist.

This is what makes Mass so special for Catholics. It's a beautiful liturgy where the central teaching of our faith—that Jesus Christ is truly present to us in the Eucharist at each and every Mass—comes to life. For many of us, the experience is too awesome to be reserved for Sundays alone. We want to be there as often as we can, basking in the glow of God's presence among us, sharing a feast with our spiritual family, soaking up nourishment for the journey.

When we enter church, we bless ourselves with holy water, a symbol of our baptism, and make that physical shift from the secular to the sacred world. As we approach our seat, we may genuflect—touch our right knee to the ground—if a tabernacle with the Blessed Sacrament is present. Or if the tabernacle is located elsewhere in the church, we may simply make a slight bow toward the altar as a sign of reverence.

Once in our seats, it's helpful if we take a minute or more to kneel in quiet prayer before Mass begins. This is a transition time from hectic outside life to quiet interior life. By taking even one minute to bow our head and say a few silent words to God, we can prepare for what is about to happen, for that moment when we will receive Jesus into our heart.

wisdom for the journey

I believe that were it not for the Holy Mass, at this moment the world would be in the abyss, unable to bear up under the mighty load of its iniquities. Mass is the potent prop that holds the world on its base.

—St. Leonard of Port Maurice, seventeenth-century Franciscan friar

Gestures of Faith

The Mass isn't a sedentary affair. The gestures, the postures, the almost-constant movement can be confusing to non-Catholic visitors, but there are reasons for all of it. The repetitive motions and liturgical responses have symbolic meaning and give us a common ground, whether we're attending Mass in our local home parish, in another state, or even in another country. The Mass is almost identical, no matter where we go.

Standing

We begin the Mass on our feet, standing as the priest enters while the opening hymn is sung. (I discuss the individual parts of the Mass in Chapters 15 through 17.) We stand on and off throughout the Mass—when we are praying or singing together or responding to the priest in some way, and when the Gospel is read. Standing is a posture of respect and praise.

Sitting

When the lector reads the first and second readings, when the cantor sings the responsorial psalm, when the priest gives his homily, and when the gifts and altar are being prepared, we sit down. This is a receptive posture, a position of listening, learning, and meditating.

Think back to when Jesus would preach to his followers. They would typically sit around him and listen. (Matthew 5:1) And so we sit down and listen to the Word of God and the words of the priest.

Kneeling

Kneeling is a posture of total reverence and adoration. We kneel at Mass during the entire Eucharistic prayer because it is then that the bread and wine become Jesus, making this the pivotal moment of the celebration.

Although it's no longer part of the Church's guidelines, Catholics in many parishes continue to kneel again after the Lamb of God is sung, in preparation for receiving Communion. The more recent directives are to remain standing after the Lamb of God and until everyone in the church has received Communion.

Using Our Hands

At specific times during the Mass, we also use our hands. These movements are gestures of faith, a way to connect our body to our prayers.

We make the Sign of the Cross at the beginning and end of the Mass. Just before the Gospel is read, we take our thumb and trace a small cross on our forehead, lips, and heart while saying "Glory to you, O Lord." During the Profession of Faith, or Creed, we bow slightly when we say the words "and by the Holy Spirit was incarnate of the Virgin Mary." After the Our Father, at the Sign of Peace, we shake hands or make some other gesture of greeting with those around us. And just before we receive Communion, we bow slightly as a sign of reverence.

Prayer Practice

We may find minor variations on basic Catholic gestures and positions from church to church. In some parishes, for example, it's common to hold hands during the Our Father. Or we may see individual people open their hands toward the priest during certain responses. These local or regional customs are not part of the Church's official directives for liturgical worship, but they can be powerful enhancements to the prayer experience at Mass.

Using our bodies, through postures and gestures, to complement our vocal prayer allows us to experience prayer on another level, a physical level because we are, after all, both physical and spiritual beings. But the gestures and postures serve another purpose as well. They unite us as Catholics, reminding us of our common bond, that we are all part of the Body of Christ.

Essential Takeaways

- The Mass is the most perfect form of prayer.
- Sunday is the Christian Sabbath, which is a day for the Lord, for family, for rest, and for recreation.
- We meet the Lord at Mass—through Scripture, through community, and especially through the Eucharist—which is why this celebration is so critical to our spiritual lives.
- Gestures and postures used at Mass allow us to connect our bodies to our prayers, making the experience more powerful.

chapter 14

New Changes to Old Language

The reasons behind the changes to the Mass translation

A line-by-line look at some of the most dramatic changes

Adapting to the new language

For more than 40 years, Catholics in the United States and Canada have been praying at Mass with the same words, the same prayers, week after week, year after year. For many of us—those of us who came of age after the Second Vatican Council—the Mass as it existed from 1970 until 2010 is the only version we've ever known.

Now English-speaking Catholics are adapting to a new translation for the first time in a long time. Old prayers, committed to memory over the course of a lifetime, have been given a few new twists. Responses have been changed. Even the Creed has been retranslated in places.

Some wonder why we need a new translation when the old one seemed to be working just fine. Others say it's about time we get the language closer to the original Latin. Whatever your point of view, the reality is that these changes are here to stay, at least for the foreseeable future.

If It's Not Broke ...

For most of us in the pews, the words of the Mass are familiar, comfortable, and clear. So it's understandable that news of the updated translation was met with more than a little trepidation by many lay Catholics, as well as some bishops and clergy. Even Pope Benedict XVI admitted, after approving the new translation, that adapting to the new language might not be easy for everyone.

wisdom for the journey

Our words in the liturgy are not simply expressions of one individual in one particular place at one time in history. Rather, they pass on the faith of the Church from one generation to the next. … The new translation provides us with prayers that are theologically accurate, in a language with dignity and beauty.

—Bishop Arthur J. Serratelli, Chairman of the United States Catholic Conference of Bishops Committee on Divine Worship

"Many will find it hard to adjust to unfamiliar texts after nearly forty years of continuous use of the previous translation. The change will need to be introduced with due sensitivity, and the opportunity for catechesis that it presents will need to be firmly grasped. I pray that in this way any risk of confusion or bewilderment will be averted, and the change will serve instead as a springboard for a renewal and a deepening of Eucharistic devotion all over the English-speaking world," Pope Benedict XVI wrote in April 2010.

So if the Church is aware that a new translation might be tough on the average Catholic, why the change at all? This process was really about returning to our Latin roots, to the language that serves as the template for the Mass in every other language.

After the Second Vatican Council (1963–1965), when the Mass went from universally Latin to the "vernacular" (that is, the native languages of Catholics across the world), Pope Paul VI promulgated a new Roman Missal, the book that contains all the prayers, chants, and instructions on the celebration of the Mass. This 1970 missal, dramatically different from its 1962 predecessor, became the official version of the Mass, called the *editio typica* (typical edition), which was then translated into various languages to serve Catholics around the world. The English version was published in the United States in 1973.

In 2000, Pope John Paul II, as part of the new millennium Jubilee Year, issued a revised Roman Missal, which set off a decade-long process of translating and approving the new text and Order of the Mass. While there had been minor changes made over the years, John Paul's revised Missal and its translation represent the most significant changes made to the Mass in English since Vatican II. The U.S. bishops approved the new translation in late 2009, and Pope Benedict XVI approved it in spring of 2010. A period of *catechesis* followed, with training in dioceses around the country to help prepare priests and parish ministers for Advent 2011, when the changes go into effect.

Definition

Catechesis comes from the Greek word *katechizo* and means "to teach orally." In Catholic tradition, catechesis is the education of children and adults in the faith.

The new translation has practical as well as spiritual implications. Music books, personal missals, parish sacramentaries, and lectionaries—every piece of printed material pertaining to the Mass—had to be updated to accommodate the changes. It's time to turn in our old missals for new versions.

The Whys Behind the Changes

In the rush to make the Mass available in the vernacular after Vatican II, liturgists now concede that the 1973 translation was not as carefully done as it could have been. The new translation brings back to the language of the Mass the prose and poetry of the original Latin, along with more concrete images and a noble tone. Experts say the updated version restores a sense of awe and mystery to the Mass, giving us a more direct connection to the words inspired by Scripture.

I have to admit that when I first heard there would be changes to the Mass, I was not happy. I didn't like the idea of needing to look at a book or a guide to get me through prayers I've been saying by heart since I was a child. I could feel myself bristle at the thought of saying certain responses, which sounded awkward to my ears, until I started reading up on the changes. Then, as I began to see the connection to words from Scripture, I could feel a shift in attitude and even began saying some of the new responses silently before they officially became part of the Mass.

wisdom for the journey

Change is never easy, especially if the change doesn't seem necessary, and right now the necessity of these changes may seem elusive at best. However, this is an opportunity for each of us to reinvigorate our own participation in the liturgy, to renew and deepen our understanding of the liturgy, to learn once again what it means for us as the Body of Christ to be drawn up into the worship of our God through the liturgy.

—Archbishop Daniel Pilarczyk, retired Archbishop of Cincinnati, twenty-first century

Learning Your Lines

As we work through the individual parts of the Mass in the next three chapters, we cover the new language of every prayer and response. But some changes really stand out as prime examples of what this new translation means for those of us praying from the pews.

One of the most dramatic and significant changes is a key bit of dialogue between the congregation and the priest. For years, when the priest has said, "The Lord be with you," we have responded, "And also with you." In the revised Missal, our response is, "And with your spirit." It sounds odd at first, but there are good reasons.

The Latin response to the priest's greeting is "*et cum spirtu tuo,*" meaning literally "and with your spirit." This is a reference to language used by St. Paul, who, in his Second Letter to Timothy, addresses him in this way: "The Lord be with your spirit." (2 Timothy 4:22) The greeting is a reminder that believers have a special closeness to God, and that the Spirit brings believers together. By using this response at Mass, we reaffirm that closeness by using St. Paul's words each time the priest says, "The Lord be with you," or "Peace be with you."

Another dramatic change comes just before Communion. In the "old" version, we would say, "Lord, I am not worthy to receive you, but only say the word and I shall be healed." With the new translation, we respond, "Lord, I am not worthy that you should enter under my roof, but only say the word and my soul shall be healed."

Again, at first blush, this seems awkward to our American ears, almost a *non sequitor*. Until we understand the context, that is. This response takes us once again back to Scripture, when the Roman centurion comes to Jesus to seek healing for his servant. (Matthew 8:8 and Luke 7:6) Jesus offers to go to the soldier's home, but the centurion responds: "Lord, I am not worthy to have you enter under my roof; only say the word and my servant shall be healed."

At that moment, as we are about to receive Communion, we, too, are preparing to welcome Jesus under the roof of our bodies. Do we have faith like the Roman soldier, believing that if Jesus but says the word we will be healed and ready to receive him? It's a beautiful translation, isn't it? This is the one that really helped me see the poetry and awe of what the Church was doing by returning the language of the Mass to its Scriptural roots.

Many other changes affect almost every prayer we say at Mass, including a shift from the communal "We believe" to the personal "I believe" when we profess the retranslated Nicene Creed.

And the priest's parts have changed as well. For example, during Eucharistic Prayer III, instead of saying, "from east to west," the priest says, "from the rising of the sun to its setting."

wisdom for the journey

For the first time we have in English a translation of the Latin prayers of the Church that are theologically accurate and communicate the mysteries of our faith as expressed for centuries in the prayers of the Mass.

—Sister Esther Mary Nickel, R.S.M., professor of sacred liturgy at St. John Vianney Theological Seminary in Denver

In the months leading up to the official switch to the new translation, the U.S. Church conducted workshops and seminars across the country to help parishes, priests, music ministers, liturgical ministers, and people in the congregation adjust to the new language. The hope is that the new translation will spark renewed excitement for and spiritual curiosity about the Mass and that, in learning our new parts, we will remember the importance of the Mass, the most beautiful and vital Catholic prayer.

Essential Takeaways

- In 2010, Pope Benedict XVI approved a new English translation of the Roman Missal, bringing the words of the Mass closer to the original Latin.
- Everything from the people's greeting to the priest, to the Creed, to the prayer before Communion has been retranslated.
- In the individual changes to various parts of the Mass, we can find direct scriptural language and imagery.
- The hope is that the new translation will reinvigorate Catholic enthusiasm for the Mass.

chapter 15

The Introductory Rites

The importance of praying together in word and song

A piece-by-piece look at the opening sequence of the Mass

Introductory prayers, from the Penitential Rite to the *Gloria*

Imagine yourself sitting in the pew of your favorite church. Some people are kneeling in prayer. Others, especially the children, are fidgeting in their seats. Candles flicker on the altar as people continue to stream in right up until the moment the Mass begins, and sometimes well after. The organist plays some background music as the priest, lectors, altar servers, and cantor get ready for the main event.

This could be Mass at any church, in this country or anywhere in the world, with minor variations on style but never on substance. This is when we come together to pray and sing, raising our voices in praise, asking for God's forgiveness, professing our beliefs. The Mass is the main celebration of our faith, the pinnacle of our prayer life.

In this chapter, we see how the Introductory Rites of the Mass unfold, according to the 2010 English translation of the Roman Missal. This portion of the Mass leads up to the Liturgy of the Word, which we look at in Chapter 16. During the opening sequence, we prepare to meet Jesus Christ in the word and sacrament that are to follow.

The Lord Be with You

Mass begins with an entrance song, except during Lent, when Mass may begin in silence. During the opening hymn, the priest, deacon (if one is serving), and ministers of the Mass process down the main aisle while the congregation stands and sings together. The entrance song reinforces the unity of the community of believers as we praise God together through music, an important part of our prayer life.

The priest and altar servers bow at the front of the altar, and the priest kisses the altar in a sign of veneration. He then proceeds to his chair. The Mass begins with the Sign of the Cross.

> Priest: In the name of the Father, and of the Son, and of the Holy Spirit.
>
> *People: Amen.*

The priest begins with a greeting. The most common one is this:

> Priest: The Lord be with you.
>
> *People: And with your spirit.*

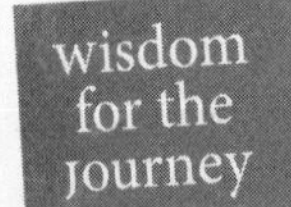

The celebration of Holy Mass is as valuable as the death of Jesus on the cross.

—St. Thomas Aquinas, thirteenth-century Dominican friar, theologian, and philosopher

I Confess ...

Before we listen to the Word of God in the readings, responsorial psalm, and Gospel, we ask for God's mercy, acknowledging our own sinfulness and expressing our remorse together.

This portion of the Mass offers three different options. The first is the prayer known as the *Confiteor,* which is a prayer of general confession. It doesn't take the place of the sacrament of confession, but it is a way for us to publicly and communally express our sorrow over our shortcomings and ask God to pardon us.

Confiteor

I confess to almighty God
and to you, my brothers and sisters,
that I have greatly sinned
in my thoughts and in my words,
in what I have done and in what I have failed to do,
through my fault, through my fault,
through my most grievous fault;
therefore I ask blessed Mary ever-Virgin,
all the Angels and Saints,
and you, my brothers and sisters,
to pray for me to the Lord our God.

At my parish, this prayer isn't used very often, but it is a favorite of mine. I love not only the cadence of it but also the sentiment that I'm confessing to God, and to my brothers and sisters in faith, that I recognize I have some spiritual work to do. I especially love the part where we say, "in what I have done and in what I have failed to do," acknowledging that sometimes our mistakes are a result of inaction rather than action. I don't see this prayer as a sign of weakness. To me, it is a sign of strength and belief, a confession but also a profession, that I believe I can do better with God's help.

And really, who among us can say we don't need to be a little humble before God? Sometimes we get caught up in the worldly notion that admitting our sins and showing humility are signs of weakness, but Jesus reminds us that, in matters of faith, it's just the opposite: "My grace is sufficient for you, for power is made perfect in weakness." (2 Corinthians 12:9)

The Church recommends a gesture to accompany this prayer. When we say "through my fault, through my fault, through my most grievous fault," we are supposed to take our right hand and gently "strike" our breast, just over our heart. Like the other gestures we use during the Mass, this one is meant to give our words a physical connection, to take our admittance of fault and give it an outward sign, a connection to our body. It was something that was done more commonly in pre–Vatican II days, although I often see older Catholics continue to do it. Now, with the new translation—and that particular line of the prayer has been changed—the gesture has been officially returned to the prayer.

Lord, Have Mercy

If the Mass doesn't include the Confiteor, it may include the following option instead:

Priest: Have mercy on us, O Lord.

People: For we have sinned against you.

Priest: Show us, O Lord, your mercy.

People: And grant us your salvation.

Or the priest may choose to use the Kyrie, Eleison (Lord, Have Mercy) for the Penitential Rite, perhaps the most common form used:

Priest: You were sent to heal the contrite of heart:
Lord, have mercy.

People: Lord, have mercy.

Priest: You came to call sinners:
Christ, have mercy.

People: Christ, have mercy.

Priest: You are seated at the right hand of the Father
to intercede for us:
Lord, have mercy.

People: Lord, have mercy.

prayer practice

On certain Sundays, during the Easter season in particular, a Rite of Blessing and sprinkling of holy water may be used in place of the Penitential Rite. The priest says a prayer blessing the water and then walks through the congregation, sprinkling holy water, a sign of our baptism, on those of us in the pews.

Gloria in Excelsis Deo

The last prayer said as a congregation in the Introductory Rites is the *Gloria,* the prayer of praise often sung with great fanfare during special feasts and seasons. I talked earlier about prayers of praise and adoration;

the *Gloria* is that type of prayer at its finest, evident in the words that proclaim God's glory. The second stanza of this prayer focuses on Jesus as Lamb of God, and, in the final stanza, we come back around to the Father, Son, and Spirit.

Gloria

Glory to God in the highest,
and on earth peace to people of good will.

We praise you,
we bless you,
we adore you,
we glorify you,
we give you thanks for your great glory,
Lord God, heavenly King,
O God, almighty Father.

Lord Jesus Christ, Only Begotten Son,
Lord God, Lamb of God, Son of the Father,
you take away the sins of the world,
have mercy on us;
you take away the sins of the world,
receive our prayer;
you are seated at the right hand of the Father,
have mercy on us.

For you alone are the Holy One,
you alone are the Lord,
you alone are the Most High,
Jesus Christ,
with the Holy Spirit,
in the glory of God the Father.

Amen.

After the *Gloria,* the priest will say, "Let us pray." He will then offer an opening prayer that concludes with us saying, "Amen." After that we sit down, ready to soak in the words of Scripture during the Liturgy of the Word.

wisdom for the journey

A sacramental celebration is a meeting of God's children with their Father, in Christ and the Holy Spirit; this meeting takes the form of a dialogue, through actions and words.

—*Catechism of the Catholic Church,* 1153

Essential Takeaways

- The beginning of Mass includes an entrance song and Introductory Rites to unite us in prayer and prepare us for what's to come.
- During the Penitential Rite, we confess our sinfulness before our brothers and sisters in faith and ask God's forgiveness.
- The Gloria is a powerful prayer of praise said or sung during the Introductory Rites.

chapter 16

The Liturgy of the Word

Meeting God in the words of Scripture

The Gospel and homily as take-home lessons for life lived out in the world

Professing our faith, and praying for others

The Catholic Mass focuses heavily on the words of Scripture. The entire first half of the Mass, in fact, revolves around the inspired words of the Bible, taken from both the Old and New Testaments, giving lie to the myth that Catholicism is not a Scripture-based faith. It is saturated in Scripture from start to finish, and the Mass is the most obvious example.

In the Liturgy of the Word, we come face to face with the written history of our spiritual journey. The pieces fit together like a puzzle, the New Testament readings showing the fulfillment of what was prophesied long before. Of course, the words of Scripture are not meant to be a history lesson. They are a living, breathing reality for us. They are not words carved in stone but words etched on our hearts, giving us direction and meaning, strength and hope.

At Mass, we are given the opportunity to sit back and listen to Scripture, as Jesus listened to Scripture in the synagogue, as the early Christians listened to the stories of their faith in small communities, as Catholics throughout our long history right up to the present have listened to these same stories in an effort to gain the insights needed to understand and absorb the truths of this faith.

Inspiration in Scripture

The Liturgy of the Word blends elements from our Jewish roots with elements from our Christian tradition, offering us a beautifully crafted tapestry of inspired words. (Catholics see Scripture as divinely inspired if not always literal. Evangelical Christians, on the other hand, believe in a literal interpretation of Scripture.)

A typical Sunday liturgy includes a reading from the Old Testament, a responsorial psalm, an "epistle" or letter from the New Testament, and a reading from one of the four Gospels—Matthew, Mark, Luke, or John. In a never-ending cycle, we hear Bible readings over and over, year after year, until they become part of our collective consciousness. These are the stories of our faith, the roots of our religion, the road to our salvation.

prayer practice

If we can find even a few minutes to read and reflect on the coming Sunday's readings before we get to Mass, it can help us get more out of the celebration of the liturgy. Knowing the focus of what's coming allows us go a little deeper into the meaning and message of what's read at Mass.

The Cycle of Readings

On Sundays, the first reading in the Liturgy of the Word comes from the Old Testament (except during the Easter season, when the first reading comes from the Acts of the Apostles). For Catholics, the selection of readings is not left to chance or to anyone's personal preference.

The Sunday readings are scheduled in a three-year rotating cycle—Years A, B, and C. Daily Mass readings are divided into liturgical years I and II. The new Church year starts on the first Sunday of Advent in late November or early December. Over the course of three years, the Catholic Liturgy of the Word gives us the chance to review much of Scripture. Then the cycle begins all over again.

We are used to hearing the words of Hebrew Scripture at Mass, even though, for many of us, the ancient meanings and connections to our modern faith are often lost on us. Still, we've become familiar with the most famous Old Testament stories—Adam and Eve, Noah and the Ark, Abraham and Isaac, Moses, Ruth and Naomi, Jacob, David, Jonah, and Job. These and all the others who dot the landscape of Hebrew Scripture are part of our family tree. And they are critical to our Catholic faith because they inform and form us, foreshadowing what is to come while reminding us of what has been.

The Second Reading of the Mass is taken from the New Testament epistles, the letters attributed to Jesus' apostles, and on occasion from the Book of Revelation. St. Paul is the premier author of the letters, credited with writing 13 of the 21 epistles that appear between the Acts of the Apostles and the Book of Revelation.

Most of the epistles were actual letters, sent to communities of believers in specific areas, such as Paul's letters to those in Corinth, Thessalonica, or Ephesus. Other letters, such as those by Peter and James, were written to a more broad and growing Christian population.

We may wonder why we need both a Gospel and a New Testament letter. Shouldn't one or the other be sufficient? Well, during weekday Masses, we don't have a second reading at all. But on Sundays, we always have a second reading. The Gospel, which we discuss shortly, gives us the teachings of Jesus direct from the source. We hear the parables, see Jesus' actions, and watch how people respond to him. In the letters, which actually predate the written Gospels, we get to hear from Jesus' earliest followers and, although we are separated by many centuries, their exhortations to those earliest Christian communities are often still very much on target for us today.

Many of the most familiar, most inspiring lines from Scripture come from St. Paul's epistles. Some are so ingrained in our culture we may not even realize their biblical roots. For example, "Love is patient, love is kind ..." (1 Corinthians 13:4) or "Pray without ceasing ...." (1 Thessalonians 5:17)

We learn from our past. And here in the first and second readings of Mass, we learn from our Jewish ancestors and then from our earliest Christian ancestors. In their experience of the faith, we find our footing and then move forward from there.

Both the first and second readings end with the lector saying, "The word of the Lord." And we respond with, "Thanks be to God."

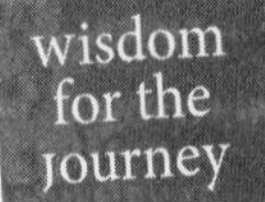

If the Scriptures are not to remain a dead letter, Christ, the eternal Word of the living God, must, through the Holy Spirit, open our minds to understand the Scriptures.

—Catechism of the Catholic Church, 108

The Responsorial Psalms

Every Mass includes a psalm sung or read after the first reading. Once again, the Liturgy of the Word takes us back to the Hebrew Scripture, to the very words that Jesus himself would have prayed.

Typically, at a Sunday Mass, the psalm is sung, which is the original way these prayers were prayed. The cantor sings the verses, and the rest of us in the congregation sing the response. Like the readings that repeat year after year, the psalms do so as well, giving them a familiar feel despite their ancient poetic cadence and their sometimes-violent or confusing content.

Over time, you're sure to develop favorites, psalms that speak to you for one reason or another or that you may have committed to memory. It may be Psalm 23, so commonly sung at funerals: "The Lord is my shepherd. There is nothing I shall want …." Or maybe it's the words of Psalm 139, with its reminders of our ever-present God: "You formed me in my inmost being; you knit me in my mother's womb. I praise you, so wonderfully you made me …."

With 150 psalms to choose from, there's sure to be something for everyone in this beautiful and lyrical Old Testament book, attributed by tradition to King David but believed by scholars to be the work of a number of individuals. Regardless of authorship, the psalms maintain a place of importance that cuts across Jewish, Christian, and Muslim faiths, all of which include these sacred poems in their inspired Scripture.

The Gospel Message

After the second reading, we stand up for the Gospel. In every season but Lent, the Gospel is greeted with an "Alleluia," which is Hebrew for "praise

Yahweh." The cantor sings it, and we respond with the same. In Lent, we refrain from saying or singing "Alleluia" because it is a song of great joy, and the Lenten journey is a penitential one. During Lent we would use a different response, typically, "Glory and praise to you, Lord Jesus Christ."

wisdom for the journey

If you believe what you like in the Gospels, and reject what you don't like, it is not the Gospel you believe, but yourself.

—St. Augustine, fourth-century philosopher and theologian

Only a priest or deacon may read the Gospel at Mass. If it is read by a deacon, the priest quietly says a prayer over him beforehand: "May the Lord be in your heart and on your lips that you may proclaim his Gospel worthily and well, in the name of the Father and of the Son and of the Holy Spirit." If the priest himself is reading the Gospel, he will quietly pray: "Cleanse my heart and my lips, almighty God, that I may worthily proclaim your holy Gospel."

Priest/deacon: The Lord be with you.

People: And with your spirit.

Priest/deacon: A reading from the holy Gospel according to [Matthew, Mark, Luke, or John].

People: Glory to you, O Lord.

As we say this, we take our thumb and trace a small cross on our forehead, our lips, and our heart, signifying our desire to know God's word, to share God's word, and to live God's word.

At the end of the Gospel, the priest/deacon says:

Priest/deacon: The Gospel of the Lord.

People: Praise to you, Lord Jesus Christ.

The Gospel, which means "good tidings" or "good news," provides us with the central teachings of Christianity, all of which spring from the words and actions of Jesus Christ. At every Mass, we hear from one of the four Gospels, each of which gives us a slightly different account of Jesus' life and work. The variations in style and storytelling are due, in part, to the time each particular Gospel was written and the audience for whom it was written. Matthew, Mark, and Luke are very similar and are known as the *synoptic Gospels.* The Gospel of John stands alone in its style.

Definition

The **synoptic Gospels** refer to the Gospels of Matthew, Mark, and Luke. *Synoptic* comes from the Greek term *syn,* meaning "together," plus *optic,* meaning "seen." These three Gospels tell most of the same stories in the same order, sometimes even with the same words. Their similarity links them. No matter which of the three synoptic Gospels you read, you come away with the same stories, parables, and people.

For example, the first three Gospels begin with some variation on the start of Jesus' life. In Matthew, we begin with the genealogy of Jesus. Mark starts later with the preaching of John the Baptist. And Luke starts with the announcement of the impending birth of John the Baptist and gives us the beautiful stories of the annunciation, visitation, Magnificat, Canticle of Zechariah, and the birth of Jesus.

John, on the other hand, begins with a beautiful and poetic Gospel in miniature:

> In the beginning was the Word,
> and the Word was with God,
> and the Word was God.
> He was in the beginning with God.
> All things came to be through him,
> and without him nothing came to be.
> What came to be through him was life,
> and this life was the light of the human race;
> the light shines in the darkness,
> and the darkness has not overcome it. (John 1:1–5)

The writer is still talking about Jesus in this passage, but it's a far cry from the much more literal versions written in the other Gospels.

The Gospels not only trace Jesus' life through his death, resurrection, and ascension, but also give us a detailed accounting of his teachings. In parables and sermons, actions and prayers, we learn our challenge: to treat others the way we want to be treated, to care for the poor and marginalized, to forgive others, to love God above all else, and perhaps most important, to follow Jesus, even when following him isn't easy.

At Mass, the Gospel serves as the center point of the Liturgy of the Word, the culmination of the message we're meant to take home with us that day. It ties into specific seasons or the feasts, reminding us of our call as Christians.

Lessons from the Homily

The homily is the part of the Mass where the priest (or deacon) preaches directly to the people. Every priest or deacon comes at Scripture and the homily from his own perspective, so this portion of the Mass can vary greatly from parish to parish and person to person.

We can't get caught up in the notion of homily as a fire-and-brimstone scolding of old. Sure, we may come across the occasional priest who still likes to give the people a little of that old-time religion, but the more common scenario is the priest who wants to give us something meaningful to take away with us, something that might affect the way we think, the way we act, and the way we live our lives in the days between Masses. According to Church guidelines, the homily should be tied to the day's readings or a particular feast being celebrated that day and should give us spiritual nourishment, a message we can take to heart.

Some homilies may have an intellectual bent, providing us with Scriptural and historical context. Others may be purely inspirational, filled with personal stories that apply the words of Scripture to everyday life. Regardless of style, we have to remember that a homily isn't meant to be a demonstration on how to give a great speech. It's meant to motivate us to live our faith day after day out in the world. Inspired by Scripture and guided by the Spirit, the priest or deacon sets out to give us a spiritual message, not a performance piece.

Not every homily is going to be an oratorical success because, as in any field, not every priest or deacon is going to be a stellar public speaker. And therein lies our challenge. When we come to Mass in hopes of deepening our prayer lives, our goal has to be to find that kernel of meaning in the homily, the thing that speaks to our souls and makes us better Christians. Sometimes it jumps out at us as if it's surrounded by flashing neon lights. Other times it's more subtle, perhaps hidden in an anecdote that seems to be off topic but turns out to be exactly what we needed to hear that day.

If we can rein in our wandering minds and stay spiritually awake, we may be pleasantly surprised to find that in even the most seemingly mundane homily is a diamond of spiritual inspiration just waiting to be mined. And if we just can't find anything in the homily to inspire us? Well, then we can find our meaning for that day or that week in the readings and the Gospel.

wisdom for the journey

The Bible tells us to love our neighbors, and also to love our enemies; probably because they are generally the same people.

—G. K. Chesterton, twentieth-century author

Credo, I Believe

After the homily at Sunday Mass, we stand to profess our faith. On most Sundays, we say the Nicene Creed, although the new translation of the Mass allows for more frequent use of the less-common Apostles' Creed.

Nicene Creed

I believe in one God,
the Father almighty,
maker of heaven and earth,
of all things visible and invisible.

And in one Lord Jesus Christ,
the Only Begotten Son of God,
born of the Father before all ages.
God from God, Light from Light,
true God from true God,
begotten, not made, consubstantial with the Father;
through him all things were made.
For us men and for our salvation
he came down from heaven,

(At the words that follow up to and including 'and became man,' all bow.)

and by the Holy Spirit was incarnate
of the Virgin Mary,
and became man.

For our sake he was crucified under Pontius Pilate,
he suffered death and was buried,
and rose again on the third day
in accordance with the Scriptures.
He ascended into heaven
and is seated at the right hand of the Father.
He will come again in glory
to judge the living and the dead
and his kingdom will have no end.

And in the Holy Spirit, the Lord, the giver of life,
who proceeds from the Father and the Son,
who with the Father and the Son is adored and glorified,
who has spoken through the prophets.
And one, holy, catholic and apostolic Church.
I confess one baptism for the forgiveness of sins
and I look forward to the resurrection of the dead
and the life of the world to come. Amen.

Both creeds spell out our basic Catholic beliefs summed up in prayer form, and both were changed ever so slightly with the new translation. (See Chapter 4 for more on the Apostles' Creed.)

Lord, Hear Our Prayer

The Liturgy of the Word concludes with the Prayer of the Faithful, also known as "general intercessions." After the Profession of Faith, we remain standing and pray for the needs of our families, our parish, our Church, and our world. These prayers of intercession can be focused on specific needs in connection to particular holidays or feasts. For example, we may pray for veterans on or near Memorial Day, for the environment on the Feast of St. Francis, for the sanctity of life from conception to natural death on Respect Life Sunday, or for high school and college graduates during the month of June.

In most parishes, the Prayer of the Faithful is a blend of universal needs, such as prayers for the poor, and localized needs, such as specific prayers for ill or deceased members of the parish family.

The priest typically introduces the intercessions with a short prayer. The lector then reads the petitions, saying after each one: "We pray to the Lord." And we typically respond: "Lord, hear our prayer."

As the Liturgy of the Word draws to a close, we shift spiritual gears and begin to settle down into the beauty and awe of the Liturgy of the Eucharist, which I discuss in detail in the next chapter. The one piece leads us naturally into the next, setting the stage for what is to come and preparing us mentally and spiritually to receive our Lord in the sacrament.

wisdom for the journey

Without prayer, you cannot be connected or you cannot remain united with the Lord. It's absolutely essential.

—Cardinal Joseph Bernardin, twentieth-century American bishop

Essential Takeaways

- The first half of every Mass revolves around Scripture, taken from the Old and New Testaments.
- The Gospel reading serves as the centerpiece of the Liturgy of the Word, providing us with the core teachings of the faith.
- In the homily, the priest or deacon, inspired by Scripture and the Holy Spirit, teaches us how to apply the teachings of the faith to everyday life.
- The Liturgy of the Word concludes with the Prayer of the Faithful, offered for the Church and the world.

chapter 17

The Liturgy of the Eucharist

Entering into Jesus' sacrifice

The Eucharistic prayer and words of "institution"

Signs of unity, signs of peace

Holy Communion—spiritual food for the journey

In the second half of the Mass, we turn our attention from Scripture to the memorial celebration of the Last Supper, when Jesus makes his own death and resurrection present to us again. The Eucharist is at the center of this portion of the Mass, book-ended by prayers of praise in the Holy, Holy and prayers of petition in the Lamb of God.

And then, of course, we receive Jesus, going forward to take in our hands this gift of our Savior and to drink from the cup just as Jesus instructed his apostles to do the night before he died.

We are invited to his table, this banquet of love, each day, each week of our lives, free to receive the food Jesus offers. When we look around at the lines of people going up to receive the host, it can make Communion seem commonplace, unremarkable. And yet what's happening is really beyond anything our human minds can comprehend. Jesus is present among us. Truly present. It doesn't get more remarkable than that.

All Good Gifts

The Liturgy of the Eucharist begins with the priest preparing the altar for the Eucharistic meal, often while the cantor or choir sings a hymn. This is followed by the offertory procession, the moment when people from the congregation bring gifts of bread and wine to the altar. And usually at this time or just before, we reach into our pocket or purse to offer a monetary gift as well. It can seem a little incongruent—the spiritual gifts of bread and wine alongside the practical gifts of money—until you trace the history.

Back in the earliest Church, Christians shared all things in common and brought offerings—chickens or sheep, eggs or fresh vegetables, as well as money—to share with their faith communities. "They devoted themselves to the teaching of the apostles and to the communal life, to the breaking of the bread and to prayers ... all who believed were together and had all things in common; they would sell their property and possessions and divide them among all according to each one's need." (Acts 2:42–45)

Our pastor might be a little stunned if we showed up in church with a hen or a basket of broccoli, or if we all started counting out our earnings and divvying them up right there in church. So these days our gifts are a little neater and easier to collect. We make a sacrificial gift in the form of cash, a check, or, increasingly nowadays, an electronic donation—something to help support our parish and other charities.

The Gospel challenges us to care for those who are needy, and so at this point of the Mass, we offer not only the bread and wine that will become food for our souls but also the monetary gifts that will become food and clothes for the poor, charitable ministries and schools, and structures that make the Gospel real. Faith and good works—the two are inseparable in Catholic life.

wisdom for the journey

What good is it, my brothers, if someone says he has faith but does not have works? Can that faith save him? If a brother or sister has nothing to wear and has no food for the day, and one of you says to them, "Go in peace, keep warm, and eat well," but you do not give them the necessities of the body, what good is it? So also faith of itself, if it does not have works, is dead.

—James 2:14–18

We remain seated for the offertory procession and for the prayers that follow immediately after it.

After the priest and altar servers have accepted the gifts of bread and wine, the priest brings them to the altar and says a prayer over them:

> Blessed are you, Lord God of all creation,
> for through your goodness we have received
> the bread we offer you:
> fruit of the earth and work of human hands,
> it will become for us the bread of life.

If the priest says the prayer out loud, we would respond:

> *Blessed be God forever.*

He pours a drop of water into the chalice to symbolize the two natures of Christ: humanity (the water) united with divinity (the wine). The priest says a prayer with the wine similar to that said with the bread, and we follow with the same response. The priest then bows and prays quietly:

> With humble spirit and contrite heart
> may we be accepted by you, O Lord,
> and may our sacrifice in your sight this day
> be pleasing to you, Lord God.

The altar servers then bring water, a bowl, and small towel to the priest. He washes his hands, saying in a quiet voice:

> Wash me, O Lord, from my iniquity
> and cleanse me from my sin.

The priest then prays aloud:

> Pray, brothers and sisters,
> that my sacrifice and yours
> may be acceptable to God,
> the almighty Father.

We stand and reply:

> *May the Lord accept the sacrifice at your hands*
> *for the praise and glory of His name,*
> *for our good*
> *and the good of all his holy Church.*

Holy, Holy, Holy

Now the priest begins the Eucharistic Prayer, which leads us into the Holy, Holy and then through the consecration. We remain standing until after we say or sing the Holy, Holy, at which point we kneel if it's possible.

> Priest: The Lord be with you.
>
> *People: And with your spirit.*
>
> Priest: Lift up your hearts.
>
> *People: We lift them up to the Lord.*
>
> Priest: Let us give thanks to the Lord our God.
>
> *People: It is right and just.*

The priest then says the preface to the Eucharistic Prayer. After the preface, which varies depending on the season or feast, we respond with the Holy, Holy, an acclamation of praise deeply rooted in Scripture, recalling the call of the prophet Isaiah and Jesus' entry into Jerusalem:

> **Acclamation**
>
> Holy, Holy, Holy Lord God of hosts.
> Heaven and earth are full of your glory.
> Hosanna in the highest.
> Blessed is he who comes in the name of the Lord.
> Hosanna in the highest.

Prayer practice

The Church recommends that we kneel after the Hosanna through the final doxology of the Eucharistic Prayer. However, we may find ourselves in churches without kneelers, or with very little space for kneeling. In these instances, it's appropriate to stand as a congregation. Or if we're too old or too ill to kneel, we may simply sit when everyone else is kneeling. The key is reverence for what is about to happen.

The Eucharistic Prayers

As we kneel in prayer, the priest begins one of the Eucharistic Prayers. The four prayers vary in length and content. All, however, include praise of the Father; intercessions for the Church, including the pope and the local bishop; prayers in communion with Mary and the saints; the calling down of the Holy Spirit; and finally, the words of "institution," or when the bread and wine become the body and blood of Jesus, known as *transubstantiation.*

Here are the words of institution, the high point of any Mass, taken from Eucharist Prayer III, which is often used at Sunday Masses:

> For on the night he was betrayed
>
> *The priest takes the bread and, holding it slightly raised above the altar continues:*
>
> he himself took bread,
> and giving you thanks he said the blessing,
> broke the bread, and gave it to his disciples, saying:
>
> *The priest bows slightly here.*
>
> Take this, all of you, and eat of it,
> for this is my body,
> which will be given up for you.

The priest then holds up the host so we can see it, places it down on the *paten,* which is a special dish usually made of silver or gold, and genuflects.

He then takes the cup of wine and continues:

> In a similar way, when the supper was ended,
>
> *The priest takes the chalice holding the wine and raises it slightly.*
>
> he took the chalice,
> and giving thanks he said the blessing,
> and gave the chalice to his disciples, saying:
>
> *The priest again bows slightly.*

Take this, all of you, and drink from it,
for this is the chalice of my blood,
the blood of the new and eternal covenant,
which will be poured out for you and for many
for the forgiveness of sins.

Do this in memory of me.

Here he shows the chalice to us, places it back on the altar, and genuflects before it.

We then join the priest in prayer:

Priest: The mystery of faith.

*People: We proclaim your death, O Lord,
and profess your Resurrection
until you come again.*

Or:

*When we eat this Bread and drink this Cup,
we proclaim your death, O Lord,
until you come again.*

Or:

*Save us, Savior of the world,
for by your Cross and Resurrection
you have set us free.*

The priest then continues with the rest of the Eucharistic Prayer. We remain kneeling through the concluding doxology:

Priest: Through him, and with him, and in him,
to you, O God, almighty Father,
in the unity of the Holy Spirit,
is all honor and glory,
for ever and ever.

People: Amen.

We then stand for the Communion Rite, which begins with the Lord's Prayer.

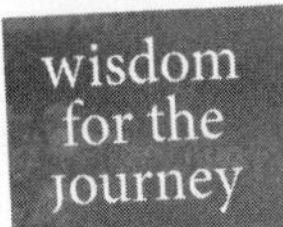

God is our Father. Even more, God is our Mother.
—Pope John Paul II, September 10, 1979, Angelus address

Our Father ...

After we have stood and the priest has placed the chalice and host on the altar, he will say:

> At the Savior's command
> and formed by divine teaching,
> we dare to say:

People and priest together:

> Our Father, who art in heaven,
> hallowed be thy name;
> thy kingdom come,
> thy will be done
> on earth as it is in heaven.
> Give us this day our daily bread,
> and forgive us our trespasses,
> as we forgive those who trespass against us;
> and lead us not into temptation,
> but deliver us from evil.
>
> Priest: Deliver us, Lord, we pray, from every evil,
> graciously grant peace in our days,
> that, by the help of your mercy,
> we may be always free from sin
> and safe from all distress,
> as we await the blessed hope
> and the coming of our Savior, Jesus Christ.

People: For the kingdom,
the power and the glory are yours
now and forever.

The Sign of Peace

Following the Our Father and final doxology, the congregation prepares for the Sign of Peace, when we greet those around us as a sign of our common brotherhood and sisterhood. We recall Jesus' words, "If you bring your gift to the altar, and there recall that your brother has anything against you … go first and be reconciled with your brother, and then come and offer your gift." (Matthew 5:23–24)

Priest: Lord Jesus Christ,
who said to your Apostles,
Peace I leave you, my peace I give you,
look not on our sins,
but on the faith of your Church,
and graciously grant her peace and unity
in accordance with your will.
Who live and reign for ever and ever.

People: Amen.

Priest: The peace of the Lord be with you always.

People: And with your spirit.

Priest: Let us offer each other the sign of peace.

We then turn to those sitting next to us, or in the pew in front or behind us, to shake hands. We may give family members or close friends a kiss on the cheek. We may simply nod to those sitting too far away to reach, although there are those who will go to great lengths to reach over people and pews to shake hands with as many people as possible.

This ritual is meant to be a respectful and spiritual exchange. I will admit, however, that on more than one occasion the Sign of Peace erupts into silent bickering among my children as they try to kiss each other—or avoid being kissed.

prayer practice

Every once in a while, we might come across a Catholic who harkens back to the pre–Vatican II days and refuses to shake hands at all. Although it can feel a little off-putting, we have to try not to take it personally if someone doesn't raise a hand or even their eyes to meet ours at the Sign of Peace. Consider, too, that during cold and flu season, the lack of physical contact could be due to a wish to curb the spread of germs.

The Lamb of God

Following the Sign of Peace, the priest will prepare for the Lamb of God and distribution of Communion. At this point, Extraordinary Ministers of Holy Communion—those who will assist with distribution of Communion—may come up to the altar.

The priest takes the host, breaks it, and places a small piece in the chalice, saying quietly:

> May this mingling of the Body and Blood
> of our Lord Jesus Christ
> bring eternal life to us who receive it.

Meanwhile, we say or sing the Lamb of God:

> *Lamb of God, you take away the sins of the world,*
> *have mercy on us.*
> *Lamb of God, you take away the sins of the world,*
> *have mercy on us.*
> *Lamb of God, you take away the sins of the world,*
> *grant us peace.*

At this point, we all kneel while the priest prays. He genuflects, raises up the host and chalice for us to see, and says out loud:

> Behold the Lamb of God,
> behold him who takes away the sins of the world.
> Blessed are those called to the supper of the Lamb.
>
> *People: Lord, I am not worthy*
> *that you should enter under my roof,*
> *but only say the word*
> *and my soul shall be healed.*

Priest: May the Body of Christ
keep me safe for eternal life.

At this point, the priest consumes the host. He takes the chalice and says:

May the Blood of Christ
keep me safe for eternal life.

Then he consumes the Blood of Christ. After this, the priest gives Communion to the extraordinary ministers, and they, in turn, bring Communion to all of us.

Receiving Communion

Depending on how your particular church organizes the distribution of Communion—front to back, the reverse, or some other configuration entirely—you may have some time before it's your turn to receive. You can remain kneeling or standing in place, praying quietly, or singing along with the Communion hymn. When it's your turn to go forward, you should do so in the most respectful manner possible.

When you stand before the priest, deacon, or extraordinary minister to receive, you can choose from one of two methods to receive the host: receiving in your hand, the most common method today, or receiving on your tongue. Regardless of which method you choose, you should make a slight bow of reverence before you receive Communion.

wisdom for the journey

When you approach, do not go stretching out your open hands or having your fingers spread out, but make the left hand into a throne for the right which shall receive the King, and then cup your open hand and take the Body of Christ, reciting the Amen.

—St. Cyril of Jerusalem, fourth-century bishop and doctor

If you're going to receive in your hand, take your dominant hand and place it under your other hand, as though you were creating a little throne. Then present your hands to the priest, who holds up the host before you and says, "The Body of Christ." You respond, "Amen," and he places the host in your hand. You then take your dominant hand out from underneath, pick up the host between your index finger and thumb, and place the host in your mouth before you step away. You can make the Sign of the Cross at this point if you choose.

If you're receiving on the tongue, after you say "Amen," open your mouth, stick out your tongue slightly, and the priest places the host on your tongue. Again, it would be appropriate here to make the Sign of the Cross.

If you're receiving from the cup, you proceed to the priest, deacon, or minister administering the precious Blood. Just as when you receive the host, the minister says, "The Blood of Christ," and you respond, "Amen." You hold the cup, take a small sip, hand back the cup, bless yourself, and return to your seat. The person administering the cup wipes the rim with a special cloth in preparation for the next communicant.

Misc.

Receiving Jesus

When you receive the host and from the cup at Mass, you are receiving Jesus under both "species." Although the Church teaches that Communion is "more complete" (*CCC,* 1390) when you receive both the precious Body and Blood, it also teaches that Jesus is fully present in each species. You receive Jesus fully even if you take Communion under only one form.

Once you're back in your pew, you can use the time to pray and reflect on what really is a momentous occasion every time it occurs. You have just received Jesus into your body, heart, and soul. There's nothing commonplace about that.

Sometimes, as I'm traipsing up to receive Communion, trying to keep my children in line, it occurs to me that if we humans could truly grasp—I mean fully, completely grasp—what is happening when we stand before the altar to receive Communion, we wouldn't stand at all. We would be prostrate on the ground, so humbled and awed by the gift of Jesus in the Eucharist. And yet, we stand, or slouch, or shuffle our way up the aisle. It's not because we don't care, but because we are human, and it's awfully hard for us humans to wrap our minds around God's gift of himself, first in Jesus who lived and died on Earth, and then in Jesus who gives himself to us again and again every time we receive Communion.

On some level, there's something to be said for the old ways of receiving Communion. We knelt down. We didn't touch the Eucharist. An altar server held a paten under our chin so there was no danger of the host dropping onto the floor. Maybe those ways were too stringent for some, but they certainly reinforced that what we were about to do was something worthy of an extra dose of care and respect and reverence.

When my middle child received her first Communion a couple years ago, I remember watching her. She held out her hands carefully, so intent on what was about to happen. I found myself longing to recapture just a little of that childlike awe and wonder because, no matter how often we receive the sacrament, this is one ritual that should never become routine.

The Final Blessing

After Communion and the meditation song, if there is one, and the Prayer After Communion, the priest says the Concluding Rite. It may start with a wrap-up of any business or brief announcements—important meetings coming up, holy days, special fund-raising appeals, or a reminder to spend some time after Mass sharing coffee and hospitality in the parish's gathering space. Then the priest says the final blessing.

> Priest: The Lord be with you.
>
> *People: And with your spirit.*
>
> Priest: May almighty God bless you:
> the Father, and the Son, and the Holy Spirit.
>
> *We all make the Sign of the Cross as he says this.*
>
> *People: Amen.*
>
> Priest (or deacon): Go forth, the Mass is ended.
>
> Or: Go and announce the Gospel of the Lord.
>
> Or: Go in peace, glorifying the Lord by your life.
>
> Or: Go in Peace.
>
> *People: Thanks be to God.*

The priest then kisses the altar as a sign of veneration. He and the altar servers bow before leaving the church as we sing the recessional hymn.

So the Mass is ended, but the work started at the Mass has only just begun.

Essential Takeaways

- The second half of the Mass revolves around the Eucharist, the most important of all the sacraments.
- Prayers of praise and petition mark our journey through the Liturgy of the Eucharist, which culminates in the consecration.
- The bread and wine offered at Mass become the Body and Blood of Jesus Christ in a memorial celebration of the Last Supper.
- We are invited to God's banquet each day, each week, to receive the Bread of Life that nourishes us for our journey.

chapter 18

Making Mass Your Own

Your role at Mass: more than just spectator

Expanding your participation beyond the pews

Allowing the Mass to resonate in your life long after the final blessing

After you receive Communion and wait for the blessing that signals the Mass has ended, you may think your work is done. You've fulfilled your "obligation" until next Sunday. But if that's your approach, you've really missed the bigger picture.

Mass is not meant to impact us for only one hour each week, and we're not meant to sit there passively waiting to be released after we've "done our time." Mass is the place where we meet Jesus, where we build up our community of faith, and where we actively participate in a spiritual feast. It's a celebration, but too often it's not viewed that way.

If we want to get something out of Mass, we have to put something into it. And that something is ourselves, our very hearts. If we go into Mass with a closed heart, as if we've got our spiritual arms folded against God, we can't truly experience Mass as the life-giving banquet it is. We've got to let down our guard and open up to the possibility that something wonderful is waiting for us just beyond the doors of that parish church.

From Your Place in the Pews

We live in a culture immersed in entertainment. From high-def TVs and unlimited Internet access to handheld devices that connect us to the world 24/7, we are surrounded by the flash of images and stories that distract us from our work, our families, and our spiritual lives.

It's no surprise, really, that when we go to Mass, we sometimes sit back and wait for the show to begin. But Mass is not a show, and we are not observers. We have a role—and a big role at that—if we are willing to step up to the spiritual plate.

You Are Not a Spectator

So if we're not meant to simply show up and watch the Mass unfold, what are we supposed to do? We can start, of course, by actually participating in the Mass—singing all the songs (even if we have a tin ear!), saying all the prayers out loud, focusing on the words and gestures.

That's not always easy. Sometimes our minds wander. We're human, after all. We can't help but wonder if we locked the front door when we left home or closed the car windows against the rain. But we can continually try to bring ourselves back to the present and find our place again within the words of the Mass.

The beauty of the Catholic Mass is that it's the same wherever we go. There's really no excuse not to participate. Even many of the hymns and sung prayers will be the same from parish to parish, state to state, country to country. It's really kind of amazing to experience that unity, to go to a church in a far-flung city, sit down, and know every word and every song. So if we can join the Mass in a physical way—through our presence and our voice—we take that first step beyond spectator to true participant.

The harder part is getting our heart and mind to cooperate, but even that comes, in time, if we are committed to upping our participation level. We can prepare in advance, read Scripture on our own, and focus all our attention on the words we hear and the prayers we say. Eventually, we'll begin to experience Mass on a whole new level.

wisdom for the journey

Unless we believe and see Jesus in the appearance of bread on the altar, we will not be able to see him in the distressing disguise of the poor.

—Mother Teresa

Building Community

I belong to a very large, suburban parish in upstate New York. When I joined 10 years ago, I felt like a little fish in a big spiritual pond. I couldn't break into the community, it seemed. My family would go to Mass each week, sometimes without saying a word to anyone save at the Sign of Peace. It got to the point where we considered looking for another parish, but then we decided we needed to make an effort to become part of our geographical faith community, the one where our children would eventually attend religious education and Catholic school. And so we volunteered for a couple of groups, and, lo and behold, we went from outsiders to insiders at breakneck speed.

When I walked into Mass on a recent Sunday morning, I greeted a friend who was serving as usher, said hello to women from my retreat team as I made my way up to the front, and gave some encouraging words to the nervous new altar girl who would be serving her first Mass with my son that morning. My family was asked to bring up the gifts at the offertory procession. A good friend with an amazing voice was serving as cantor. Even during Communion, an older woman who is battling cancer touched my arm as she went by and whispered that she had been praying for me every morning because a few weeks ago I told her I was struggling with something and could use some prayers. As I sat in my pew, it dawned on me that in this parish that once felt so big and so unfeeling, I was at home and surrounded by an ever-growing spiritual family that lifts me up week after week.

We may build community in our neighborhoods, in our schools, and in our athletic clubs, but the community we build in our parish church is unlike any other because it's built on faith. If we're willing to put ourselves out there, to volunteer for a ministry or join a parish group, we'll quickly learn that every parish—even those that are big and seemingly faceless—has a real heart and soul waiting to welcome us in and claim us as its own.

Praying together at Mass and other spiritual services is meant to strengthen that sense of community in ways that social events and even service programs cannot. As we stand side by side, singing and praying, we build up our local Church, which, in turn, builds up the universal Church. We are the Church, and we can never forget that or minimize its importance.

One Body, Many Parts

St. Paul's famous discourse on the body and how all its parts are important to the whole is a concrete reminder of how we are all important to the Body of Christ. No part is insignificant; no part unnecessary. And just as each part of our body has a specific talent or function, so, too, are our roles as parts of the Body of Christ. Maybe we are particularly good at singing and so we give our time to the parish choir. Maybe we have the organizational skills to administer parish-wide programs or help round up volunteers for various ministries. Maybe we are deeply prayerful and can lead a weekly prayer group or Scripture study.

We are all called to serve God and the Church in different ways. "Now you are Christ's body, and individually parts of it. Some people God has designated in the church to be, first, apostles; second, prophets; third, teachers; then, mighty deeds; then gifts of healing, assistance, administration, and varieties of tongues. Are all apostles? Are all prophets? Are all teachers? Do all work mighty deeds? Do all have gifts of healing? Do all speak in tongues? Do all interpret? Strive eagerly for the greatest spiritual gifts." (1 Corinthians 12:27–31)

It's because of our differences, not in spite of them, that we build a stronger faith community. If we were all the same, we couldn't have the diversity of talents and gifts, programs, and ministries. We just need to recognize our particular gifts and seek out ways to serve.

Misc.

Women in the Church

Although women cannot be ordained priests or deacons, they have critical roles in their local churches and beyond. Stop by any parish, and you're likely to see women at the helm of many ministries—charitable, spiritual, social, and educational.

Taking on a Greater Role

Once we figure out where we feel our greatest talents lie, we can decide if we'd like to take on a role that allows us to participate in the liturgy in an expanded way. Look at any parish, and you'll find a long list of ministries that offer something for just about everyone—from greeters who stand at the front door and hand out song sheets, to ushers who take up the collection, to extraordinary ministers of the Eucharist.

Lectors, Cantors, and Choirs

Some people shine when it comes to reading out loud or singing. If you have been given the gift of a beautiful voice and the desire to share it, you can sign on for one or several liturgical ministries.

Every Mass has one or two lectors, those who read the first and second readings from the altar. A clear and loud speaking voice is really all that's required for this ministry.

The cantor is the leader of song. He or she usually stands at the front of the church and sings the hymns, responsorial psalm, and prayers of the Mass, guiding the congregation by lifting his or her hands when it's our turn to sing.

wisdom for the journey

Singing is the sign of the heart's joy. Thus St. Augustine says rightly, "Singing is for one who loves." There is also the ancient proverb: "One who sings well prays twice."

—General Instruction on the Roman Missal

Many parishes have a traditional choir and sometimes a "contemporary" or folk choir. Some even have a children's choir. There may be additional opportunities to play guitar, piano, trumpet, flute, or other accompanying instruments. It's a great way to get involved in liturgical ministry if we have musical ability but aren't quite ready or willing to take on a solo position as cantor.

Extraordinary Ministers

At a Sunday Mass, the priest typically needs the assistance of a number of Extraordinary Ministers of Holy Communion, sometimes referred to as "eucharistic ministers," to help with the distribution of Communion. These men and women come up to the altar and receive Communion immediately after the priest does. Then they help distribute Communion to the rest of us, some offering the host and others the cup.

If we feel called to this ministry, we'll need some basic training on the practical aspects of distributing Communion, including how to place the host in someone's hand or on the tongue, offer and wipe the rim of the cup, and assist the priest after Communion. We may also receive some theological and spiritual training to help us prepare to handle and distribute the Body and Blood of Christ with proper reverence.

Some extraordinary ministers may sign on for the additional role of bringing Communion to shut-ins or hospitalized parishioners. Once again, we are all part of one body, so even those who are separated from us physically remain part of us and need to be nourished by the gift of Christ in the Eucharist.

prayer practice

Every once in a while, someone may drop the host when receiving or distributing Communion. If the priest or extraordinary minister has not noticed this, be sure to let them know so the host can be picked up and consumed, typically by the priest although there's no hard-and-fast rule about who must consume it. Bottom line: a consecrated host can never be thrown away. Similarly, if the precious Blood is spilled, it must be cleaned up with "purificators," or linen cloths used to wipe the chalice or dry the celebrant's hands and mouth. Every church has a special sink that drains directly into the ground rather than a sewer so vessels and linens used for Eucharist can be washed in a way that sends any possible remnants back to the earth.

Serving at the Altar

Back in the day, altar servers were known as altar boys because only males were permitted to serve in this role. But since 1994, when this ministry was opened to girls, altar boys have been known as altar servers or even acolytes, a ministry formerly reserved to those preparing for ordination but now popularly used in parishes. It's up to the local bishop's discretion whether girls can participate in this ministry, although nowadays it's an almost universally accepted practice in the United States.

Altar servers assist the priest throughout Mass from start to finish. Typically, two servers help with Mass, but there may be more or fewer depending on availability and the size of the parish. They process up the aisle with the priest; hold the sacramentary as he reads the prayers of the Mass; and assist with the gifts, hand-washing, and altar preparations for the Liturgy of the Eucharist.

An altar server is usually young—anywhere from about 10 years old through high school age. But sometimes an adult might be an altar server at a daily Mass or certain Sunday Masses. My grandfather was once known as the "oldest altar boy" at his parish because he served at morning Mass every day. So although this ministry is typically reserved for young people, there are sometimes opportunities for adults to serve.

Go Now to Love and Serve

Before the new translation was issued, the traditional words that ended Mass were "The Mass is ended. Go in peace to love and serve the Lord." Even though the specific words have changed a bit, the sentiment is the same. "Go and announce the Gospel of the Lord" or "Go in peace, glorifying the Lord by your life." In other words, we're supposed to take what we've heard and the presence of Christ we've received at Mass and let them influence our behavior outside the church doors.

The message and spiritual graces received during Mass are meant to resonate throughout our lives. By attempting to put the words of the Gospel into action on a daily basis, we become witnesses to the very faith we profess. It may sound cliché, but actions really do speak louder than words. Or to put it another way—in wording that is often attributed to St. Francis of Assisi—"Preach always. When necessary, use words."

Through our very actions and words, we are meant to pass on the teachings of our faith, letting others see the power of Christian love through the way we treat others, friends and strangers alike; through our generosity to those in need; and through our prayerfulness and faithfulness. And we have to do all that without becoming self-righteous and judgmental or overly pious for piety's sake. We are called to serve, the way Jesus served. At the Last Supper, he washed his apostles' feet as a model of what they would then be called to do: serve others. And we are challenged to do the same.

Aftereffects of Mass

In a perfect world, Mass would also impact our lives in a deeply personal way on a full-time basis. If we allow the Scriptures and the Eucharist to seep deep down into our souls, we'll eventually start to notice a change of heart and a change of attitude. Spending time with God at Mass gives us a spiritual center that cannot be shaken by the frustrations and challenges in our lives.

Clearly, if we leave Mass only to rush out into the parking lot and cut off a fellow parishioner, we've missed something along the way. Mass cannot be confined to one hour each week within the four walls of our parish church. Its meaning has to emanate outward, shining a light on our home life, our work life, and our community life. If we take the Gospel message to heart, if we enter into the Eucharist open to God's graces, we cannot help but see our world, our family, even strangers on the street through new eyes, eyes of compassion and mercy and love.

wisdom for the journey

In Louisville, at the corner of Fourth and Walnut, in the center of the shopping district, I was suddenly overwhelmed with the realization that I loved all those people, that they were mine and I theirs, that we could not be alien to one another even though we were total strangers. … I suddenly saw the secret beauty of their hearts, the depths of their hearts where neither sin nor desire nor self-knowledge can reach, the core of their reality, the person that each one is in God's eyes. If only they could all see themselves as they really are. If only we could see each other that way all of the time.

—Trappist Monk Thomas Merton, twentieth century, *Conjectures of a Guilty Bystander*

The Big Picture

The Catholic faith is also "catholic," with a small c, meaning "universal." And so we Catholics are part of something that reaches far beyond our town, our state, or even our country. And the Mass connects us to our brothers and sisters in faith around the world. We are one in the Eucharist. Even when we're separated by thousands of miles, even when our languages and our cultures and our traditions are drastically different, our faith remains the same.

Some in our Catholic family are desperately poor and struggling day to day just to survive. Some are fabulously wealthy and living in near-perfect conditions. In this Church, we are called to serve one another, to ensure that our poor brothers and sisters are not abandoned or forgotten. (I discuss this in more detail in Chapter 23.)

That challenge, that Gospel message, is so much at the core of what we as individual Catholics do, what our local churches and dioceses do, and what the universal Church does on a regular basis. But none of it can happen without prayer. We need to meet Jesus, to talk to Jesus on a daily basis, if we want to take this faith he gave us beyond our homes and local churches and out into the world at large.

Essential Takeaways

- We are called to be active participants in the Mass, not merely spectators.
- Various ministries—lector, cantor, Extraordinary Minister of Holy Communion—allow us to take on an even greater role in the liturgy.
- Mass is not a self-contained experience that ends with the final blessing. We are meant to take its message out into our daily life in the world.

chapter 19

Moving Ever Outward

Finding companions and support for the spiritual journey

Establishing common bonds with those of other faiths

Using technology to expand and strengthen prayer life

As we move deeper into our prayer lives, we're likely to find that we need some outside support, other like-minded Catholics who will pray with us, talk with us, walk with us on our spiritual journey.

One of the great things about Catholicism is that everything is interconnected, giving us the ability to find people who share our interest in a particular style of prayer or a specific approach to spirituality.

If we know where to look—and often it's just a matter of making a phone call—we can surround ourselves with spiritual friends who help us expand our prayer life beyond the walls of our home and parish church.

Strength in Numbers

If you want to begin to build a spiritual support team of sorts, the best place to start is at your parish. It's close to home and, if you're a regular there, you probably already know the people and programs. If not, joining a group is a great way to become better acquainted.

You can check your parish bulletin for starters. There you're likely to find listings for any parish prayer groups,

Scripture study programs, adult faith formation sessions, and, of course, dates and times for Mass, confession, the Rosary, the Liturgy of the Hours, and more.

Parish Prayer Groups

Many parishes have some sort of prayer groups, whether formal or informal. If you don't see any obvious signs of an existing group, check with the parish office or pastor. Sometimes people may meet weekly in small groups, or they may gather informally before First Friday Mass or at other times that aren't always advertised.

In addition, if you know others who share your desire to become part of a prayer group, you can always take the initiative to start your own group.

A few years back, a woman I met through my parish invited me and several other moms of toddlers to meet at her house once a week to read the Scriptures for the coming week, talk about them, and pray together. It was perfect for us. Our children would play together and share snacks while the mothers talked and prayed. It wasn't always the most peaceful prayer group, but it got us through a Lenten season in a very special way.

Parish-based prayer options are vast. We may be able to join in more traditional devotions such as the Rosary or the Divine Mercy Chaplet. Or we may find groups that focus on specific types of prayer. For example, some parishes may have "charismatic" prayer groups, something that came into vogue in the 1970s and remains strong in some areas. This type of prayer is much more free-flowing and spontaneous than traditional Catholic prayer, with a heavy emphasis on the movement of the Spirit.

Another possible option is a small faith community. Many parishes have multiple communities to suit people of different ages, backgrounds, and callings—single, married, with children, seniors. These groups often meet in a member's home to pray, share spiritual reading and conversation, and socialize. Over time, these small faith communities can develop into close-knit groups akin to families. Your parish office can tell you if existing communities are available or if there is the possibility of starting a new one.

wisdom for the journey

Without some form of community individual prayer cannot be born or developed. Communal and individual prayer belong together as two folded hands.

—Henri J. M. Nouwen, twentieth-century Catholic priest and spiritual writer

And if we can't find a prayer group or small faith community in our own parish, there's nothing wrong with checking into neighboring parishes to see what they might have to offer.

Associations for Lay People

Beyond the boundaries of our local parish are almost endless options for lay men and women interested in exploring their spirituality in a deeper way with other Catholics. No matter what our interest, we are likely to find an association or organization that suits our style.

There are too many to list individually, but here are some of the more widely recognized groups:

- The Catholic Worker Movement, dedicated to serving the poor
- The Legion of Mary, focused on prayer and spiritual works of mercy
- Worldwide Marriage Encounter, which strengthens Christian marriages through weekend retreats
- The Cursillo Movement, another retreat-focused program designed to strengthen relationships with God
- The Community of Sant'Egidio, which works for peace and living out the Gospel through prayer and service to the poor

These are just a handful of the hundreds of associations available for Catholic men and women. Appendix C at the back of the book contains more information on lay associations and how to find them.

Tapping Into Religious Communities

Perhaps we want to take our spiritual connections to even greater heights. If so, we might want to explore the possibility of becoming affiliated with a religious community in a formal way. Many communities of religious sisters, brothers, and priests have programs that allow lay men and women to become "associates," meaning we can align ourselves with a particular community while living out in the world.

For example, we may have a particular affinity for the Sisters of Mercy. If so, there's an associate program that allows men and women to make a formal covenant with the Sisters. Associates share in prayer, friendship, and celebrations with the Sisters and also participate in their service to the poor and sick.

Many religious communities offer this option for lay people, but because it typically involves some sort of formal commitment, it requires some discernment on our part. We don't just sign up for any associate program. We need to find a community whose mission and spirituality best suit us.

Taking that commitment to an even deeper level is the option of public and permanent profession to a religious community while remaining out in the world. One popular example is the Secular Franciscans—lay men and women who go through a lengthy study and discernment process to become vowed lay members of the order founded by St. Francis of Assisi. Similar options exist with the Benedictines, Carmelites, Dominicans, Salesians, and others.

Another option is to join a "secular institute," which can also provide a more structured way to seek spiritual growth through prayer and charity. The U.S. Conference of Secular Institutes describes these lay men and women as "in the world and not of the world, but for the world." In other words, if we choose to commit ourselves in such a way to a secular institute, we remain in the world while living out the "evangelical counsels" of poverty, chastity, and obedience within our circumstances, whether we are married or single, rich or poor, young or old. (See Appendix C for general contact information for secular institutes.)

prayer practice

If you're considering a commitment to a religious community, the best place to start is with spiritual reading. Read the writings of St. Francis of Assisi, the Rule of St. Benedict, or the writings associated with whatever community you'd like to explore. The first step is discerning which philosophy and mission best suits your spirituality and lifestyle.

Making such a commitment to a religious order or secular institute allows us to immerse ourselves in a true community devoted to prayer and service. But it's not something to be undertaken lightly. It requires prayer, discernment, and deep understanding of the mission and charism of the order we choose and its founder. I cover the big four of religious orders—Franciscan, Benedictine, Dominican, and Jesuit—in Chapter 22.

Unity in Diversity

Perhaps you don't want to pray with Catholics only. After all, can't all people of faith—any faith—pray together for the good of each other and the good of our world? Yes, although sometimes it's easier than other times. Obviously, Catholics and other Christians have some strong common bonds that allow us to pray together in ways that simply aren't possible when we move beyond the Christian fold.

When Catholics and other Christians pray together and "dialogue," it's called ecumenism. When Catholics and people of faiths outside Christianity pray or dialogue together, it's called interfaith.

Ecumenism: Different Paths, One Goal

As Catholics, we are called to work toward ecumenism, to pray with and talk to other followers of Jesus in the hope that one day there will be unity among all Christians. After all, we were one Church in the earliest days of Christianity. Through ecumenical prayer, we can benefit from and share in the best of each other's traditions.

Many parishes and dioceses host ecumenical events, from seminars on topics that reach across Christian denominations, to joint concerts, to charitable efforts that bring people of different faiths together to work toward a common goal on behalf of others.

Every January, for example, the Franciscan Friars of the Atonement, based in Garrison, New York, sponsor the worldwide Week of Prayer for Christian Unity designed to focus the prayers of the global Christian community on the fulfillment of Jesus' words that "they all may be one." (John 17:21)

Ecumenical efforts started in earnest after the Second Vatican Council. One Council document, "Decree on Ecumenism," said:

> All the faithful should remember that the more effort they make to live holier lives according to the Gospel, the better will they further Christian unity and put it into practice. For the closer their union with the Father, the Word, and the Spirit, the more deeply and easily will they be able to grow in mutual brotherly love.
>
> This change of heart and holiness of life, along with public and private prayer for the unity of Christians, should be regarded as the soul of the whole ecumenical movement, and merits the name, "spiritual ecumenism."

Although we can pray with each other and for each other, there are still limits to just how far we can go in ecumenical worship. The Catholic Church does not usually permit "inter-Communion." This means non-Catholics are discouraged from receiving the Eucharist at Mass, and Catholics are not permitted to receive Communion at non-Catholic services. The reason is that the Eucharist has always implied a complete unity of belief. As St. Paul wrote, "Because the loaf of bread is one, we, though many, are one body, for we all partake of one loaf." (1 Corinthians 10:17) Extending Eucharist to non-Catholics or receiving Communion in a non-Catholic church presumes a unity that, unfortunately, does not yet exist and that all Christians are called to work toward.

Still, when it comes down to it, we all believe Jesus Christ is the Son of God sent to Earth to save us. That's a pretty strong starting point for unity. So we can pray with our Christian friends, knowing that whatever we do together strengthens not only our individual relationships but also the larger Christian community around the world.

Here's a prayer for Christian unity from *Catholic Household Blessings and Prayers,* published by the U.S. Conference of Catholic Bishops, a great book to have on your spiritual bookshelf:

Prayer of Christian Unity

Lord Jesus Christ,
you call us together in faith and love.
Breathe again the new life of your Holy Spirit
among us
that we may hear your holy Word,
pray in your name,
seek unity among Christians,
and live more fully the faith we profess.
All glory and honor be yours
with the Father, and the Holy Spirit, forever and ever.

Amen.

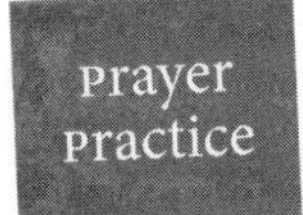

Taizé is an ecumenical monastic community made up of Catholic and Protestant religious brothers based in France but with outreach worldwide. Focused on the work of peace and justice through prayer and meditation, Taizé has become—in Catholic parish circles—synonymous with ecumenical worship services centered around prayer, music, and chant.

Interfaith Prayer

Interfaith prayer takes the idea of ecumenism to a different level. Obviously there are more difficult divisions that separate Christians and Jews or Christians and Buddhists. So we have to reach back further, to our common belief in a Higher Power, a being who created our world and us.

Both Pope John Paul II and Pope Benedict XVI made special efforts to foster interfaith dialogue during their papacies. John Paul II, who traveled to Israel and visited the Western Wall, was the first pope in history to visit a synagogue, which he did in Rome in 1986. He later became the first pope to visit and pray in a Muslim house of worship when he visited Syria in 2001. Pope Benedict XVI, who also traveled to the Holy Land and visited the same synagogue in Rome, continued his predecessor's interfaith efforts, visiting the famed Blue Mosque in Turkey in 2006 and the Hussein bin-Talal mosque in Amman in 2009.

On more localized levels, dioceses and parishes may hold occasional interfaith prayer services or events that highlight the common values and bonds shared by all people of faith.

Interfaith prayer, however, cannot rely on the Bible or the holy book of any particular faith. We also can't use words to describe God according to our own beliefs, such as Heavenly Father or Lord. The same holds true for other faiths involved in an interfaith service as well. For instance, it also would not be appropriate to call on Allah, Buddha, or Krishna in an interfaith prayer. So how can we pray together across drastically different faith lines? We can focus on blessings, prayers of thanksgiving, prayers asking for protection, and prayers focusing on our common humanity.

wisdom for the journey

On this path we can walk together, aware of the differences that exist between us, but also aware of the fact that when we succeed in uniting our hearts and our hands in response to the Lord's call, his light comes closer and shines on all the peoples of the world.

—Pope Benedict XVI, during a visit to Rome's main synagogue, January 2010

My son is the associate chaplain for his Boy Scout troop, meaning he is occasionally called upon to write invocations to open an event or say a blessing before a meal. Having prayed certain prayers his whole life, particularly our nightly Grace Before Meals, he has to be very conscious of the way he writes these public interfaith prayers. Although he is allowed to refer to God, because the Boy Scouts openly acknowledge and worship God (their promise even starts with duty to God), he cannot mention Jesus Christ. It's an interesting exercise in inclusiveness whenever he's called on to do something like this, always sparking a conversation not only about what divides us but about what unites us. And that's where our focus in interfaith prayer needs to be.

Prayer in the Digital Age

Talking about prayer probably makes us think of ancient words, images, and rituals. But increasingly in our modern world, prayer is taking on new forms. The Internet has really changed the prayer landscape. Years ago, if we needed someone to pray for us, we'd have to write a letter or make a phone call. Today, it's as simple as posting a status update on Facebook or Twitter or sending an e-mail to family and close friends.

Although it may seem somewhat faceless and rather superficial at first, social networking sites and online communities actually allow us to build up a network of spiritual friends who are available at the click of a mouse. Granted, we need to foster those friendships in deeper ways—through visits and phone calls—but it really helps to have the immediate connection that our high-speed world provides.

I write a blog (Not Strictly Spiritual) and regularly post to Facebook and Twitter. I did so reluctantly at first, figuring it was just one more time-waster in my already-jam-packed life. And at first it was. But then what happened was amazing. I started connecting with old friends and making new friends, without ever leaving my home. Through my posts about prayer and spiritual life, I created a small community of people who regularly discuss their spiritual struggles, their prayer needs, and their willingness to keep me in their prayers. It's been a remarkable development, one that has been pleasantly surprising and spiritually rewarding.

So if we have access to the Internet and aren't afraid of dipping our toes into the fast-moving waters of social networking and other online communities, we will soon have a whole new world of prayer partners—literally at our fingertips!

The Internet, too, is a great source for exploring different types of prayer and approaches to Catholic spirituality. Appendix C provides some links that serve as a great launching pad for using technology to aid your spirituality.

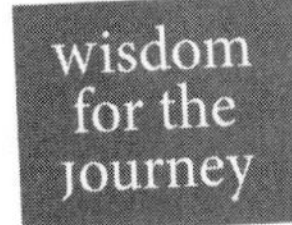

Authentic prayer is not detached from reality. If prayer alienates you, removes you from real life, be aware that it is not authentic prayer ....

—Pope Benedict XVI

Essential Takeaways

- We can find spiritual support through parish prayer groups and other spiritual organizations.
- Lay associations and religious orders offer us the opportunity to deepen our prayer lives according to a specific mission in a community setting.
- We are called to build spiritual bridges through both ecumenical and interfaith prayer.
- The digital world is a doorway to a whole new way of praying and meeting spiritual friends.

Part 5

Following the Path of Prayer

Now that we have all the basic background information—the hows and whys of particular prayers and devotions—it's time to set off on the final part of our journey to a place where we can explore new rituals and bask in old spirituality.

Catholic tradition offers so many ways to weave prayer into daily life, from the feasts and seasons of the liturgical year and the classic spirituality of the great spiritual masters to the more esoteric approaches of the mystics and the seemingly simple yet powerful methods of incorporating prayer into the most mundane moments of our lives.

It's all there before us, waiting to be explored, tasted, savored, and absorbed. We can try one approach and enter deeply into it with single-minded focus, or we can create a blend of styles that offer us an array of prayer options, depending on our mood or the moment.

In Part 5, we look at the seasons of the Church year, ancient traditions that can be adapted to modern life, particular types of spirituality that may allow us to go further down our prayer path, and finally, simple ways to incorporate regular prayer into the rhythm of our days.

chapter 20

Prayer Through the Year

Aligning prayer with the seasons of the Church year

Celebrating special seasons with new rituals and old traditions

Seeking out the beauty of "ordinary time"

For everything there is a season, and when it comes to the Catholic faith, we can take that Scripture-based quote literally. The Church year is divided into seasons—Advent and Christmas, Lent and Easter. Thrown into the liturgical march through the calendar is "ordinary time," which sounds rather dull but includes plenty of feasts and celebrations of its own.

These times of year can give our prayer lives a special depth and tone, bringing beautiful rituals and faith traditions into our everyday routines. Week by week, month by month, our spiritual lives are enriched as we worship and pray through the different feasts and holidays.

Advent: The Season of Light

The Church year starts with the first Sunday of Advent, which falls in late November or early December. This four-week season emphasizes the need to not only prepare for the celebration of the birth of Christ, but also ready ourselves for when he comes again. We immerse ourselves in readings and rituals that remind us to be hopeful but also to be vigilant.

Although the specifics of our Advent Scripture readings change depending on which liturgical year we're in, the general tone and focus remain the same:

> You know what time it is, how it is now the moment for you to wake from sleep. For salvation is nearer to us now than when we became believers; the night is far gone, the day is near. Let us then lay aside the works of darkness and put on the armor of light; let us live honorably as in the day, not in reveling and drunkenness, not in debauchery and licentiousness, not in quarreling and jealousy. Instead, put on the Lord Jesus Christ, and make no provision for the flesh, to gratify its desires. (Romans 13:11–14)

From there we move progressively closer to the main event, hearing from John the Baptist, who was sent to prepare the way of the Lord.

> In those days John the Baptist appeared in the wilderness of Judea, proclaiming, "Repent, for the kingdom of heaven has come near." This is the one of whom the prophet Isaiah spoke when he said,
>
> "The voice of one crying out in the wilderness:
> 'Prepare the way of the Lord,
> make his paths straight.'"
>
> … I baptize you with water for repentance, but one who is more powerful than I is coming after me; I am not worthy to carry his sandals. He will baptize you with the Holy Spirit and fire. His winnowing fork is in his hand, and he will clear his threshing floor and will gather his wheat into the granary; but the chaff he will burn with unquenchable fire. (Matthew 3:1–12)

Fire and threshing floors? That doesn't sound very jolly, does it? The truth is, Advent isn't the spiritual equivalent to the secular preparation for Christmas. It is penitential—although not as much so as Lent—hence the deep purple, verging-on-midnight-blue liturgical color. Light and darkness—and which side we will choose—are center stage as we approach the birth of the Savior.

Advent is a season rich in both imagery and substance. Of course, sometimes it's hard to recognize the spiritual beauty amid the chaos of our Christmas shopping and wrapping and get-togethers. If we can find a way to spend a little time each day focusing on Advent, we just may become the calm at the center of the holiday storm swirling around us.

Candles in a Wreath

Probably the most recognizable symbol and ritual of Advent is the Advent wreath. Parishes place a wreath in the sanctuary during Advent and celebrate by lighting the appropriate candle before the start of Mass each week. Many families have Advent wreaths in their homes, too, and light candles each evening to keep the essence of this season burning brightly in daily life.

The Advent wreath is a circle of evergreen (although there are many modern variations) with four candles—three purple and one rose. On each Sunday of Advent, we light another candle until, just before Christmas, all four candles are burning. The circle of the wreath represents eternal life, and the evergreens and candles represent life and light in the darkness.

The purple candles put us in a penitential frame of mind. As mentioned earlier, Advent is a time to reflect on our sinfulness and prepare our souls for Christ's coming.

The rose-colored candle represents joy and is lighted on the third Sunday of Advent. It's not uncommon for folks to think this one should be lighted last as a final buildup to the big day. Instead, falling in the calendar where it does, this candle is almost like a wake-up call. It snaps us to attention and reminds us that although Christmas is very near, there's still time to get spiritually prepared for it if we haven't done so already. So when using an Advent wreath, you light two purple candles, then the rose candle, then the final purple one.

On Christmas, you can remove the purple and pink candles and put a white candle, known as a "Christ candle," in the center.

In our house, we set the Advent wreath on the kitchen table and light it each night before dinner. Typically I get a small book of Advent reflections geared toward children, and the little ones take turns lighting candles (or blowing them out) and reading from the brief reflections. After we say our Advent prayer, we say Grace Before Meals.

This ritual has become as much a part of our pre-Christmas lives as shopping and decorating. Even when the kids are fighting over whose turn it is to blow out the candles, it's clear that the Advent wreath tradition brings a much deeper spiritual dimension to a season that is becoming increasingly secularized.

Advent Wreath Prayer

Heavenly Father,
as we light these candles
against the darkness of winter,
we pray for the strength
to throw off the things that
keep us from loving you as we should.
Kindle in us a spiritual fire
that fills our souls with the light
of your Son, Jesus Christ,
so that we may share it with others
and renew the face of the earth.

Amen.

—Mary DeTurris Poust

prayer practice

It's easy to add other inexpensive and simple Advent rituals into our family's daily life. We always have an Advent calendar featuring a Nativity scene (as opposed to the countless Advent calendars decked out with snowmen and Santas). The kids take turns opening one of the little doors on the calendar each day from December 1 until Christmas. It's one more little way to focus their attention on Jesus rather than on their lengthy Christmas lists.

From the Root of Jesse

Less common than the Advent wreath but just as beautiful is the tradition of the Jesse tree. Starting with a bare tree or branch, we work our way through the Old Testament, placing symbols of Jesus' lineage and our faith on the tree day after day. It's an especially good way to help children connect the Old Testament figures to Jesus.

Relying on the prophecies of Isaiah, the tree starts with Jesse, the father of King David: "But a shoot shall sprout from the stump of Jesse, and from his roots a bud shall blossom." (Isaiah 11:1)

There is no standard set of ornaments, so you can get creative. Here are some suggestions:

- Globe or moon and stars for creation
- Apple for Adam and Eve
- Ark or rainbow for Noah
- Ram for Abraham and Isaac
- Ladder for Jacob
- Six-pointed star for David
- Burning bush for Moses

Then you can add some New Testament symbols:

- Hammer for Joseph
- Lily or crown of stars for Mary
- Shell for John the Baptist
- Manger scene for Jesus

Some parishes may set up a Jesse tree near the altar, but it's also something you can do at home. The tree can be as simple as paper ornaments glued or taped to a construction paper tree or as elaborate as a real tree with wooden or cloth ornaments. In my parish, every third year, depending on the liturgical cycle, our pastor hangs a floor-to-ceiling banner of the Jesse tree behind the main altar. The first time I saw it, it took my breath away. I loved seeing our lineage, from creation through Jewish history to Jesus' birth, on display before our church community throughout Advent.

You can read Scripture stories that correspond to each of the ornaments, or you can say a simple prayer, depending on the ages of your children and how complex you want your Jesse tree tradition to be.

Jesse Tree Prayer

As we add this ornament to our Jesse tree,
we recall our spiritual ancestors,
whose stories provide a firm foundation
for the lives of faith
we continue to build each day.
May we find in these holy men and women
of sacred Scripture
a pathway to peace, hope, and love—
a spiritual road map that leads
to the God of all creation.

Amen.

—Mary DeTurris Poust

Misc.

Little Old St. Nick

Although my children believed in Santa Claus when they were young, I was never really comfortable focusing too much energy on that story. As a balance, I tried to make them familiar with the story of the "real" Santa—St. Nicholas, Bishop of Myra, whose feast is December 6. Legend has it that this fourth-century saint often left secret gifts in shoes. Do you recognize something of our Christmas stocking tradition there? My kids will leave their shoes near the door on the eve of St. Nicholas' feast day and come down the next morning hoping to find some little trinket—something small, like a ball or candy or a tiny doll. I have to admit I love the tradition as much as they do.

O Antiphons

During the last days of Advent, those of us praying the Divine Office add what are called the "O Antiphons" to our evening prayers. These prayers are short responses based on the Scriptures for each day and are included in the Liturgy of the Hours for that week. The O Antiphons are similar to the Alleluia verse sung at that day's Mass and are said before and after the Canticle of Mary (the *Magnificat*). We can also add the O Antiphons to our Advent wreath reflections or any other daily prayers.

Each antiphon addresses Jesus by a particular title. These are taken from the Liturgy of the Hours:

December 17: Wisdom:

> O Wisdom, O holy Word of God, you govern all creation with your strong yet tender care. Come and show your people the way to salvation.

December 18: Lord of Israel

> O sacred Lord of ancient Israel, who showed yourself to Moses in the burning bush, who gave him the holy law on Sinai mountain: come, stretch out your mighty hand to set us free.

December 19: Root of Jesse

> O Flower of Jesse's stem, you have been raised up as a sign for all peoples; kings stand silent in your presence, the nations bow down in worship before you. Come, let nothing keep you from coming to our aid.

December 20: Key of David

> O Key of David, O royal Power of Israel controlling at your will the gate of heaven: come, break down the prison walls of death for those who dwell in darkness and the shadows of death; and lead your captive people into freedom.

December 21: Dayspring, Radiant Dawn

> O Radiant Dawn, splendor of eternal light, sun of justice; come, shine on those who dwell in darkness and the shadow of death.

December 22: King of All Nations

> O King of all the nations, the only joy of every human heart; O Keystone of the mighty arch of man, come and save the creature you fashioned from dust.

December 23: Emmanuel, God with Us

> O Emmanuel, king and lawgiver, desire of the nations, Savior of all people, come and set us free, Lord our God.

Blessing the Christmas Tree

In our house, decorating the Christmas tree can deteriorate quickly into bickering and frustration, what with the lights that don't work and the ornaments that don't have hooks for hanging. So we have to work hard to make this annual tradition not only fun but meaningful as well.

The Christmas tree as a Catholic-Christian tradition is fairly modern, originating in Germany in the 1600s, although the practice of putting lights on an evergreen tree as a sign of hope dates back thousands of years to pagan celebrations of the winter solstice. The evergreen represents eternal life, and the lights represent Christ as light of the world. Ornaments can range from religious to ridiculous these days. Although we adorn the top of our tree with an angel, mixed in among the Nativity scenes and stars that decorate the branches are rocket ships and baseballs, chile peppers and reindeer. The tree, especially in modern American culture, is an amalgam of spiritual and secular.

We can return our tree to a more religious realm by starting our decorating session with a Christmas tree blessing. Once the tree is in its stand, we can gather around it and pray:

Christmas Tree Blessing

Lord God, we ask you to bless this tree as a sign of our faith. May the twinkling lights be a reminder to us of the One who is to come: Jesus Christ, the Light of the World.

Bless our family and our home. May the joy and peace of Christmas take root in our hearts and make our lives an outward sign of your love. We ask this through Christ our Lord. Amen.

—Mary DeTurris Poust

We light the tree at the conclusion of our prayer. We can even sing "O Come, O Come, Emmanuel," the words of which echo the prayers of the O Antiphons.

Catholic tradition suggests that the tree be put up close to Christmas, at least after the O Antiphons have begun on December 17, and remain up until the feast of the Epiphany, which falls on a Sunday between January 2 and 8.

wisdom for the journey

Christmas is the season for kindling the fire of hospitality in the hall, the genial flame of charity in the heart.

—Washington Irving, nineteenth-century American author

Christmas Joy

The build-up of Advent culminates in the celebration of Christmas and the Christmas season, which starts on Christmas Eve and continues until the feast of the Baptism of the Lord. The spectacular spiritual celebration announces the birth of our Savior, a moment in time that changed the course of history and continues to impact individual lives the world over.

The penitential purple is put away during the Christmas season, replaced by the bright white of joy and hope and peace. The Baby Jesus finds his place in the manger. Shepherds bow before him. Magi make their way from distant lands—or from across the living room to the family *crèche* scene.

Definition

Crèche is a French term meaning "manger" or "crib" and is another name for a Nativity scene that represents Christ's birth in Bethlehem—a stable, animals, Jesus, Mary, Joseph, shepherds, kings, and an angel. St. Francis of Assisi created the first Nativity scene or crèche—a living one—in 1223, using real people and animals from the town of Grecio, Italy, as a way to commemorate the birth of the Savior.

I collect Nativity scenes, so we've got more than our fair share of crèches around the house—big ones across the entire dining room buffet, little ones that fit in the palm of your hand, and everything in between. We set up all but one Nativity scene in its entirety before Christmas. But the crèche in our living room near our tree—the one my own parents placed in my living room as a child—is left with an empty space where Jesus will be placed on Christmas.

When the kids come downstairs on Christmas morning to open their gifts, they head to the Nativity scene, put Jesus into it, and sing, "Happy Birthday." When my son was very young, this event had to be accompanied by an actual birthday cake, although I think he may have had some ulterior motives there. This little ritual still brings tears to my eyes every Christmas—my children gathered around the crèche, singing to their Savior.

For us Catholics, our prayer lives of course reflect this same joy. From Liturgy of the Hours to Christmas Mass to the prayers said around our holiday dinner table, this is a time to allow the light of this season to seep into the nooks and crannies of our souls and nourish us for the year ahead.

Celebrating the Holy Family

On the Sunday after Christmas (or December 30, if Christmas is a Sunday), the Church celebrates the feast of the Holy Family. This is a day to celebrate not only the deep relationship among Jesus, Mary, and Joseph, but also the special relationships that exist within our own families. We can look to the Holy Family as a model of what we can strive to achieve: nurturing and encouraging the spiritual formation of our children, sacrificing for one another, and serving God above all else.

The Holy Family provides us with a true example of grace under pressure. The lives of Jesus, Mary, and Joseph were filled with struggle, disappointment, and outright danger. And yet they persevered—together. So can we.

Praying together as a family (see Chapter 6 for more on that) is the best way to strengthen our spiritual bonds. Praying to the Holy Family, not only on the annual feast day but frequently, can help us remain focused on our vocations as parents and our roles as spouse, parent, child, or sibling.

The Feast of the Epiphany

Although the traditional date of the feast of the Epiphany is January 6, it's typically celebrated on the Sunday between January 2 and 8. Why? Because most Catholics can't or won't get to Mass on January 6 if it falls on a weekday, so the celebration is moved to Sunday—as is done with other Church feasts in the United States—to allow more Catholics to join in the spiritual festivities.

This day is not just a celebration of the Magi's visit to the Christ Child in the manger, as often comes to mind at the mention of this feast. Epiphany is a celebration of the manifestation of Christ among us and of the fulfillment of the Old Testament promise that the Savior would be a light to all peoples and nations.

prayer practice

In some countries around the world—Italy, Russia, Mexico—Epiphany is the day children receive gifts. In Italian legend, La Befana is an old woman who met the Magi and was invited to join them on their journey to Bethlehem, but she had to finish cleaning her house and never caught up with them. As the story goes, she's been wandering around searching for the Christ child ever since, leaving gifts for children on the night of January 5. We can explore some of these other traditions—and the spiritual significance behind them—and incorporate elements into our own rituals to add another layer of richness.

The Baptism of Jesus

We may hear of the baptism of Jesus and think of this as chronologically falling at this time of year much the same way our own baptism would be celebrated soon after our birth. But we have to remember that Jesus was baptized by his cousin John the Baptist in the Jordan River as an adult at the outset of his public ministry.

This feast is celebrated by the Western Church the Sunday after Epiphany and marks the end of the Christmas season. (The Eastern Church celebrates this feast on Epiphany.)

Lent: Through the Desert

Lent is another season of preparation, although it's very different in tone from Advent. During Lent, we enter into the sparseness of spiritual life, stripping away the things that get in the way of our prayer and spiritual growth in an effort to encounter Jesus during the pivotal and final moments leading up to his crucifixion.

This 40-day season in anticipation of Easter is marked by the deep purple of penance, by altars stripped of flowers, and songs and prayers stripped of "alleluias." This is a time to dig deep down into the core of our being and work toward true transformation.

The Stations of the Cross

Although we can pray the Stations of the Cross—or Way of the Cross—any day of the Church year, this devotion that commemorates the Passion of Jesus Christ takes on deeper significance and is more popular during Lent, when it's typically prayed on Fridays.

If we pray the Stations of the Cross at a church or shrine, whether individually or as a group, we would pray in front of a series of pictures or sculptures depicting scenes from Jesus' final hours leading up to his death and burial. Before each station, we repeat the following prayer:

> We adore you, O Christ, and we praise you, because
> by your holy cross you have redeemed the world.

If we pray as a group, the priest would move from station to station, often accompanied by altar servers carrying a cross. A short reflection might be read to help us focus on each station.

> *First Station:* Jesus is condemned to death.
>
> *Second Station:* Jesus takes up his cross.

Third Station: Jesus falls the first time.

Fourth Station: Jesus is met by his mother.

Fifth Station: Simon of Cyrene helps Jesus carry his cross.

Sixth Station: Veronica wipes the face of Jesus.

Seventh Station: Jesus falls a second time.

Eighth Station: The women of Jerusalem mourn for our Lord.

Ninth Station: Jesus falls a third time.

Tenth Station: Jesus is stripped of his garments.

Eleventh Station: Jesus is nailed to the cross.

Twelfth Station: Jesus dies on the cross.

Thirteenth Station: Jesus is taken down from the cross.

Fourteenth Station: Jesus is placed in the tomb.

Fasting, Prayer, and Almsgiving

Woven into the fabric of many of the world's religions in one fashion or another are the practices known as the three "pillars" of lent: fasting, prayer, and almsgiving. The three are meant to hold equal weight for us, although Catholics of the past focused more attention on the fasting element than on the other two. These days of prayer and almsgiving, which includes charitable donations of time and talent as well as treasure, are emphasized. In fact, it could be said that prayer is the foundation that holds up the other two pillars.

wisdom for the journey

The ancients, we realize, were correct in their conviction that prayer and fasting are needed if true charity, unhindered by our selfishness, is to take place at all.

—Msgr. Charles M. Murphy, *The Spirituality of Fasting*

For Catholics, fasting has been cut back to a fairly minimal practice in terms of what we are *obliged* to do. Fasting, which in contemporary Catholic tradition means taking no more than one full meal in a day and two other very small meals that don't add up to one, is only required on Ash Wednesday and Good Friday. Abstinence, which means refraining from meat, is required only on Ash Wednesday and the Fridays of Lent. But for those of us looking to deepen our prayer lives, fasting can become a conduit to spiritual growth.

Learning to do without, especially when our sacrifice is made on behalf of others, helps us move beyond earthly wants and needs to focus our energy on something bigger, deeper. Fasting (as I discuss in more detail in Chapter 21), when combined with prayer, creates a physical void that is then filled by God.

Similarly, almsgiving, when approached not from a place of obligation but a place of true generosity, can plant seeds of transformation that blossom into a Gospel-centered life, not just during Lent, but year-round.

Often in our modern world, giving has been divorced from prayer and fasting. We may give each week to our parish, each month to a special charitable cause, or each year to a diocesan appeal. And yet, prayer may never enter the picture. Too often giving to our church has become similar to giving to any charitable organization—generous, perhaps, but separated from the thing that turns plain old philanthropy into Gospel-inspired almsgiving. So this practice is meant to *be* a prayer that leads to a new perspective and perhaps even to a permanent change of heart.

Prayer, of course, seems obvious, and yet during Lent we are supposed to focus our prayer more intensely on Jesus and his sacrifices. Grounded in the messages of the Lenten season, we are challenged in prayer to reach inward and outward all at once. Our Lenten prayers should not remain in the vocal realm alone but should include silent times spent in quiet conversation with God, listening for His word to us. (See Chapter 8 for more on silent prayer.)

The High Holy Days

As Lent ends, we move into the holiest days in the Church year, the Triduum: Holy Thursday, Good Friday, and Holy Saturday. These days are marked with special liturgies and services to help us enter deeply into Christ's Passion in preparation for the Easter Vigil Mass.

On Holy Thursday, one Mass is celebrated in a parish: the Mass of the Lord's Supper. During this liturgy, which celebrates Jesus' institution of the Eucharist, the presiding priest or a deacon often washes the feet of 12 parishioners, mirroring Christ's own actions and his teaching that his followers must serve rather than be served. It's a beautiful liturgy that ends in silence and without the traditional final blessing. Instead, following Communion, the priest carries the Blessed Sacrament to a chapel or place on the altar so people can spend time before it in quiet prayer throughout the night.

Good Friday, the day we commemorate Christ's death on the cross, is the one day in the Church year when no Masses are celebrated. (On Holy Saturday, there's no Mass until the Easter Vigil, which is the next day in liturgical time.) Typically, on Good Friday, parishes have one or two opportunities for Stations of the Cross and a Communion service with the reading of the Lord's Passion and veneration of the cross, a time when we come forward and bow before or kiss a cross. At these services, hosts that were consecrated the evening before are used for communion.

This most solemn day in the Church year is meant to be a time of deep interior prayer, a day when we set aside work or unnecessary activities to really focus on Christ's sacrifice on our behalf and our response to him. If we are working on our prayer lives, this is the day to move deep into the still waters of spiritual reading, meditation, and devotional prayer.

The quiet continues on Holy Saturday, as spiritually we remain in the tomb with Jesus. It is only when the sun goes down and the Easter Vigil Mass begins that the darkness of Lent fades and we emerge into the light of new life.

Easter: Alleluia, Alleluia

Easter brings with it a truly joyous celebration. Christ is risen from the dead! He has taken the cross and transformed a symbol of death into a symbol of salvation. This is the pinnacle of the Church year, the most important day in the liturgical calendar, and rightly so. Our God, who came down from heaven and became man, died for our sins and rose from the dead to open the gates of heaven. Understandably, this is an incredibly big deal in our spiritual lives.

The Church is decked out in the bright white of resurrection. The Easter candle is lighted. Every prayer and song is laced with "alleluias." Joy is everywhere!

Fire, Water, and Light

The Easter Vigil, beyond a shadow of a doubt, is the ultimate liturgy of the Church year. Starting just after nightfall, with a church submerged in darkness, a "new fire" is lighted outside the church to signify new light and life in Christ. From that the Paschal candle is lighted, and the deacon processes up the aisle with it. As he moves forward, people in the pews light their candles, gradually brightening the church until the Paschal candle is placed on the altar and the church is flooded with light.

Then we work our way through seven Old Testament readings, each followed by a Psalm or canticle, until we get to the New Testament readings and Gospel. It's at this Mass that adults who have been preparing to enter the Church receive the sacraments of initiation, baptism (if they have not already been baptized), confirmation, and Holy Communion, thereby becoming fully Catholic. Baptism, Holy Communion, and confirmation are celebrated there before the entire congregation. It is a powerful liturgy, one every Catholic should experience at least once. It's hard not to get caught up in the beauty and splendor of the liturgy, the Scripture, the songs, and the celebration.

The symbolism of fire, light, and water echoes throughout the Easter season, which lasts for 50 days.

Ascent to Heaven

After he rose from the dead, Jesus appeared to his disciples in different forms but was always recognizable in the breaking of the bread. He remained with them for a while, continuing his teaching and preparing them for when he would return to his Father.

Ascension Thursday is celebrated 40 days after Easter and is a holy day of obligation. However, in many dioceses throughout the United States, the feast has been moved to the following Sunday, again to accommodate those who cannot get to Mass during the week.

Descent of the Spirit

Before Jesus ascended into heaven, he promised his disciples he would send them—and therefore us—a helper, or "advocate." Fifty days after Easter, on the feast of Pentecost, we celebrate the day when the Spirit of God descended upon Jesus' disciples, giving them the ability and the courage to go out and spread the Good News. All these many centuries later, we look to the same Spirit to guide our prayers and our lives.

Pentecost marks the end of the Easter season and a return to "ordinary time."

All Saints and All Souls

Two key feast days that fall outside any of the special seasons are the Solemnity of All Saints, celebrated on November 1 and a holy day of obligation, meaning Catholics are required to attend Mass that day, and the Commemoration of All Souls, celebrated on November 2.

These two days in ordinary time are like a mini season of their own, connecting us in a focused way with the communion of saints. When we celebrate All Saints Day, we look to those men and women from throughout our Church history who now share in heavenly glory. We celebrate their lives and ask for their intercession in a special way.

All Souls Day is dedicated to all those who have died but who may not yet be in heaven. It's a time to pray for those loved ones who have gone before us in faith in a special way, asking God to take them to heaven.

Prayer Practice

In the Mexican tradition, All Souls Day is known as *Dia de los Muertos*—Day of the Dead—and is marked not by somber services but by parties, sometimes held graveside at a cemetery. The food, photos, and memorabilia placed on homemade altars are seen as a way to build a connection to the other side so the dead can hear the prayers of the living. The celebration is a blend of Catholic and indigenous traditions.

"Ordinary Time" Isn't So Ordinary

Any days outside the special seasons of the Church year are part of "ordinary time." We know it's ordinary time when we walk into church and see a green cloth on the altar or the priest wearing green vestments. The title actually belies the literal translation of the Latin words for this season: *Tempus per annum,* which means "time through the year."

Ordinary time runs sporadically throughout the year—after Advent and Christmas until Lent, and then after Easter all the way up to Advent again. And yet this season is filled with special occasions. Ordinary time is the "season" of the feasts of the Body and Blood of Christ, the Assumption of Mary, and St. Francis, as well as other holy days. It's the season of secular holidays with spiritual ties, such as Thanksgiving Day.

Ordinary time is filled with liturgies and rituals that can make our prayer lives full to overflowing, if we seek them out and dive in. A quick check of the Church calendar shows that whether it be a saint's feast day or a day to honor Mary, more often than not, even the most ordinary of days has special significance when it comes to faith.

Essential Takeaways

- The feasts and rituals of the Church year can bring an added richness to our daily prayer lives.
- Advent marks the start of the Church year and the spiritual preparation time for Christmas.
- Through prayer, fasting, and almsgiving we move through Lent in anticipation of Easter, the pinnacle of the Church year.
- Ordinary time is filled with its own special feasts, including All Saints Day, that provide opportunities to explore new avenues of prayer and devotion.

chapter 21

Ancient Traditions for Modern Times

- Iconography: windows to heaven
- Praying without ceasing through the Jesus Prayer
- Growing in faith through pilgrim journeys
- Finding a spiritual desert amid the lushness of daily life

Sometimes, despite all the modern conveniences and high-tech possibilities, the most effective and powerful thing we can do for our spiritual lives is to return to the ancient prayer traditions of our faith. Like an oasis in a spiritual desert, these practices—icons and repetitive prayer, solitude and fasting—can become a gateway to contemplation.

We can trace many of these traditions back to the Desert Fathers and Mothers, those men and women who lived in prayerful solitude in the deserts of Egypt around the third century A.D. In an attempt to imitate the ways of Jesus and John the Baptist, they stripped away the distractions of life in the world to confront themselves—their spiritual distractions and personal demons—in powerful ways. Through their ascetic practices, they forged a deeper connection with God and left a road map for us to do the same, even when we can't literally roam the deserts of North Africa.

Although these practices can seem somewhat foreign to us if we've never tried them before, they provide a whole new way of approaching prayer. Through these ancient traditions, we can discover interior places we've never been before and spiritual connections that seem to buzz with new life and depth.

Praying with Icons

Our spiritual brethren in the Eastern Church have long recognized religious icons as a pathway to prayer, a door to eternity. For many of us westerners, however, icons can be discomforting. The perspective, facial features, and penetrating stares often feel strange to those of us who have spent our spiritual lives surrounded by statues of smiling saints.

wisdom for the journey

Icons are not just artwork and they're not just there to remind you of something, but in a mysterious way they make a connection for you. The usual phrase is that icons are "windows into heaven," and that is the role they're supposed to fill.

—Frederica Mathewes-Green,
The Open Door: Entering the Sanctuary of Icons and Prayer

Iconography originated in the earliest days of Christianity. In fact, iconographers credit St. Luke with "writing" the first icon, an image of the Virgin Mary holding the Christ child. True icons are said to be "written" instead of painted because they are like a theological text, exact representations of teachings of the faith, not an artist's interpretation of a teaching.

Where statues and stained glass attempt to bring God into our space, icons do the opposite, attempting to bring us into God's space. Hence the idea of an icon as a doorway into heaven. It's as if we are going *through* the icon to reach God.

Among the most popular icons are *Christ Pantocrator* (*Universal Ruler or Almighty*), the oldest known icon of Christ, and the *Old Testament Trinity* by famed Russian iconographer Andrei Rublev. *Christ Pantocrator* was written in the sixth or seventh century and is preserved at St. Catherine's Monastery in Sinai. The commanding but unsettling figure of Christ has a penetrating stare that seems to beckon us even as it makes us feel as though it's aware of all our weaknesses.

The *Old Testament Trinity,* written around 1410, is also known as the *Hospitality of Abraham.* It shows the three angels who appeared to Abraham in

Mamre, giving us a kind of Trinity, gathered around an altar table on which sits a cup filled with wine. These icons and so many others give us a starting place for deeper prayer.

Once we've chosen an icon, we set it before us and begin to pray. We don't pray *to* the icon but rather *in the presence of* the icon. Instead of closing our eyes, as we often do in quiet prayer, we keep our eyes wide open to take in all the icon puts before us. We don't focus on the artistic aspects of the icon but instead on what it means, and how it depicts God's love for us and for all creation.

There is no vocal praying involved in this method, which instead is a pathway to meditation and contemplation. And so we would pray before an icon the way we would pray any silent prayer—in our sacred space or a church with icons, in silence, surrounded by things that help us forget the world around us and move inward.

The Jesus Prayer

One of the oldest prayers in Christian tradition, the Jesus Prayer attempts to put into practice St. Paul's admonition to "pray without ceasing." (1 Thessalonians 5:17)

> Lord Jesus Christ, Son of God, have mercy on me, a sinner.

This simple but powerful prayer is intended to be repeated over and over, almost unconsciously, until it begins to work in mysterious ways, serving as a jumping-off point for a much deeper type of prayer than what we hear on the surface.

You begin praying the Jesus Prayer with your lips, repeating it regularly throughout the day, maybe dozens or even hundreds of times, quietly but still vocally. The hope is that as this prayer becomes engrained in your thought process and in our daily life, it starts to change you and make you more aware of God on a constant basis.

Eventually, as you get used to saying the Jesus Prayer, you no longer need to move your lips. Instead, you say the prayer with your heart. When you take this prayer to its deepest level, you say it without needing to move your lips or even consciously focus on the words because it becomes part of your soul, one with your breath, and propels you toward God with each moment of the day. The words, "Lord Jesus Christ, Son of God, have mercy on me, a sinner," become part of your being and shape your words and actions.

Prayer Practice

You must try continually to make all of your actions, without distinction, a sort of little conversation with God—not in a rehearsed way but just as they happen, with purity and simplicity of heart.

—Brother Lawrence, seventeenth-century French monk and spiritual writer

This prayer is taken from the New Testament story of two blind men. As Jesus passes by, they cry out: "Lord, Son of David, have pity on us!" (Matthew 20:30) And in his mercy, Jesus heals them. Some say the prayer is a summation of the Gospel, declaring Jesus to be Lord, begging for his forgiveness and compassion, and acknowledging our own human weakness in his sight.

Over time, what seems so simple, a few words uttered now and then throughout our day, becomes transforming, giving us an entirely new outlook on our relationship with God and with others. It can be said anywhere, any time—alone or in a crowd, at work or at rest, in a sacred space or a crowded subway, with no study or reading or outside guidance. We can simply begin right now, today.

I have tried to say the Jesus Prayer and have not always been successful, despite how simple it seems. It really does require us to be constantly aware of God's presence, to pray without ceasing, which isn't always easy when the kids have the TV blaring or the neighbors are revving a chainsaw outside our window.

The key is to keep saying the prayer, even if we have to say it out loud to make it sink in. It is, in effect, a spiritual distraction, giving our minds and lips something to do while we prepare our hearts for the message. The goal is not simply to *say* the prayer but to *become* the prayer. This prayer practice may not be for everyone, but Catholic tradition is a big tent with something for everyone.

Misc.

Not a Mantra

On the surface, the Jesus Prayer might seem like a "mantra" from Eastern meditative traditions, the repetition of a word or sound over and over in an attempt to empty the mind and focus on the breath. Because the Jesus Prayer is just that—a prayer—it sets it apart from a mantra, which doesn't necessarily have a faith element to it.

The Pilgrim's Journey

When we think of pilgrimage, it's likely we imagine a journey to some far-off land. It's true that a pilgrimage in the traditional sense is a long journey, but our entire lives are meant to be a pilgrimage—both physical and spiritual—leading us ever closer to God.

We can trace the tradition of pilgrimage back to our Jewish forebears and even to the ancient Greeks, Egyptians, and Aztecs. For people of faith, pilgrimage is often an important, sometimes required element of spiritual practices. It has stood the test of time, certainly, in our own faith tradition. Since the beginning of Christianity, believers have traveled to places of religious significance for spiritual nourishment and inspiration.

Visiting Sacred Places

Our Christian pilgrimage tradition starts with the Holy Family and continues from there. We know Jesus, Mary, and Joseph made an annual pilgrimage to Jerusalem. Jesus was crucified during a time of pilgrimage. The early Christians made pilgrimages to the tombs of martyrs. Later Christians made pilgrimages back to the Holy Land.

And today the tradition continues, with Catholics making pilgrimages to churches and shrines around the world to walk in the footsteps of the great saints and to be near to places where God's presence is felt in abundant, sometimes mystical ways.

Of course, pilgrimage is not just about the destination; both the journey and the companionship are critical. Even if we go on pilgrimage without any friends or family, we won't be alone. We'll be surrounded by other pilgrims seeking what we're seeking—a deeper connection to God.

If we have the ability and desire to make a traditional pilgrimage, we have plenty of options from which to choose. From the obvious places such as the Holy Land, Rome, and Lourdes, to lesser-known pilgrim spots around the world, we can find something to suit our spiritual style, our travel interests, and our physical abilities. We can join a prearranged tour that directs us throughout our pilgrimage, or, if we're more adventurous, we can do something more grueling and independent, such as the famed Camino de Santiago Compostela, the Way of St. James, a 1,200-mile route that weaves its way through Europe, ending in Spain. Pilgrims walk for hundreds of miles stretched over weeks, carrying nothing more than a backpack.

Misc.

Not Just Another Vacation

A pilgrimage can easily turn into just another vacation, as you run from one scenic church or shrine to another. To keep it from losing its spiritual focus, try to connect with people and events that make the spiritual places come alive. On a recent trip to Rome, one of the most moving moments occurred in a neighborhood church where I joined in nightly vespers. Sitting in the darkened church filled with icons and statues, as Italian chants echoed off the ancient walls, I felt a deep spiritual connection that took me far beyond anything the guidebooks said about the place. Pilgrimage is not only about the destination but about the human encounters we have along the way.

St. Peter's Basilica in Rome, shown here, and other holy places in the Holy Land are key pilgrimage destinations for Catholics who want to connect with the earliest foundations of the faith.

Photo courtesy of Mary DeTurris Poust

Pilgrim Spots Near Home

For many of us, a pilgrimage to a foreign country for weeks at a time simply isn't feasible. Perhaps we don't have the money or the time or the ability. That doesn't mean we can't find pilgrim spots within driving distance, or sometimes right around the corner.

We can visit local shrines in our state or province or take a road trip to another part of the country. Even a visit to a nearby historic church can be a pilgrimage of sorts if we approach it with a pilgrim's heart and spirit.

Only 45 minutes from my home in upstate New York is the Shrine of the North American Martyrs in Auriesville. There, on the beautiful land in view of the Mohawk River, Blessed Kateri Tekakwitha was born. Known as the Lily of the Mohawks, she is the first Native American on the road to sainthood. The shrine also marks the spot where Jesuit missionaries St. Isaac Jogues and St. Rene Goupil and lay missioner St. John Lalande were martyred.

Although this picturesque and peaceful shrine is so close to home, it took me eight years to set out and explore it. Even at that, I only did so because I was going on a Boy Scout camping retreat with my son. When I walked the grounds of Auriesville, I could feel a holy presence, a sense that something awful but awesome happened in that place. It is sacred to be sure, and that sacredness seeped into my heart and helped me understand the importance of pilgrimage in our spiritual lives.

Misc.

Beat the Clock

If you go on a guided pilgrimage, one problem you might encounter is the "group mentality." And typically all the pilgrimage groups have the same idea. That means when you visit a cathedral or shrine, you may be shoulder-to-shoulder with other pilgrims, creating a less-than-spiritual experience. Ask some locals or pilgrimage-savvy friends about good times to visit scenic spots, and try to go in off hours. St. Peter's Basilica can feel like any other overcrowded museum if you go there at noon, but stop in at 7 A.M., when all the chapels are filled with Masses being celebrated in different languages, and you'll have the place to yourself.

Walking in the footsteps of holy men and women surrounded by other pilgrims breathed new life into my spirit and filled me with a sense of oneness—oneness with the strangers who prayed beside me, oneness with the saints who lived and died there, oneness with God in the majesty of the natural beauty of the land.

So whether we live in the city, suburbs, or country, we can seek out sacred places that can provide us with a pilgrim experience without traveling far from home.

A Pilgrimage of the Heart

Pilgrimage doesn't have to be a physical journey at all. All of life can be a pilgrimage, and *should* be a pilgrimage. But certain key moments lend themselves to this type of inward journey—an illness, a crisis, a joyful event, any moment when we sense God's presence in a particular way.

wisdom for the journey

We need not travel to southern France to encounter God's presence in our lives. God dwells within us already, and just as important as the grotto of Lourdes, where Mary spoke to Bernadette in 1858, is the grotto of our hearts.

—Father James Martin, S.J., *Lourdes Diary: Seven Days in the Grotto of Massabielle*

The goal of pilgrimage is not to reach a physical destination but rather a spiritual one. Without leaving home, we can make a pilgrimage of the heart, an interior journey where we hope to meet God. Through our various methods of prayer—vocal and silent, communal and private—we make this pilgrimage with countless others around the world. We simply have to look at our very lives as pilgrim journeys, guided by the Spirit, our destination being the heart of God. It's a pilgrimage that often takes the better part of a lifetime.

Finding Our Own Desert

Throughout Jesus' public ministry, we see him retreat to the desert to pray in solitude. The *Desert Fathers and Mothers* did the same, as do modern-day hermits and even monks and nuns who live in community but spend long hours in silence in their cells. For those of us living out in the noisy workaday world, it can seem as if we don't stand a chance. We can't retreat to the desert, so how can we achieve those same levels of holiness?

The truth is, we have to make our own desert, maybe right there in the lush green of our backyard. It may take some creativity on our part, but it can be done. And the rewards are well worth the effort.

Definition

The **Desert Fathers and Mothers** were those holy men and women who lived as hermits, monks, and nuns in the deserts of Egypt, mainly Scetes, beginning in the third century A.D. Although they originally fled to the desert because of persecution, their focus on solitude, self-discipline, and constant prayer later became the model for monasticism. St. Antony of Egypt is the most famous of the Desert Fathers.

Going on Retreat

The best way to give ourselves a short stay in the "desert" is to go on retreat—once a year if possible. That can be difficult for busy moms and dads with little ones at home or those with stressful jobs and little vacation time, but even one or two days away from the world can re-energize us for the long months ahead.

Retreats come in all shapes and sizes—one day, two days, one week, even an entire month or longer in special circumstances. They can be silent or filled with dialogue sessions, in shrines and churches, by the ocean, in the mountains, and of course, in the desert. If you're new to the retreat world or haven't been on one in a while, you may want to start with a directed retreat with a group of people and work toward a silent, self-directed retreat. The possibilities are almost limitless.

I went on my first silent retreat about two years ago. I couldn't imagine how I would keep myself from talking for two days. To top it off, this particular retreat in camp-style lodging in the Adirondack Mountains also forbade reading, writing, and "casual eye contact." They might as well have said, "No breathing." I went because I felt drawn to it, but I really didn't know if I would make it.

I needn't have worried. Rather than struggle with it, I basked in the glow of silence, freed from the need to make small talk, even at the communal dinner table. It was a revelation. My "monkey mind" was in full swing as I sat in silence, always trying to distract me with things I needed to do or worry about, but slowly, over the course of two days, it settled down and I found myself sorry that the silence couldn't go on a little bit longer.

Misc.

A Monkey on Your Back

Monkey mind is a Buddhist term used to describe the constant distractions that crop up when we try to enter into meditation. It's a perfect fit for the distractions of Catholic meditative prayer as well. Imagine a monkey jumping from tree to tree, never letting up with its constant movement and chatter. That's what your mind will do when you try to quiet down and spend time in silent prayer, especially at first. Slowly, and with practice, the monkeys settle down and the stream of random thoughts and worries slows to a trickle.

The reverberations were obvious, too. At home I sought out silence amid the chaos of family life. I drove with the car radio off and just let the silence fill me with God's presence and soothe my soul. I ate in silence when I was home alone. I walked in silence when I went out at night for some exercise. It proved to me that even a short spiritual retreat could have a long and powerful impact on my prayer life.

Prayer Through Fasting

I talked a bit about fasting in Chapter 20 when I discussed Lent, but the kind of fasting I'm referring to now is different. This isn't the obligatory fast of a specified day or season; this is a fasting mind-set, a conscious decision to make due with less—less talking, less television, less food, whatever it is we need less of—on a regular basis in order to have more space and time for God.

Like pilgrimage, fasting has a long history in our faith tradition as well as in the traditions of many other faiths. On the surface, fasting can seem like punishment, making people see it as a negative rather than positive spiritual practice. But the doing without is not supposed to be punishment but rather a way to free our bodies and spirits from the worldly desires that threaten to pull us off our spiritual path. By fasting, we open up a space, both literally and figuratively, and allow God to squeeze in among all the other things that lay claim to our attention.

Fasting doesn't have to be extreme to be effective. We don't have to go for days or even for one full day without food, although that's an option as long as we are healthy enough to handle it. Fasting can be as simple as giving up a particular meal on a particular day on a regular basis, or giving up something else that gets too much of our energy and attention.

One man I know eats only one slice of toast for breakfast and one slice of toast for lunch on Fridays, and he never eats meat with Friday dinner, his one real meal of the day. It's his way of living in solidarity with those who are hungry every day. His minor hunger pangs remind him to work for a more just society. Fasting is a prayer, he says.

By learning to do without food, we become more adept at doing without other things. And freeing ourselves from those earthly desires allows us to put our focus on spiritual matters.

Extended Silence

A few years ago, I went to see a beautiful but long movie about the Carthusian monks in the French Alps. *Into Great Silence* was, in some ways, a spiritual endurance test: three hours of almost total silence interspersed by a few lines in French with subtitles. There were moments when the only sound or visual was water dripping. For three hours, I got the chance to experience vicariously a life without talking, without much noise at all, save for the ringing of church bells and the chanting of psalms.

Such deep and extended silence is something typically reserved for those living away from the world in the strictest monasteries. After all, the rest of us wouldn't get very far if we suddenly stopped talking to our spouse, children, boss, and friends. But we can learn an important lesson from the Carthusians and others who ground their spiritual lives in silence so profound it's deafening.

We all need silence in our spiritual lives, something I covered in Chapter 8 when I talked about silent prayer. However, extended silence takes the silent prayer discussed earlier to a much deeper level. Through the extended silence of a retreat or time away at a monastery or spirituality center, we give ourselves enough time to get our monkey mind under control and really hear God speaking to our hearts.

Although I've never done it, my goal is to go on a weeklong silent retreat sometime soon. Having done a two-day silent retreat, I realize it takes about that much time to get used to the silence and stop giving our random thoughts so much attention. After those initial days of adjustment, we settle into the silence where our souls are refreshed, our spirits renewed, and our spiritual "hearing" heightened.

prayer practice

We can work our way up to some of these more extreme spiritual practices. We can pick one day a month and fast from food or talking. Or we can choose to cut out all *unnecessary* talking or eating one day or weekend a month. Even that's not easy, especially when those around us are going about life as usual. But it's a good way to get a taste of what we might like to explore in a more extended way on retreat.

Essential Takeaways

- By praying in the presence of icons, we attempt to enter into God's space.
- The Jesus Prayer, said repeatedly each day, helps us pray without ceasing.
- Both traditional pilgrimage to a sacred place and interior pilgrimage to our own spiritual center are meant to lead us closer to the heart of God.
- We can create a desert experience despite our busy worldly lives through annual retreats, occasional fasting, and extended periods of silence.

chapter 22

Going Deeper Still

Different prayers for different times of life

Seeking guidance from saintly spiritual masters

Women mystics' perspective

Hitting a prayer dry spell

Getting help from a spiritual director

It always helps to have companions on a journey, and a spiritual journey is no exception. We can, of course, seek out family members and friends who share our spiritual hunger, but there's a long list of prayer masters who have left words, letters, rules, and guidelines that remain relevant today, centuries later.

Throughout history and right up to this moment, we have been given abundant examples of holy men and women who have been gifted with special spiritual insights. Some were founders and leaders of religious communities. Others were mystics who had visions and experienced spiritual ecstasy. And some are "regular" people who were simply a little further down the very same path we're on.

We can benefit from all of them. Reading their words, understanding their lives, and experimenting with the kinds of prayers and practices they developed can give us a new outlook on prayer life, especially when we find ourselves falling into a rut or dry spell.

Different Styles for Different Stages

One thing we have to realize is that no one prayer style is likely to fit us for a lifetime. We change, we grow, we find ourselves in different places and circumstances, and all those things influence how we pray and what we pray about.

The beauty of Catholic prayer is that so many options are available. At times, we might find ourselves drawn only to traditional vocal devotions like the Rosary, something we can pray with our family or a group. At other moments, we might need the quiet of *Lectio Divina* or contemplation. Just because we start with one type of prayer doesn't mean we have to stay there.

Changing our prayer routine can reinvigorate us and renew our enthusiasm for our spiritual journey. Going outside our prayer comfort zone just might open an interior door we've never looked behind before. As long as we're guided by the Spirit and within the realm of authentic Catholic spirituality, we are on safe ground and can explore and experiment with new and intriguing prayers and approaches.

Lessons from Spiritual Masters

If we want to incorporate a little more classic Catholic spiritual tradition into our everyday prayer lives, a number of options have been laid out for us by some of the spiritual giants of Catholic history—St. Benedict of Nursia, St. Francis of Assisi, St. Dominic of Guzman, St. Ignatius of Loyola, and many others. It would be impossible to cover them all in this book, so we'll focus on the spiritualities of these four leading saints. Just keep in mind that other spiritualities—Carmelite, Trappist, Redemptorist, Passionist, and on and on—might be a better fit for you. We'll briefly review some of them as well in the pages that follow.

wisdom for the journey

Over and over, the Rule calls us to be more mindful of the little things, even as it reminds us of the big picture, allowing us a glimpse of who we can be when we remember to love.

—Kathleen Norris, *The Cloister Walk*

Benedictine by the Rule

Benedictine spirituality is grounded in the mission of St. Benedict of Nursia, the sixth-century Italian monk whose "Rule" has been the basis for nearly all of Western monasticism for the last 1,500 years. St. Benedict—and Benedictines who continue to follow his path today—set out a basic mission of prayer and work, *Ora et Labora,* meaning that spiritual life and practical life are totally intertwined.

While the Rule of St. Benedict covers everything from how much wine the monks were allowed to drink with dinner to receiving guests at the monastery, it's still very much relevant to our lives today. Even the parts about moderation in food and drink can be adapted to our modern lives.

St. Benedict opens the Rule with these words: "Listen with the ear of your heart." That's a favorite quote of mine, and it hangs on a stone plaque in my office. It gets to the heart of prayer life, and the heart of life in general. We're not meant to run from one thing to another without focus, without peace, without direction. We need to stop, breathe, be quiet, and listen with our hearts.

Misc.

Seeking Solitude in a Cave

In the cliffs of Subiaco, Italy, about 30 miles outside Rome, you can visit the cave where St. Benedict lived as a hermit for three years. A medieval monastery now sits directly on top of it, but the cave is still there and open to pilgrims. Benedict lived there in prayerful solitude, receiving food from a basket lowered into the cave by Romanus, another monk. Eventually Benedict's followers clamored for his guidance and wisdom, and he founded 12 monasteries. The Monastery of St. Scholastica, named for his twin sister, is still in operation just down the hill from his cave. You can visit and even eat lunch in an adjoining monastery restaurant. Despite being only an hour's drive from the bustle of Rome, you are a world away when you step into the quiet cloisters and fresco-covered hallways of the monastery that looks out on a sprawling valley below.

He then goes on to outline all the things that will lead to a balanced life grounded in God. Through prayer, work, study, and community we can re-create a Benedictine lifestyle out in today's world. St. Benedict's Rule can help us find the key to true happiness and freedom, not a freedom based on doing what we want when we want, but a freedom that comes from breaking free of all the earthly ties that bind us—materialism, power, vices, excesses of any kind.

A stone carving at the entrance to the Monastery of St. Scholastica in Subiaco, Italy, expresses the heart of Benedictine spirituality: *Pax* means "peace"; *ora et labora* means "work and pray."

Photo courtesy of Mary DeTurris Poust

St. Benedict teaches us to live an integrated life. So prayer is woven into the work we do each day, whether we drive a bus, balance budget sheets, or care for our children. Our community is our family, our friends, our parish, our workplace. And our study? Well, we're doing that right now as we attempt to learn more about faith and prayer in order to grow closer to Christ.

So if we lean toward a holistic view of spirituality, of our faith as intricately woven into every moment and event of our lives, then Benedictine spirituality could be a path to explore. We can study the Rule, which is short and easy to understand, as well as other Benedictine writings on our own (Appendix C has resources), or we can contact a Benedictine monastery for guidance, retreats, and possibly even entrance into a program to become a Benedictine Oblate, someone who makes a formal commitment to a particular Benedictine monastery while living out in the world.

Franciscan Spirituality

St. Francis of Assisi is, without question, one of the most well-known and beloved saints of all time. Even non-Catholics can't get enough of this eccentric friar recognized for his love of animals, the earth, the poor, and peace. But we have to be careful not to compartmentalize Francis into single issues or causes. This was a saint whose work and teachings went far beyond the poetry of the *Canticle of Brother Sun,* a song in praise of God's creation.

Would those St. Francis lawn statues that dot suburban landscapes be as popular if we really stopped to reflect on what they stand for? Francis' life was one centered on his love of Christ, his commitment to a radical living out of the Gospel, and his "marriage" to the bride he dubbed "Lady Poverty." The path St. Francis chose was not an easy one. He was ridiculed and mocked as a madman for what appeared to be an extreme response to his conversion experience. He renounced his family's fortune, fasted for days on end, heard the Lord speak to him from a cross in the church of San Damiano, and bore the stigmata (the wounds of Christ). He lived and died for Christ.

And so if we are drawn to Franciscan spirituality, we need to go forward with eyes wide open, recognizing that this path is not focused on one cause or one slice of God's creation. Franciscan spirituality is Christ-centered and Gospel-focused. It honors the sacredness of all creation, all humanity.

St. Francis lived out the Gospel in true imitation of Christ, giving away everything he had, living in poverty, waging peace even at the risk of his own life. Can we who live out in the world be Franciscan in our spirituality if we don't do the same? Yes, we can do so in a modified way more suitable to our modern lives. Maybe we can't give away everything, but we can live simply, learning to do with less in order to bring a piece of "poverty" (and peace of poverty!) into our lives.

Prayer Practice

We can practice "detachment" in our daily lives as a way to create an interior poverty in the spirit of St. Francis. This doesn't mean giving away our possessions but rather giving up our attachment to our possessions, as well as to people, places, and events in our lives. When we stop clinging to earthly things, we cling to God instead. When we detach ourselves from material wants, we begin to desire only God.

We can use the writings of St. Francis—his rule, his prayers, his canticles—to form a foundation for daily living and allow the example of his life to inspire us in our own.

Order of Preachers

The Dominicans, also known as the Order of Preachers, were founded by St. Dominic of Guzman, a thirteenth-century *friar* who started his religious community in an attempt to combat heretical Albigensians of his time; these were people who believed in a "dualism" that set the material world against the spiritual world. Even the body was seen as evil.

Dominic's order continues to this day with communities of men and women around the world committed to spreading the Gospel through words and ministries. Like the Franciscans, the Dominicans were founded as a "mendicant" movement, meaning that rather than remain in their monasteries, these friars were called to take their faith out into the world.

Dominican spirituality is grounded in seeking the truth through study and sharing that truth through preaching and other ministries. Lay associates do not make vows but rather make a commitment to partner with vowed members—friars and sisters—in prayer, study, and ministry.

Definition

A **friar** is a man who has made religious vows to a "mendicant" order such as the Franciscans or Dominicans. He may or may not be an ordained priest. Some friars remain "brothers," called to religious life but not the ordained ministry. In fact, St. Francis of Assisi was a friar but not a priest.

An Ignatian Approach

St. Ignatius of Loyola is known most famously as the founder of the Society of Jesus—or the Jesuits, as they are more commonly known. But this sixteenth-century Spaniard, who experienced a spiritual conversion while recovering from a war wound, gave us a transforming practice: his "Spiritual Exercises."

Originally designed to be prayed over the course of one month in a secluded retreat house or monastery, the prayers, meditations, and mental exercises that make up this practice can be spread over several months or even a full year in order to complete them while going about daily life.

I once inquired about the "Spiritual Exercises in Daily Life," which required a commitment of at least one full hour of prayer each day and a weekly meeting with a spiritual director over a nine-month period. I was ready to submit my application when I learned I was pregnant and in no position to make that kind of spiritual commitment. But I plan to do it when I once again feel called to this intense experience of prayer and reflection. (We all feel called to different spiritual experiences depending on where we are on our life journey.)

Ignatian spirituality challenges us to put ourselves into Scripture passages and imagine how the scene plays out before our eyes. We attempt to smell the smells and walk through the stories of Scripture in an effort to better understand how those stories relate to our own lives. This is not Scripture study but Scripture-based prayer.

The Spiritual Exercises are divided into four "weeks" or stages that are meant to lead us to spiritual freedom. The first week focuses on God's love for us, our own patterns of sin, and Christ's call to follow him. The second week focuses on how to be a true disciple of Jesus Christ. The third week's focus is on Christ's Passion and death and the gift of the Eucharist. The final week's focus is on Christ's resurrection, His appearance to His disciples, and how we might walk with Christ today.

The Spiritual Exercises should be done with the aid of a spiritual director, something I discuss in more detail a little later in this chapter.

Other Spiritual Options

If you feel you're called to a specific type of ministry or spirituality, continue looking at various communities until you find a good match. It's not something to be undertaken lightly. In addition to the orders mentioned previously, there are many others that focus on various aspects of Catholic life and teaching.

The Trappists, a branch of the Cistercians, are known for their silent prayer and work. They are contemplatives who follow the Rule of St. Benedict. Thomas Merton is the most famous Trappist, writing on everything from his own spiritual conversion in *The Seven Storey Mountain* to his later interest in Zen and Eastern meditation.

Although Trappists do not have lay associates or oblates in the same way other orders do, there are often opportunities to align yourself with the spirituality of a particular community and share in their prayers and abide by the same simplicity in your own daily life and work.

Carmelites are also a contemplative order with a strong Marian devotion whose ranks include St. Therese of Liseux, St. Teresa of Avila, and St. John of the Cross.

Passionists, founded by St. Paul of the Cross in 1741, attempt to reach out to those who are suffering through preaching and missionary work, with a focus on the Passion of Jesus Christ.

Hundreds of other religious communities of men and women exist in the United States and around the world. Check Appendix C for more information on how to locate a community in your area.

Through the Eyes of Women Mystics

Mystics have that otherworldly aura about them. We think of mystics as great saints from a long-ago time, and, in some ways, that description would be on target. The Middle Ages saw the peak of mysticism in the Catholic Church, particularly among women, leaving us with stories, visions, and spiritual messages to ponder.

The mystics' lives were marked by deep inner prayer, service to others, and visions or messages received from God. During their lives, they were often seen as mentally unstable, and yet their words were heeded by everyone from popes and priests to people on the streets.

Hildegard of Bingen

She may have lived during the Middle Ages, but Hildegard of Bingen was the classic Renaissance woman. A twelfth-century German mystic, this

Benedictine nun founded a religious community in Bingen, composed music that some consider genius, wrote poetry, understood the medicinal use of plants, and was as comfortable talking about science as she was talking about the Spirit. Hildegard, with her love for creation and her understanding of the environment, was "green" long before anyone even knew about the ozone layer.

In Hildegard, we can experience a kind of cosmic connection to God that seems beyond anything our modern world has to offer. Hildegard reminds us that even when others doubt our devotion, even when others don't understand our desire for union with God or our single-minded pursuit of prayer, we need to carry on and trust in our calling. Her visions of God's light inspired her writing and her music, which we can use to inspire our own prayer lives today.

Julian of Norwich

Julian of Norwich was a Medieval English mystic known as an *anchoress,* one who lives and prays in solitude and yet is still connected to the world. Anchoresses of old had three windows in their *cells*—one through which they received Communion, one through which they received food and other necessities, and one through which they could counsel people who sought their wisdom.

Definition

When we hear the word *cell,* we think of prison, or perhaps biology class. In the spiritual world, however, *cell* refers to a monk's or nun's room. For the ascetical orders, like the Carthusian monks, the cell really is a place where the monk is, in a sense, "held." He eats there except for maybe one meal a week. He studies there. He may even have his own small garden plot to tend. In other, less-strict communities, the cell refers to a simple room. To be sure, there are no luxuries. We're talking about a simple bed, dresser, desk, and chair. Typically there are no mirrors, no televisions, no phones. Just a crucifix and a clock and maybe some other spare sacred art for decoration.

Very little is known about Julian's life outside her writings. She had a series of visions during a near-death illness, and these were the source of her greatest work, *Sixteen Revelations of Divine Love.* Her revelations focus on the idea that "everything will be all right," meaning that God looks on all the moments of our lives, great and small, and doesn't miss even the tiniest thing.

Julian, who wrote about God the Father, God the Mother, and God the Lord, emphasized God's love and compassion rather than His wrath. She talked about the fact that God "dwells in our soul" and that our soul "dwells in God's substance."

wisdom for the journey

The contemplative spirit requires not so much a change of life as a change of awareness, an interior change. It is not the outward circumstances of life that make a contemplative, but the inner intention of the soul.

—Peggy Wilkinson, Third Order Carmelite, *Finding the Mystic Within*

Catherine of Siena

The youngest of 25 children, Catherine of Siena was said to have had her first vision of Christ when she was only 6 years old. At age 16, this fourteenth-century Italian mystic became a member of the lay Order of St. Dominic. She cared for the sick, counseled popes, and bore the stigmata (the wounds of Christ). She is one of three women named "Doctor of the Church," someone recognized by the Church as an outstanding teacher. (Teresa of Avila and Therese of Lisieux are the other two female Doctors of the Church.)

Catherine was not just deeply spiritual but politically active as well, urging Pope Gregory XI to return the papacy from France to Rome and attempting to bring peace to warring principalities in Italy. She suffered much in her life—loss, sickness, spiritual dryness—but she learned to retreat to an interior place of strength, an inner "cell." Her life of prayer focused on the sufferings of Christ, and she willingly accepted suffering into her own life as a way to grow in faith.

In Catherine, we can learn to serve others as a way to serve Christ and to see the suffering that life brings as a pathway to deeper spiritual understanding and strength.

The body of St. Catherine of Siena is buried under the main altar of the church of Santa Maria Sopra Minerva in Rome, although her head is kept in Siena.

Photo courtesy of Mary DeTurris Poust

Teresa of Avila

One of the most influential mystics of her time, or perhaps of any time, Teresa of Avila was born in 1515 in Avila, Spain, and developed a special devotion to the Blessed Mother after her own mother died. She became a Carmelite nun in 1536 and lived a life of deep mental prayer, fueled by spiritual visions and voices. She and St. John of the Cross reformed the Carmelite order into the Discalced (barefoot) Carmelites, and she founded convents all over Spain. She was a teacher, a poet, and a contemplative who reached the highest levels of spiritual union with God.

Among the best-known writings of this Doctor of the Church are *The Way of Perfection*, which offers practical instruction on prayer, and *The Interior Castle*, which uses a castle to represent our interior spiritual life with seven separate dwelling places. The gate of entry to this castle is prayer.

Prayer of St. Teresa of Avila

Let nothing trouble you,
let nothing make you afraid.
All things pass away.

God never changes.
Patience obtains everything.
God alone is enough.

MISC.

Hermit Living in the World

When we think of "hermits," we typically think of someone living alone in a cave or on a mountain or, at the very least, in a really simple cell. But today, more and more "regular" people are seeking the simplicity and spirituality of the hermit even as they live in the world, maybe even as part of a family. Is it possible to be a hermit and not live in total solitude? Some say yes, that it's an interior attitude not an exterior place. St. Francis of Assisi once said: "The world is my cloister, my body is my cell, and my soul is the hermit within!"

Dry Spells and Dark Nights

Inevitably, as we progress along our spiritual path, we will come up against times of dryness and darkness, moments or months or maybe even years when we pray and pray but don't feel any connection to God. It's not unusual. In fact, it's rather common. Many of the great saints and sages have written about these times of spiritual despair, when our heart longs to be with God but no matter how hard we try or how long we pray, we feel alone, abandoned.

The term "dark night" comes from St. John of the Cross, the sixteenth-century Spanish mystic whose classic "Dark Night of the Soul" chronicles the difficult, sometimes painful experience of trying to forge a true union with God.

A dry spell or dark night is like a spiritual roadblock. It makes us want to give up on prayer just when we need it most. So the key to getting through the dry spell is to keep praying, even if it feels totally pointless at the time.

Some spiritual "experts" say these dry spells and dark nights are meant to strengthen our resolve, to help us depend more completely on God, to trust in him even when we cannot feel his presence.

The world was stunned when the book *Come Be My Light: The Private Writings of the "Saint of Calcutta"* revealed the prolonged dark night of Blessed Mother Teresa. Some cynics took it as a sign that the saintly Missionary of

Charity wasn't what she appeared to be on the surface, but it's evident in her writing that in her prolonged spiritual darkness, she did not give up on God, even when she felt that perhaps he had given up on her.

"No, Father, I am not alone. I have His darkness—I have His pain—I have the terrible longing for God—to love and not to be loved. I know I have Jesus—in that unbroken union—for my mind is fixed on Him and in Him alone, in my will," she wrote, and yet day after day, she continued to smile, continued to serve the poor, continued to believe even while she grew to love the darkness.

"If I ever become a saint—I will surely be one of 'darkness.' I will continually be absent from Heaven—to light the light of those in darkness on earth," Mother Teresa wrote.

That may seem like small comfort to us as we struggle in our own darkness, but we need to remember that we are not alone and that the dryness and darkness are a sign of our closeness with God. Our longing for God is evidence that we are connected. Just showing up for prayer is a reminder that, despite any dryness, we know God is present in our lives.

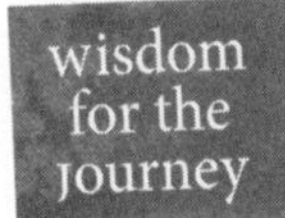

Pray inwardly, even if you do not enjoy it. It does good, though you feel nothing; yes, even though you think you are doing nothing.

—Julian of Norwich, fourteenth-century mystic

Seeking Spiritual Direction

When I first considered formal spiritual direction, I imagined it was something for someone who had already "arrived" in terms of prayer. I felt too low on the spiritual ladder to consider myself ready for spiritual direction. But that was a backward way of thinking. During the early stages of our spiritual journey, we need someone to talk to, someone to offer insights, someone to guide us and give us instructions on how to keep moving forward. A spiritual director can be just the person to do that.

Finding a spiritual director is not like finding a hair stylist or medical doctor. We don't just want someone who's good at what he or she does; we want someone who complements our personality, someone with whom we feel comfortable sharing our deepest, darkest spiritual questions and thoughts.

We may find a spiritual director by accident or "organically," meaning we meet someone with whom we are spiritually at ease, and spiritual direction grows out of it. Or we can take up a more concerted and formal search for a director, interviewing different people, calling our local diocese for resources, or visiting monasteries or retreat houses to meet with potential candidates.

Depending on where we go, there may or may not be a cost associated with this. Some places, such as spiritual direction centers in dioceses, may have sliding fees for individual direction. Some "freelance" spiritual directors may have a per-session fee, and others—priests or religious from a parish or monastery—may not charge anything at all. We may meet with a spiritual director more frequently at first—maybe every two weeks—and then monthly once we get to know one another.

Spiritual direction can provide a structure or path for our journey. Directors can suggest spiritual reading, talk to us about devotions or prayer practices that might suit our spiritual style, and walk with us as we experience the highs and lows of our faith journey.

Essential Takeaways

- Our prayer style may change and expand over the course of our lifetime, giving us the opportunity to explore new paths and prayer methods.
- The great spiritual masters and mystics have much to offer in terms of prayer content, style, and daily living.
- It's not unusual to experience periods of dryness or darkness in prayer, times when we cannot feel God's presence.
- A spiritual director can offer guidance on our prayer path, whether we're just starting out or have been hard at work for years.

chapter 23

Seeing All of Life as Prayer

Weaving prayer into every day

How inward prayer can inspire outward service

Surrendering to the transforming power of daily prayer

We've come a long way since our first conversations about basic Catholic prayers, creating sacred spaces, and learning the words and motions of Mass. And now we are here, ready to embark on a lifetime of prayer in a real and practical way.

You can put away the books, stop reading about prayer, and just start praying, in whatever way suits you right now. Sometimes it's tempting to keep reading more and more, thinking it will make us better pray-ers, but I've found that excessive reading about prayer is just one more thing our mischievous mind does to keep us from actually being quiet and listening for God.

If you can see prayer not as something you do at a certain time or in a certain place, but something you *are,* something that centers you at every moment, you'll find yourself and your daily grind transformed.

Beyond Words

Whether we say vocal prayers every morning, sing our prayers at night, or sit in silence after dinner, our communication with God goes far beyond what we see on the surface. From our vantage point, we are moving our lips in praise or quieting our minds in hopeful expectation. But as discussed at the beginning of this book, God was there all the time, inviting us, waiting for us, longing for us. Prayer is just our human way of finally accepting his unconditional and eternal invitation.

When we pray regularly, we begin to long for God in the same way he longs for us. As St. Augustine wrote in his famous *Confessions,* "You have made us for yourself, O Lord, and our hearts are restless until they rest in you." We become restless for God, and the only thing that brings peace, that settles our soul, is the regular rhythm of prayer. But we don't want peace for only the few minutes we pray each day; we want to *be* peace, and so prayer must become a way of life.

When you say "Jesus" the word is already a prayer.

—Servant of God Catherine Doherty, twentieth century

Finding Prayer Everywhere

Many of the great saints remind us that we do not have to pray in a cathedral or live in a monastery to pray well and pray deeply. Prayer is not a place. It comes from within, which means we can lay a template of prayer over anything and everything in our lives.

We have a choice. We can approach our daily obligations, chores, and activities as a long to-do list that must be completed before we can pray. Or we can turn the items on the to-do list into opportunities for prayer.

This is where we begin to see the transforming power of prayer: when we stop seeing a chore as a chore and start seeing it as a path to prayer, we shift our worldview, and that has powerful repercussions that echo throughout the rest of our lives.

Chores as Prayer

For a long time, I understood the idea behind what's known as the "Little Way"—a phrase referring to St. Therese of Lisieux's spirituality of infusing the little events of our lives with prayer—but I never seemed to get around to actually doing it.

I finally got a taste of what this spiritual practice is all about when I decided to try it out on one of my least favorite chores—putting away the laundry. I do laundry for an active family of five, so the hampers are always full, the piles always high. It wasn't the washing and drying that got to me. It wasn't even the folding that took its toll. It was the putting away. Don't ask me why I drew the line at putting away. I would sort and wash and dry and fold. Then I would cart the baskets up to my bedroom and wait. And wait. And the longer the baskets sat there, untouched by anyone else in the family, the more the resentment would build.

So one day I decided to try the Little Way approach. I started a new routine. As soon as I folded the laundry, I took it upstairs and put it away, seeing it not as one more chore but as a way to serve my family with love. I went from steaming about the piled-up laundry to trying to surprise everyone by putting it all away before they realized it was even missing. This approach has turned an obligation into an act of love, and I find myself surprised by the simple power of it.

The Little Way approach can work with any chore we face, especially those we have to do on a daily basis, from making beds to mowing the lawn. And there are many different ways to approach chores as prayer. We can pray for the person who will benefit from the chore—for our family as we chop onions for the night's dinner, for our husband as we fold his shirts, for our neighbors as we take in their mail or newspapers.

Or we can allow the rhythm of a chore to take us into a deep inner prayer. Washing the dishes, for example, with our hands in the warm soapy water, is a meditative action that lends itself to the repetition of a vocal prayer, such as the Jesus Prayer or the Rosary, or to a silent interior prayer where the movement occupies our body, freeing our mind to travel inward.

Eating as Prayer

Like daily chores, eating is one of those things that can become a mindless rush of activity as we try to finish one thing to get to another. But eating is a wonderful example of how we can enter into prayer through the most mundane moments of life.

I experienced this firsthand when I went on my short silent retreat. At first I found it a bit awkward to sit directly across a narrow table from someone during dinner and not talk or resort to some sort of busywork, like reading. By the second meal of the retreat, however, it became obvious that this was yet another opportunity to explore an inner place I'd never been to before. As I stared into my bowl of corn chowder, I let go of that need to fill every silent space, to make small talk even when I don't feel like it. Instead, I reflected on my retreat experience and tasted every bite of food, thanking God for the abundant blessings I was receiving.

In the mornings, I would take a cup of coffee and sit in an Adirondack chair looking out at the lake, listening to the gurgle of a little stream, the crunch of gravel underfoot as another participant walked silently by, the rhythmic clunk of oars against a boat as someone paddled on the water. By focusing on my eating and drinking in silence, I opened a door to another place where my spiritual senses were heightened.

This isn't always so easy to do at home, however. With family buzzing around us and e-mails dinging and phones ringing, eating can often become a blur of hands passing bowls, forks banging against plates, mouths chewing mindlessly as we worry about what's next on our to-do list. In fact, for too many of us, breakfast or dinner around a family table is a dying tradition. Meals grabbed on the go are often the norm nowadays. By beginning our meal with a prayer, and by finding a way to have a quiet meal every now and then, we can reclaim mealtime as sacred time.

Prayer Practice

You can easily experiment with eating as a path of prayer. First you need to find a time when you'll be eating alone. Turn off all exterior sounds—TV, music, cell phones. Put away books, magazines, and anything that will distract you. Prepare the food carefully, even if it's just a bowl of cereal. Clear the table of clutter, and set a place, perhaps even lighting a prayer candle. Begin with a quiet prayer and then let your mind slip silently into your meal. You can end the meal with similar care, not rushing to and fro, but basking in the simple but sacred task of mealtime.

Walking as Prayer

As someone who has both lived in and commuted to New York City, I know the true meaning of a power walk. My walk from subway to office was probably more like a jog or run, complete with the bobbing and weaving that's required to make good time on city sidewalks. Even in my suburban neighborhood, I rarely go for a walk that's not meant to get my heart rate up to an aerobic level. But if we can get past the idea of walking only as exercise or transportation, we can begin to see it as a physical way to reach a spiritual place.

Walking without purpose, without an end goal or destination, can be a meditative movement that provides the perfect backdrop for prayer. We can concentrate on our steps, walking more slowly than we normally would, to say the Rosary or some other devotion in time with our pace. Or we can bask in the natural beauty around us, perhaps taking a new route to appreciate God's creation while becoming more peaceful, more centered with every step.

Maybe we need a little accompaniment, which is fine. In that case, we can load up our MP3 player with a Rosary recording, religious music, or perhaps even a spiritual talk that gives us a focus as we put one foot in front of the other. Whatever our approach, walking—like so many other common activities—can be blended with prayer to give us a new way to experience and connect with God.

Walking a Labyrinth

The ancient tradition of walking a labyrinth has made a strong comeback in spiritual circles, including many Catholic churches and retreat houses. A labyrinth is not a maze but rather a single path with no wrong turns that winds slowly toward a center and then winds slowly back out. Some traditional Catholics are wary of the labyrinth, saying it's a pagan tradition, while others emphasize its usefulness in teaching pray-ers to slow down and focus their thoughts not on achieving a spiritual goal, but on the journey itself.

Breathing as Prayer

We breathe, usually without thinking. In and out, fast or slow, rhythmic and constant. It's a perfect gateway for prayer, this built-in metronome that keeps our physical body going. We can say something on an inhale, say something on an exhale, and suddenly prayer becomes a constant in our life rather than a variable that always seems to get dropped when things get busy.

Praying with our breath doesn't mean we're constantly saying the words to a particular devotion or even that we're constantly and consciously focusing on God. As I discussed in Chapter 21 in the section on the Jesus Prayer, we may need to be very aware of this kind of prayer at first, but over time, as it becomes part of our normal routine, it settles down to a different level. At that point, every breath becomes a prayer. Even when we're not focusing all our energy on it, it has become so engrained in us, so much a part of our words, thoughts, and actions, that the simple act of breathing is wrapped up in prayer. It's as though we're breathing in the Spirit and letting it fill us with God's goodness.

And of course, this kind of prayer works in conjunction with the other types of prayer I've just talked about. We can match our breath to our walking, our breath to our eating, our breath to our sweeping or lawn mowing, and in doing so, slow ourselves down long enough to let God in. He breathed life into us and brought us into being. What better way to connect with Him than through our breath?

Prayer Through Service

Prayer can do a lot of things for us—calm us down, free us from worry, center us on God, give meaning to seemingly meaningless moments of our days. But when prayer really takes root in us, it does something even greater: it inspires us to go out and serve others.

We see that kind of prayer in action in the lives of great saints and holy men and women. Therese and her Little Way used prayer to turn every action into a way to serve. Blessed Mother Teresa once said, "In this life we cannot do great things. We can only do small things with great love." Dorothy Day, founder of the Catholic Worker Movement, allowed her love for God and her deep spiritual life to lead her out into a world that desperately needed her love and compassion.

As we grow closer to God in prayer, we will discover the desire, the need, maybe even the urge, to go out and serve His people, to strive to live the Gospel lessons of love and service, mercy and generosity. The Catholic Church includes a huge network of organizations, agencies, foundations, communities, and individual Catholics dedicated to serving the poor, the suffering, and the forgotten.

If we build our prayer life on a solid foundation—grounded in Scripture, guided by the Spirit, inspired by God's love—we will likely want to take the next logical step by being Christ to those we meet.

St. Teresa of Avila said:

> Christ has no body
> on Earth now but yours;
> no hands but yours;
> no feet but yours.
> Yours are the eyes
> through which the compassion of Christ
> must look out on the world.
> Yours are the feet
> with which he is to go about doing good.
> Yours are the hands
> with which he is to bless his people.

Prayer is the fuel that energizes our spirit, that gives us the courage and strength to be Christ to a world in need. If we want to take that next step, all we have to do is look around and find the cause or the organization that best suits our talents, our longings, our vision of living the Gospel in a practical way. (Appendix C has resources for connecting with various charitable agencies.)

Changed from the Inside Out

Prayer is about inner transformation. That doesn't mean we pray in hopes of becoming someone else. It means we pray in order to reveal and become our true selves, the people God created us to be. Through prayer—by talking to God and listening for the whisper of the Spirit—we strip away our outer shell of self-protection, all those things that we put on to make ourselves appealing or acceptable to the world but that ultimately keep us from finding true peace and joy in our lives. What we're left with is this shining inner light that's a source of clarity and calm even in the midst of crises or confusion.

We can't set out on the pathway of prayer hoping to become a particular kind of person or trying to force a change. What happens in prayer happens from the inside out. If we are faithful to our prayer routine and spend time each day conversing with and listening for God, a transformation will begin, one that may surprise us. We're likely to discover aspects of ourselves we never knew or understood. We're sure to find a source of inner strength that never wavers.

The further we progress down the pathway of prayer, the closer we will get to our true home, a destination that does not exist somewhere "out there," but that resides deep within us, a destination that starts and ends with God.

wisdom for the journey

Start by doing what's necessary; then do what's possible; and suddenly you are doing the impossible.

—St. Francis of Assisi, twelfth century

Essential Takeaways

- A daily prayer routine will grow into a prayerful perspective that provides us with calm and strength even during difficult times.
- By weaving prayer into even the most mundane events of our days—cleaning, gardening, commuting to work—we create a life flooded with an awareness of God's presence.
- Prayer often leads to a desire to live the Gospel more fully through service and kindness to others.
- If we let down our defenses and surrender to God during our deepest moments of prayer, we will be changed from within and discover our true self.

Appendix A

Glossary

absolution When a priest, through the power given to the Church by Jesus Christ, forgives a penitent's sins during the sacrament of reconciliation.

Advent The four-week season of preparation before Christmas.

Amen Said at the end of most prayers, this Hebrew word means, "I believe."

angel A free spiritual and intellectual creature who never had mortal body and serves as God's messenger and servant.

Annunciation The moment when the angel Gabriel appeared to the Blessed Virgin Mary and announced that she would bear the Christ child through the power of the Holy Spirit.

Anointing of the sick One of the seven sacraments, this sacrament of healing provides spiritual comfort and strength to those who are seriously ill or in danger of death.

antiphon A response during prayer, often taken from a psalm. Common in the Liturgy of the Hours.

Apostles' Creed A profession of faith or "symbol of faith," it summarizes the beliefs of the Catholic Church in prayer form and is recited during the sacrament of baptism, during the renewal of baptismal vows, and at certain liturgies.

Ascension The moment when Jesus ascended bodily into heaven 40 days after Easter.

Assumption Church teaching that the Virgin Mary was taken up to heaven body and soul at the end of her earthly life. The feast day marking this event is August 15.

baptism The first of the seven sacraments, it frees believers from original and actual sin.

beatify The third step in the canonization process leading to sainthood. Typically requires approved miracles. When a person is beatified, he or she is declared "blessed."

beatitudes A series of teachings Jesus gave during the Sermon on the Mount (Matthew 5:3–12). The word *beatitude* means "happiness" or "blessedness."

bishop A successor to the apostles, a bishop is a member of the college of bishops and typically is head of a particular diocese, or local church, assigned him by the pope.

Blessed Sacrament Another name for Eucharist, which is the body and blood of Christ under the species of bread and wine. It often refers to the reserved Eucharist kept in the tabernacle for adoration by the faithful.

canon law The official laws and rules of the Catholic Church. Officially known as the Code of Canon Law.

canticle A scriptural "song"—the *Magnificat,* for example—that is not a psalm. Canticles are said during Morning, Evening, and Night Prayer during the Liturgy of the Hours.

catechism A manual of Church doctrine used to teach the faith.

catholic With a lowercase *c,* this word means "universal." Eastern Orthodox Churches and some Protestant denominations use the word *catholic* in their creeds.

centering prayer A silent prayer method that begins with the repetition of a sacred word and leads the pray-er toward contemplation.

Communion The body and blood of Jesus Christ received by the faithful.

communion of saints All members of the Church—souls in heaven, people on Earth, and all those caught somewhere in between (purgatory).

confession Refers to the sacrament of reconciliation through which sins are forgiven in the name of the Father, the Son, and the Holy Spirit.

confirmation A sacrament of initiation that completes the grace received at baptism and marks the confirmation with the indelible seal of the Holy Spirit.

contemplation Deep, silent prayer that leads to spiritual union with God. Requires being in a "receptive" state and listening for God rather than speaking to him.

creed A statement of a community's belief, also known as a symbol of faith.

deacon A member of the ordained clergy, who has the capacities to baptize, bless marriages, distribute Communion, proclaim the word of God, preach, and preside at funerals. Deacons may not celebrate Mass, hear confessions, confer holy orders, or administer the anointing of the sick. Transitional deacons are men working toward the priesthood; permanent deacons are men who will remain deacons for the rest of their lives. Unlike priests, permanent deacons may be married.

Decalogue Another name for the Ten Commandments given to Moses on Mount Sinai.

devotions Particular "private" prayers with a specific focus. The Rosary is the most popular Catholic devotion. Although devotions are private, meaning they are not part of the Church's official liturgies, they are often prayed in community.

diocese A community of the faithful in a particular geographic area, headed by a bishop.

disciple A follower of Jesus Christ.

Divine Office Another name for the Liturgy of the Hours, which is a Scripture-based prayer that gives a spiritual rhythm to the entire day.

Eucharist One of the seven sacraments, Eucharist is the body and blood of Jesus Christ under the appearance of bread and wine. It is the "source and summit" of the Christian faith. Eucharist also refers to the action at Mass through which bread and wine become the body and blood of Jesus Christ.

evangelization To proclaim the Gospel in order to bring others to Jesus Christ.

excommunication A penalty that removes a Catholic from communion with the Church, excluding him from participating in the Eucharist and other sacraments due to a grave offense against the faith.

Good News The teachings of Christianity as found in the New Testament, especially the four Gospels: Matthew, Mark, Luke, and John.

Gospel The teachings of Jesus Christ, also known as the "Good News," as revealed in the books of Matthew, Mark, Luke, and John in the New Testament.

grace A supernatural gift God bestows on men and women to help them live as children of God and achieve eternal salvation.

holy orders One of the sacraments of commitment or service, holy orders is when a man is ordained a bishop, priest, or deacon.

Holy Spirit The third person of the Holy Trinity. When Jesus ascends to his Father, he leaves the Spirit—also known as the Paraclete, the Advocate, and the Consoler—to dwell on Earth and guide his followers.

Immaculate Conception Catholic dogma that states that the Blessed Virgin Mary was conceived without original sin in anticipation of the role she would play in bringing God's Son into the world. The feast day for this event is December 8.

Incarnation The reality that Jesus Christ assumed human form and was at once truly human and truly divine.

Lent The 40-day season in preparation for Easter, usually marked by fast, abstinence, and prayer.

liturgy Refers to official public worship, separating it from private prayer. The Catholic Mass is a liturgy.

magisterium The Church's teaching authority, which rests with the pope and the college of bishops.

Mass A public liturgy where Catholics gather to pray, receive the word of God, and celebrate the Eucharist.

matrimony One of the sacraments of commitment or service, matrimony (or marriage) is a covenant relationship between a man and a woman. To be a sacrament a marriage must be between two baptized Christians.

meditation A form of silent prayer that focuses the mind on a particular Scripture passage, scene, or image as a pathway to closer union with Jesus Christ.

miracle An inexplicable and unexpected event that can be attributed only to divine intervention or the intercession of the Blessed Mother or a saint.

mission A particular spiritual goal or calling that drives a person's or group's words and actions. The mission of the Church is to spread the Gospel and bring others to Jesus Christ. Most religious communities have a particular "mission."

missionary Someone who travels to a specific area to spread the message of Jesus and minister to others—teaching, providing medical care, feeding the poor, building houses, etc.

Nicene Creed A profession of faith recited by the faithful during liturgy.

novena A devotional prayer said nine days in a row, or nine weeks in a row on a specific day; for example, every Monday for nine weeks.

original sin Humanity's fall from grace, attributed to Adam and Eve when they disobeyed God in the Garden of Eden. All people (except the Virgin Mary) inherit this sin, which is washed away during baptism.

Passion Refers to the suffering and death Jesus Christ endured, from the Last Supper to his Crucifixion.

penance Another name for the sacrament of reconciliation, *penance* is also used to describe either an interior or exterior action that moves a person away from sin and closer to God.

Pentecost Commemorates the day when the Holy Spirit descended upon the apostles, which was about 50 days after Easter.

pope The bishop of Rome and head of the college of bishops and successor to St. Peter, the first pope, he is the vicar of Christ on earth and head of the universal Church.

priest A man ordained by a bishop through the sacrament of holy orders to serve the Church by guiding the faithful, celebrating the sacraments, and serving in various charitable ministries.

prophet Someone sent by God to proclaim God's word and to speak in God's name.

psalm One of 150 Scriptural songs that make up the Old Testament Book of Psalms.

purgatory A place of purification where souls land before proceeding to heaven.

reconciliation Through this sacrament Catholics confess their sins, receive absolution, and complete penance in order to cleanse their souls of sin. Also known as the sacrament of penance or confession.

Resurrection Can refer to the resurrection of Jesus Christ from the dead three days after his crucifixion or the resurrection of all people after death. Resurrection of the body means our mortal bodies will be reunited with our risen souls at the end of the world.

Rosary Both a prayer devoted to Mary—made up of a series of Hail Marys and Our Fathers and other prayers recited in a repeated pattern—and the string of beads used to count the prayers.

sacramental A prayer or object that makes a person more open to God's grace. Holy water, a blessing, and a religious medal are all sacramentals.

sacraments Instituted by Christ, there are seven sacraments that are signs of grace: baptism, confirmation, Eucharist, reconciliation or penance, anointing of the sick, holy orders, and matrimony.

saint A holy person who has lived an exemplary life of faith while on earth and now resides in heaven with God for all eternity. The pope can canonize a deceased person as a saint of the Church, but any deceased person who is in heaven is a saint, whether the Church officially declares it to be so or not.

Scripture The writings contained in both the Old and New Testaments.

Servant of God The first step in the canonization process that leads to sainthood. At this level, the person is recognized as a potential saint and an investigation into his or her life begins.

Sign of the Cross A common Christian prayer that honors the Holy Trinity. A person forms a cross by marking forehead, heart, and each shoulder, first the left and then the right, with the right hand while saying the following words: "In the name of the Father and of the Son and of the Holy Spirit."

soul The spiritual part of human beings, the soul lives on after the body dies.

Stations of the Cross A devotion that commemorates the Passion of Jesus. It's more popular during Lent, when it's prayed on Fridays.

Ten Commandments Also known as the Decalogue, the Ten Commandments make up the essence of the "Old Law" given to Moses by God on Mount Sinai.

Transfiguration The moment when Jesus was transformed and appeared between Elijah and Moses in the presence of the apostles Peter, James, and John. A voice from heaven spoke, revealing Jesus' divinity.

transubstantiation The term used to describe the change of bread and wine into the body and blood of Jesus Christ during the Eucharistic celebration.

Trinity The central teaching of the Christian faith, the Trinity is the belief that there are three persons in one God: Father, Son, and Spirit. Each person of the Trinity has existed since the beginning of time, and each is fully divine and distinct from the others, and yet they are one.

venerable The second step in the canonization process, when a person is recognized for his or her life of heroic faith and virtue.

Virgin Mary The Mother of Jesus Christ, who was conceived without sin and chosen by God to bear his son through the power of the Holy Spirit. She is known by many names, including Mother of God.

vocation Signifies whatever calling a person has. The Church teaches that every person has a vocation, or destiny.

Word of God All of God's revelations to humanity as recorded in the Bible.

Appendix B

A Treasury of Prayers

Certain prayers are considered essential to Catholic life. In this appendix, I've pulled together a collection of prayers I hope you'll find useful.

Traditional Prayers

The prayers in this section are basics you might want to include in your daily prayer life regardless of any additional prayers or devotions you develop over time. These are the backbones of Catholic prayer life.

Sign of the Cross

In the name of the Father
and of the Son
and of the Holy Spirit.

Amen.

Our Father (Lord's Prayer)

Our Father, who art in heaven,
hallowed be thy name;
thy kingdom come;
thy will be done on Earth as it is in heaven.
Give us this day our daily bread,
and forgive us our trespasses,
as we forgive those who trespass against us;
and lead us not into temptation,
but deliver us from evil.

Amen.

Hail Mary

Hail Mary, full of grace,
the Lord is with thee.
Blessed art thou among women,
and blessed is the fruit of thy womb, Jesus.
Holy Mary, Mother of God,
pray for us sinners,
now and at the hour of our death.

Amen.

Glory Be

Glory be to the Father
and to the Son
and to the Holy Spirit,
as it was in the beginning,
is now, and ever shall be,
world without end.

Amen.

Apostles' Creed

I believe in God,
the Father Almighty,
creator of heaven and earth,
and in Jesus Christ, his only Son, our Lord,
who was conceived by the power
of the Holy Spirit,
and born of the Virgin Mary.
He suffered under Pontius Pilate,
was crucified, died, and was buried.
He descended into hell.
On the third day he rose again.
He ascended into heaven and
and is seated at the
right hand of the Father.

He shall come again to judge
the living and the dead.
I believe in the Holy Spirit,
the holy catholic Church,
the communion of saints,
the forgiveness of sins,
the resurrection of the body,
and life everlasting.

Amen.

Prayer to the Holy Spirit

Come, Holy Spirit,
fill the hearts of your faithful,
and enkindle in them the fire of your love.
Send forth your Spirit and they shall be created.
And you shall renew the face of the earth.
Let us pray.
O God, who has taught the hearts
of the faithful by the light of the Holy Spirit,
grant that by the gift of the same Spirit
we may be always truly wise and
ever rejoice in his consolation.
We ask this through Christ our Lord.

Amen.

Act of Contrition

O my God, I am heartily sorry
for having offended Thee,
and I detest all of my sins
because of thy just punishments,
but most of all because they offend Thee,
my God, who art all good
and deserving all of my love.
I firmly resolve with the help of Thy grace

to sin no more and
to avoid the near occasion of sin.

Amen.

Alternate Act of Contrition

O my God, I am sorry for my sins
with all my heart.
In choosing to wrong
and failing to do good,
I have sinned against you
whom I should love above all things.
I firmly intend, with your help,
to do penance,
to sin no more
and to avoid whatever leads me to sin.

Amen.

Hail, Holy Queen

Hail, Holy Queen,
Mother of Mercy,
our life, our sweetness, and our hope.
To thee do we cry,
poor banished children of Eve.
To thee do we send up our sighs,
mourning and weeping in this valley of tears.
Turn then, most gracious advocate,
thine eyes of mercy toward us,
and after this our exile
show unto us the blessed fruit of thy womb, Jesus.
O clement, O loving, O sweet Virgin Mary.
Pray for us, O holy Mother of God.
That we may be made worthy of the promises of Christ.

Amen.

The *Magnificat*

My soul proclaims the greatness of the Lord,
my spirit rejoices in God my Savior,
for he has looked with favor on his lowly servant.
From this day all generations will call me blessed.
The Mighty One has done great things for me and holy is his name.
He has mercy on those who fear him in every generation.
He has shown might with his arm;
he has scattered the proud in their conceit.
He has cast down the mighty from their thrones,
and has lifted up the lowly.
He has filled the hungry with good things,
and the rich he has sent away empty.
He has come to the help of his servant Israel
for he has remembered his promise of mercy,
the promise he made to our fathers,
to Abraham and his children forever. (Luke 1:46–55)

The Memorare

Remember, O most loving Virgin Mary, that never was it known that anyone who fled to your protection,
implored your help or sought your intercession
was left unaided.
Inspired by this confidence,
I fly unto you, O virgin of virgins, my mother.
To you I come, before you I stand,
sinful and sorrowful.
O Mother of the Word Incarnate, despise not my petitions,
but in your mercy hear and answer me.

—St. Bernard

Angel of God

Angel of God,
my guardian dear,
to whom God's love
commits me here,
ever this day be at my side,
to light and guard,
to rule and guide.

Amen.

Jesus Prayer

Lord Jesus Christ,
Son of God,
have mercy on me,
a sinner.

Prayer for Peace (Prayer of St. Francis)

Make me an instrument of your peace.
Where there is hatred, let me sow love.
Where there is injury, pardon,
where there is doubt, faith,
where there is despair, hope,
where there is darkness, light,
and where there is sadness, joy.
O Divine Master, grant that I may not
so much seek to be consoled,
as to console;
to be understood, as to understand;
to be loved, as to love.
For it is in giving that we receive;
it is in pardoning that we are pardoned,
and it is in dying that we are born
to eternal life.

Amen.

Traditional Morning Offering

O Jesus,
through the Immaculate Heart of Mary,
I offer you my prayers, works,
joys, and sufferings of this day
in union with the holy sacrifice
of the Mass throughout the world.
I offer them for all the intentions
of your Sacred Heart: the salvation
of souls, reparation for sin,
the reunion of all Christians.
I offer them for the intentions
of our bishops and of all
the apostles of prayer,
and in particular for those recommended
by our Holy Father this month.

Amen.

Grace Before Meals

Bless us, O Lord,
and these thy gifts
which we are about to receive
from thy bounty
through Christ Our Lord.

Amen.

Prayer to St. Michael the Archangel

Saint Michael the Archangel,
defend us in battle.
Be our protection against
the wickedness and snares of the devil.
May God rebuke him, we humbly pray;
and do Thou, O Prince of the Heavenly Host
by the Divine Power of God

cast into hell, Satan
and all the evil spirits,
who roam throughout the world
seeking the ruin of souls.

Amen.

How to Pray the Rosary

The Rosary is the most popular Catholic devotion. The word *Rosary* can refer to the devotion itself or to the beads used to say the prayers. When praying the Rosary, you say the Our Father, Hail Mary, and Glory Be in a repeating pattern, keeping count with the beads.

For each of the five "decades" of the Rosary, you meditate on a "mystery"—joyful, luminous, sorrowful, or glorious. Although this devotion is most closely associated with the Blessed Mother, it is meant to be a meditation on the life of Jesus Christ and to lead pray-ers closer to him through is mother.

1. Holding the cross on your Rosary beads, make the Sign of the Cross and recite the Apostles' Creed.
2. On the first separate bead, say the Our Father.
3. On each of the next three beads, say a Hail Mary.
4. On the next separate bead (or medal, depending on your Rosary beads), announce the first mystery and say an Our Father.
5. On each of the next 10 beads, say a Hail Mary. End the decade with a Glory Be.
6. Repeat the process: announce a mystery and say an Our Father, 10 Hail Marys, and a Glory Be for the next 4 decades until you go around the entire set of beads. While saying each decade, reflect on the principal mysteries of Christ's life and humanity's salvation.
7. End with the Hail Holy Queen.

All the Rosary prayers can be found in the previous section of essential Catholic prayers.

Mysteries of the Rosary

When we pray the Rosary, although we say the words of specific prayers, our hearts and minds are supposed to be focused on the events of Jesus' life, as outlined in the joyful, luminous, sorrowful, and glorious mysteries. According to tradition, certain mysteries are prayed on specific days.

Joyful Mysteries (recited Monday and Saturday)

- The Annunciation
- The Visitation
- The Birth of Our Lord
- The Presentation in the Temple
- The Finding of the Child Jesus in the Temple

Luminous Mysteries (recited Thursday)

- The Baptism in the Jordan
- The Wedding at Cana
- The Proclamation of the Kingdom of God
- The Transfiguration
- The Institution of the Eucharist

Sorrowful Mysteries (recited Tuesday and Friday)

- The Agony in the Garden
- The Scourging at the Pillar
- The Crowing with Thorns
- The Carrying of the Cross
- The Crucifixion

Glorious Mysteries (recited Wednesday and Sunday)

- The Resurrection
- The Ascension of our Lord
- The Descent of the Holy Spirit
- The Assumption of Our Lady into Heaven
- The Coronation of the Blessed Virgin Mary

The Stations of the Cross

Stations of the Cross, also known as the Way of the Cross, is a devotion that commemorates the Passion of Jesus Christ—from his condemnation before Pilate to his being placed inside the tomb. Although many Catholics might pray the stations regularly throughout the year, it's most popular during Lent, when it's often prayed in parishes on Fridays.

Typically, you meditate on each of the stations before a physical depiction—picture or sculpture—of the scene, an actual "station" located in a church, shrine, or garden. If you pray the stations as a community, you not only say the prayer and think about each station, but you may also reflect on a specific Scripture reading for each station or listen to a brief reflection.

Before each station, recite the following prayer:

> We adore you, O Christ, and we praise you. Because
> by your holy cross you have redeemed the world.

First Station: Jesus is condemned to death.

Second Station: Jesus takes up his cross.

Third Station: Jesus falls the first time.

Fourth Station: Jesus is met by his mother.

Fifth Station: Simon of Cyrene helps Jesus carry his cross.

Sixth Station: Veronica wipes the face of Jesus.

Seventh Station: Jesus falls a second time.

Eighth Station: The women of Jerusalem mourn for our Lord.

Ninth Station: Jesus falls for the third time.

Tenth Station: Jesus is stripped of his garments.

Eleventh Station: Jesus is nailed to the cross.

Twelfth Station: Jesus dies on the cross.

Thirteenth Station: Jesus is taken down from the cross.

Fourteenth Station: Jesus is placed in the tomb.

Catholic Basics

Although the following Catholic teachings may not fall directly under "prayer life," they certainly infuse all Catholic life and cannot be ignored or denied. They are elemental to Catholic spirituality.

The Ten Commandments

Given to Moses on Mount Sinai, the Ten Commandments provide the basic structure for how Catholics—like their Jewish ancestors before them—should act. The first three commandments focus on our relationship with God; the next seven commandments focus on our relationships with other people.

1. I am the Lord your God, I brought you out of the land of Egypt, you shall have no other gods before me.
2. Do not take the name of the Lord your God in vain.
3. Keep holy the Sabbath.
4. Honor thy father and mother.
5. You shall not kill.
6. You shall not commit adultery.
7. You shall not steal.
8. You shall not bear false witness against your neighbor.
9. You shall not covet your neighbor's wife.
10. You shall not covet your neighbor's goods.

Jesus' "New" Commandment

Jesus took the Ten Commandments and expanded them. They were no longer literal teachings only but broad, compassionate teachings on how to treat all those we meet along life's way. Jesus summed up this "new" commandment like this:

> You shall love the Lord your God with all your heart,
> with all your soul, and with all your mind, and you
> shall love your neighbor as yourself.

The Beatitudes

The Beatitudes are a series of key teachings Jesus gave during his Sermon on the Mount (Matthew 5:3–12):

> Blessed are the poor in spirit,
> for theirs in the kingdom of heaven.
> Blessed are they who mourn,
> for they will be comforted.
> Blessed are the meek,
> for they will inherit the land.
> Blessed are they who hunger and thirst
> for righteousness,
> for they will be satisfied.
> Blessed are the merciful,
> for they will be shown mercy.
> Blessed are the pure of heart,
> for they will see God.
> Blessed are the peacemakers,
> for they shall be called children of God.
> Blessed are those who are persecuted
> for the sake of righteousness,
> for theirs is the kingdom of heaven.
> Blessed are you when they insult you
> and persecute you and utter every kind of
> evil against you falsely because of me.
> Rejoice and be glad, for your reward
> will be great in heaven. (Matthew 5:3–12)

The Corporal and Spiritual Works or Mercy

Catholics believe they have a Gospel call—given to them by Jesus—to care for others, both physically and spiritually. This mission is outlined in the Corporal and Spiritual Works of Mercy:

The Corporal Works of Mercy

1. Feed the hungry.
2. Give drink to the thirsty.
3. Clothe the naked.
4. Shelter the homeless.
5. Visit the sick.
6. Visit the imprisoned.
7. Bury the dead.

The Spiritual Works of Mercy

1. Counsel the doubtful.
2. Instruct the ignorant.
3. Admonish sinners.
4. Comfort the afflicted.
5. Forgive offenses.
6. Bear wrongs patiently.
7. Pray for the living and the dead.

Appendix C

Resources

When it comes to a life of prayer, it's not simply a matter of sitting down—or kneeling down—and getting to work. Sometimes you need outside support and resources. Fortunately, plenty of additional resources are available to guide you, no matter what style of prayer interests you. Check the following books, websites, and applications for practical support and general encouragement along the way.

Recommended Reading

A multitude of printed material exists to help you further along your spiritual path.

Catholic Basics

Bishops' Committee on Liturgy, National Conference of Catholic Bishops. *Catholic Household Blessings & Prayers*. The Liturgical Press, 1989.

Christian Prayer: The Liturgy of the Hours. Catholic Book Publishing Corp., 1976.

The New American Bible (Holy Bible). Iowa Falls: World Bible Publishers, Inc., c1970, c1986, 1991.

Vaticana, Libreria Editrice. *Catechism of the Catholic Church*, Second Edition. USCCB Publishing, 1994, 1997.

——— *Essentials for Christian Living*. USCCB Publishing, 2008.

Classic Spirituality

Bangley, Bernard, ed. *Nearer to the Heart of God: Daily Readings with the Christian Mystics*. Paraclete Press, 2005.

Merton, Thomas. *Seven Storey Mountain*. Harcourt, Brace & Co., 1948.

———. *Thoughts in Solitude*. Farrar, Straus, Giroux, 1956, 1958.

Mottola, Anthony, ed. *Spiritual Exercises of St. Ignatius of Loyola*. Image Books, 1964.

Murphy, Charles M. *The Spirituality of Fasting: Rediscovering a Christian Practice*. Ave Maria Press, 2010.

St. Benedict of Nursia. *The Rule of St. Benedict*. Image Books, 1975.

St. Francis de Sales. *Introduction to the Devout Life*. New York: Vintage Books, 2002.

St. Teresa of Avila. *Interior Castle*. Paulist Press, 1979.

St. Therese of Lisieux. *The Story of a Soul*. Image Books/Doubleday, 1957, 2001.

Contemporary Inspiration

Bernardin, Joseph Cardinal. *The Gift of Peace*. Loyola Press, 1997.

Keating, Thomas. *Open Mind, Open Heart: The Contemplative Dimension of the Gospel*. Continuum Publishing, 1986, 1992.

Kolodiejchuk, Brian, MC, ed. *Mother Teresa: Come Be My Light: The Private Writings of the Saint of Calcutta*. Doubleday, 2007.

Martin, James SJ, ed. *Awake My Soul: Contemporary Catholics on Traditional Devotions*. Loyola Press, 2004.

———. *My Life with the Saints*. Loyola Press, 2006.

Norris, Kathleen. *The Cloister Walk*. New York: Riverhead Books, 1996.

Nouwen, Henri J.M. *Beloved: Spiritual Living in a Secular World*. Crossroad Publishing Company, 1992.

Poust, Mary DeTurris. *Walking Together: Discovering the Catholic Tradition of Spiritual Friendship*. Ave Maria Press, 2010.

Scaperlanda, Maria Ruiz, and Michael Scaperlanda. *The Journey: A Guide for the Modern Pilgrim*. Loyola Press, 2004.

Straub, Gerard Thomas. *The Sun & Moon Over Assisi: A Personal Encounter with Francis and Clare*. St. Anthony Messenger Press, 2000.

Talbot, John Michael, with Steve Rabey. *The Lessons of St. Francis: How to Bring Simplicity and Spirituality into Your Daily Life*. Plume Publishing, 1997.

Taylor, Brian C. *Spirituality for Everyday Living: An Adaptation of the Rule of St. Benedict*. The Liturgical Press, 1989.

Vest, Norvene. *No Moment Too Small: Rhythms of Silence, Prayer, and Holy Reading*. Cistercian Publications, 1994.

Walters, Kerry. *A Retreat with Brother Lawrence and the Russian Pilgrim*. St. Anthony Messenger Press, 1989. (Check out the many offerings in the A Retreat with … series.)

Websites Worth a Visit

In this age of immediate access, you can find just about anything you need to explain or promote your prayer life by visiting various websites dedicated to Catholic prayer, teaching, and spirituality.

General Reference

Holy See
www.vatican.va
The Vatican's official site, available in six languages, provides links to everything from papal encyclicals and messages to news photos and archives.

United States Conference of Catholic Bishops (USCCB)
www.usccb.org
Statements of the U.S. bishops, links to American Catholic dioceses, the New American Bible, and numerous other resources.

Canadian Conference of Catholic Bishops
www.cccb.ca
Includes access to documents and statements by the bishops of Canada as well as links to dioceses throughout that country.

USCCB/Roman Missal
www.usccb.org/romanmissal
Provides information on the revised Missal, including the General Instruction on the Roman Missal (GIRM) and the Order of the Mass, with resources for teaching.

Bible Search Engines
www.usccb.org/nab/bible
Allows you to look up passages in the New American Bible by book, chapter, and verse.

Bible Gateway
www.biblegateway.com
Scripture search engine that allows you to use key words, topics, or specific passages to locate Bible verses. Provides 100 different Bible translations.

Daily Scripture Readings
www.usccb.org/nab
Here you'll find the Scripture readings for each day in the Catholic liturgical cycle, New American Bible translation.

Magnificat
www.magnificat.com
A subscription publication that provides monthly booklets (as well as special seasonal issues) with readings for Mass, reflections, and more. A children's version is also available.

Mass Times
www.masstimes.org
Find Mass times at any parishes across the country or around the world, searching by zip code, city, and/or country.

Prayer Sites

The Divine Mercy
www.thedivinemercy.org
Prayers, events, and links related to the Divine Mercy devotion, sponsored by the National Shrine of the Divine Mercy in Stockbridge, Massachusetts.

General prayers and devotions:

Catholic Teaching and More
www.ewtn.com/faith/index.asp
Sponsored by the Eternal Word Television Network, this website provides links to everything from traditional Catholic prayers to breaking Catholic news, with web links to live events and more.

American Catholic
www.americancatholic.org
A website of St. Anthony Messenger Press, this link offers not only general information on the Catholic Church and Catholic teaching, but features on saints, seasons, prayer, and more.

Catholic Mom
new.catholicmom.com/faith
A "go-to" website for Catholic parents, faith formation teachers, and general Catholics who want articles, projects, suggestions, and advice when it comes to living the Catholic faith in the day-to-day world.

Liturgy of the Hours:

eBreviary
www.ebreviary.com
Provides daily readings and prayers for the Liturgy of the Hours.

Universalis
www.universalis.com
Also provides prayers and meditations for the Liturgy of the Hours.

Association of the Miraculous Medal
www.amm.org/prayers/prymnov.asp
Find prayers, novenas, and historical information related to Our Lady of the Miraculous Medal.

The Sacred Heart of Jesus
www.ewtn.com/Devotionals/Heart/meditation.htm
Provides background information, prayers, novenas, and other devotions associated with the Sacred Heart.

Sacred Space
www.sacredspace.ie
This site provides daily online guided prayer from the Jesuit Communication Centre in Ireland.

Word of God Every Day
www.wordofgodeveryday.com
Free daily Scripture quotes, accompanied by related saint quotes, sent by e-mail.

Prayer Apps for Download

The digital age meets the spiritual age in a series of apps for iPhones and other personal "assistants." The following applications are among the most popular for using a handheld device to further prayer life.

Liturgy of the Hours
Universalis
iPhone/iPad application
Univeralis Publishing
Daily psalms, prayers, and readings for the Divine Office seven times a day.

Rosary
Rosary Miracle Prayer
iPhone/iPod application
Pauline Books and Media
Audio Rosary with accompanying music, artwork, and icons.

Missal
IMissal

iPhone application
Cantcha, Inc.
Provides daily Scripture readings and prayers for Mass.

Daily Reflections
Pray-as-You-Go
free download for MP3 players
Jesuit Media Initiative
Includes music, Scripture, and reflections for every day.

Associations and Organizations

Most religious communities have websites and even blogs to support their mission and ministries. Explore those that interest you via web search and then make personal contact for further information.

Benedictine Oblates
www.osb.org/obl

Carmelite Third Order
www.ocarm.org/en/category/carmelite-family/lay-people

Dominican Associates
www.domlife.org/BeingDominican/WhoWeAre/Associates.htm

Ignatian Associates
www.ignatianassociates.org

Secular Franciscans
www.nafra-sfo.org

United States Conference of Secular Institutes
www.secularinstitutes.org

Service Opportunities

Catholic teaching says that faith is not enough. Good works must be part of the mix. Service opportunities abound in the Catholic Church. Consider the following organizations, or conduct your own web search to find something that suits your needs, interests, and talents. Some of the agencies are general Catholic service organizations; others are religious community-based groups that require a specific time commitment from volunteers.

Catholic Charities USA
www.catholiccharitiesusa.org

Catholic Relief Services
www.crs.org

Catholic Worker Movement
www.catholicworker.org

Claretian Volunteers
www.claretians.org

Jesuit Volunteer Corp
www.jesuitvolunteers.org

Society of St. Vincent de Paul
www.svdpusa.org/default.aspx?tabid=66

Index

B

D

E

I

J

L

N

O

S

T